THE CHILD AT PSYCHIATRIC RISK

The Child
at Psychiatric Risk

Edited by

Ralph E. Tarter

Associate Professor of Psychiatry and Neurology
Western Psychiatric Institute and Clinic
University of Pittsburgh School of Medicine

New York   Oxford
OXFORD UNIVERSITY PRESS
1983

Library of Congress Cataloging in Publication Data
Main entry under title:

The Child at psychiatric risk.

  Bibliography: p.
  Includes index.
  1. Child psychopathology. 2. Psychology,
Pathological. I. Tarter, Ralph E. [DNLM:
1. Mental disorders—In infancy and childhood.
2. Child psychiatry—Methods. WS 350 C53505]
RJ499.C4824 1983   618.92′89   82-8207
ISBN 0-19-503241-1

Printing (last digit): 9 8 7 6 5 4 3 2 1

Printed in the United States of America

Preface

In shifting the emphasis of health care from treatment to prevention, one must consider the mounting evidence that not all individuals are at equal risk for a psychiatric or behavioral disorder. Some individuals, because of biological predisposition are at *increased* risk. This book addresses the methods and findings pertaining to the study of psychiatric risk. The focus is primarily on the genetic and biological factors that are responsible for the major disorders found in children and adults. Hence, the reader will find, after the introductory chapters on methods and issues, discussions of the various disorders—hyperactivity, developmental disabilities, affective disorders, alcoholism, antisocial personality, neurotic disturbances, and schizophrenia. Although these conditions do not, by any means, comprise the total range of psychiatric disorders, they are, nonetheless, the disorders for which there is a body of information, and that most frequently constitute the conditions routinely encountered in clinical practice.

Research on psychiatric risk is relatively recent, most of the major investigations having been published within the last decade. Hence, the reader will discover large gaps in our understanding of most of the disorders. It is hoped that this book will encourage the reader to either participate in the research enterprise or to develop clinical applications. Considering the clinical, financial, and social ramifications of learning about the characteristics that place individuals at heightened risk, the topics covered should interest psychiatrists, neuroscientists, psychologists, educators and epidemiologists, as well as policy analysts and administrators who are charged with the difficult task of dispensing monies to the most potentially fruitful projects and agencies.

The realization of this project is due in large measure to the cooperation of a number of individuals. Particularly, I extend my gratitude to the authors for their contributions, and for their enthusiasm and openness in responding to editorial input. My appreciation is also extended to Grace Allen, Jeanne Odenheimer, Andrea Hegedus, and Mary Ann Kelly for their secretarial, proofreading, and library assistance. A special note of thanks is expressed to Kathy Lou Edwards for her editorial assistance.

Pittsburgh, Pennsylvania   R.E.T.
February 15, 1983

CONTRIBUTORS

ROBERT A. ASARNOW, Ph.D.
Department of Psychiatry
University of California at Los Angeles
Los Angeles, California

OLIVER CHADWICK, Ph.D.
Gertrude H. Sergievsky Center
Columbia University
New York, New York

RAYMOND R. CROWE, M.D.
Department of Psychiatry
The University of Iowa Hospitals
    and Clinics
Iowa City, Iowa

ROBERT CUDECK, Ph.D.
Social Science Research Institute
University of Southern California
Los Angeles, California

HANS J. EYSENCK, Ph.D.
Institute of Psychiatry
University of London
London, England

DONALD W. GOODWIN, M.D.
Department of Psychiatry
University of Kansas
Kansas City, Kansas

ANDREA M. HEGEDUS, B.S.
Department of Psychiatry
Western Psychiatric Institute
    and Clinic
University of Pittsburgh
Pittsburgh, Pennsylvania

SARNOFF MEDNICK, Ph.D., Dr. Med.
Social Science Research Institute
University of Southern California
Los Angeles, California

TERRIE E. MOFFITT, M.A.
Social Science Research Institute
University of Southern California
Los Angeles, California

ROBIN MORRIS, Ph.D.
Department of Clinical Psychology
University of Florida
Gainesville, Florida

THEODORE REICH, M.D.
Department of Psychiatry
Washington University
St. Louis, Missouri

JOHN P. RICE, Ph.D.
Department of Psychiatry
Washington University
St. Louis, Missouri

MICHAEL RUTTER, M.D.
Institute of Psychiatry
University of London
London, England

PAUL SATZ, Ph.D.
Department of Psychiatry
University of California at Los Angeles
Los Angeles, California

RUSSELL SCHACHAR, M.D.
Department of Psychiatry
Hospital for Sick Children
Toronto, Ontario

ROBERT E. SMITH, M.D.
Department of Psychiatry
The University of Iowa Hospitals
    and Clinics
Iowa City, Iowa

BRIAN K. SUAREZ, Ph.D.
Department of Psychiatry
Washington University
St. Louis, Missouri

RALPH E. TARTER, Ph.D.
Department of Psychiatry
Western Psychiatric Institute
    and Clinic
University of Pittsburgh
Pittsburgh, Pennsylvania

GEORGE WINOKUR, M.D.
Department of Psychiatry
The University of Iowa Hospitals
    and Clinics
Iowa City, Iowa

Contents

THE CHILD AT PSYCHIATRIC RISK

1. Vulnerability and risk: Assessment and prediction of outcome

Ralph E. Tarter

Many disorders result from the interaction of biological and psychosocial factors, but for a factor to have causal influences, it must act on a vulnerable organism. Thus, although many individuals who smoke cigarettes, abuse alcohol, or follow a high fat diet do not develop lung cancer, cirrhosis, or coronary disease, respectively, the finding that many individuals who do have these habits succumb to these disorders suggests that they may be at high risk. Similarly, prematurity at birth, widowhood, or alcohol abuse do not invariably result in developmental disability, clinical depression, or alcoholism.

As discussed throughout this book, there are numerous factors that increase the risk of a behavioral or psychiatric disorder. These include genetic, physiological, neuropsychological, and behavioral factors, which define *vulnerability; risk* is the degree of probability of an unfavorable outcome. *Proband* is the individual being studied, the subject. Because of the many factors that act to determine vulnerability, research strategies are complex, and before they are discussed (Chapters 2 and 3), it is important to consider the clinical issues involved in the assessment of vulnerability.

Assessment of vulnerable children

Where

Academic underachievement or a conduct disorder are typical reasons for bringing a child to the attention of health professionals. School is usually the first institution in which the young child must adapt to a structured environment, achieve criterion levels of performance in diverse learning tasks, and behave in a socially skillful and age-appropriate fashion. Thus through periodic evaluations conducted in the school setting, it is possible to detect early signs of emotional disturbance as well as to monitor the development of competence in academic and social skills.

Teachers often can identify children who are at increased risk for developing a psychiatric disorder, and Mulligan, Douglas, Hamond, & Tizard (1963) have found that teachers were able to predict future delinquency. Weintraub, Liebert, and Neal (1978) reported that male children of depressed mothers and female children of schizophrenic mothers were described by their teachers as inattentive, impatient, and withdrawn. In addition, the children of psychiatrically disturbed mothers had a lower comprehension capacity and behaved more disruptively and were more defiant to authority than were their peers.

High risk children can also be detected from peer ratings. Sociometric ratings identified children who subsequently developed a psychiatric disturbance (Cowen, Pederson, Babigian, Izzo, & Trost, 1973) and who became delinquent (Skaberne, Blejec, Skalar, & Voopivec, 1965). Interestingly, sociometric ratings are better predictors of maladjustment than either self-ratings of behavior or withdrawal from school (Ullman, 1957).

Psychometric tests are good predictors of learning disability. Ferinder and Jacobson (1970) found that the Wide Range Achievement Test and the Evanston Early Identification Scale identified children who subsequently developed a reading disability. Serwer, Shapiro, and Shapiro (1972) observed that numerical ability was a good predictor of learning disability, although teacher ratings were almost as good. This study underscored the need to develop instruments to predict a specific type of impairment, inasmuch as the label "learning disabled" encompasses a heterogeneous population of individuals (see Satz & Morris, Chapter 6). As a group, however, learning disabled children are at appreciably higher risk than their peers for developing an antisocial disorder (Clark, 1970; Rutter, Tizard, & Whitmore, 1970). Children with a speech or language disturbance are also at increased risk for developing emotional problems (Cantwell & Mattison, 1979).

Child guidance clinics are another institutional resource for the identification of high risk children. For example, Ricks and Berry (1970) distinguished two types of antecedents of schizophrenia. One type was primarily antisocial and exhibited destructiveness, delinquency, truancy, lying, and low self-esteem. The second type was marked by withdrawal, acquiescence, and obsessional symptoms. Children who were violent toward their parents had a poorer prognosis than those who were violent toward their peers. In another study, Mellsop (1972) found that children who required psychiatric services were also at risk for psychiatric problems. Children who did not subsequently require psychiatric treatment could not be differentiated from those who did.

What

A comprehensive assessment, of all levels of biological organization, is necessary to understand the reasons for such vulnerability. Vulnerability can exist at morphological, biochemical, physiological, or behavioral levels of biological organization and can be either inherited or acquired. To begin an evaluation, information about family background is obtained, bearing in mind that a positive history of a disorder does not necessarily implicate a genetic etiology. Nonetheless, it is often possible to project the risk of an unfavorable outcome from a family history. For example, Goodwin (Chapter 8) reports that approximately 20% of male offspring of alcoholic fathers become alcoholic themselves. Higher rates of neurological disturbance and psychopathology are found in children whose parents are schizophrenic (Asarnow, Chapter 7). These latter studies indicate that a history of a psychopathological disorder in the family can provide useful leads concerning the areas to assess for current status as well as enable predictions regarding long term prognosis.

Certain genetically mediated characteristics, such as physique and temperament are related to emotional and social adjustment. Children with an ectomorphic physique are more prone than mesomorphs and endomorphs to be shy, anxious, and hypersensitive (Walker, 1962), and they are more inclined to need psychiatric help (Parnell, 1957). Activity level during infancy is predictive of emotional status in adulthood. Adults who were either very active or very inactive as infants are more likely to suffer psychological problems than their cohorts who were moderately active (Fries & Woolf, 1971). Temperament is another constitutional dimension that is largely inherited (Buss, Plomin, & Willerman, 1973) and measurable soon after birth (Plomin & Rowe, 1979). It is also related to behavioral adjustment in adolescence (Thomas, Chess, & Birch, 1968).

Neurochemical, endocrinological, and metabolic disturbances may place the child at risk for a psychiatric disturbance. Individuals with close relatives who are alcoholic metabolize alcohol differently than individuals without a family history of alcoholism, which suggests that there may be a metabolic factor underlying this disorder (Shuckit & Rayes, 1979). Buchsbaum, Coursey, and Murphy (1976) found that neurochemical characteristics, inferred by platelet monoamine oxidase (MAO) levels, are related to the psychiatric status of children and their families. Family members of male probands with low MAO levels, compared to those with high MAO levels, are eight times more likely to attempt or to succeed at committing suicide. Low MAO probands are also more likely to be convicted of a crime and to seek psychiatric counseling.

The number of known biochemical disturbances that affect psychological status is quite extensive. Some of these conditions, such as phenylketonuria (PKU), are easily detectable and if treated by an appropriate diet, can be effectively counteracted. Other disorders are not so easily identified, or they are routinely overlooked. Endocrinological disturbances, nutritional deficiencies, and liver malfunction, for example, have cognitive and emotional sequelae.

When

The time in life in which vulnerability is established is a critical factor in determining the probability of an unfavorable outcome. A genetic predisposition has been found for alcoholism (Goodwin, 1976), sociopathy (Crowe, 1974), affective illness (Winokur, Cadoret, Dorzab, & Baker, 1971), and neurosis (Fulker, 1980). In addition, temperament (Buss, Plomin, & Willerman, 1973), personality (Floderus-Myrhed, Pederson & Rasmuson, 1980), hyperactivity (Cantwell, 1975), and learning disability (Mathey, Dolan, & Wilson, 1976) are genetically influenced traits that can place the person at high risk for a psychiatric or behavioral disorder. Thus, for a number of disorders, vulnerability is established at the moment of conception.

Events occurring during intrauterine development can substantially increase the risk for an unfavorable outcome. Even a relatively common occurrence such as sharing the intrauterine environment with a twin has been reported to be associated with temporary postnatal developmental retardation (Dales, 1969), although this may be due in part to restricted parenting opportunities available to each child (Costello, 1978). Inadequate nutrition in (Omolulu, 1974) and alcohol consumption (Streiss-guth, Landesmann-Dwyer, Martin, & Smith, 1980) by a gestating woman increases the risk for postnatal cognitive, behavioral, and neurological disturbances in the offspring.

The outcome of fetal and perinatal stress includes such diverse conditions as learning disabilities, schizophrenia, tics, infantile autism, and mental retardation. These disorders have been described along a continuum of severity of "reproductive casuality" (Pasamanick & Knoblock, 1961). The demographic and medical status of the mother are also related to neurological disturbance in the offspring (Niswander & Gordon, 1972; Heineman, Slone, & Shapiro, 1977). Thus, factors that directly affect the fetus, as well as the psychosocial characteristics of the mother, influence the outcome of pregnancy.

Infection and nutritional deprivation during postnatal development can have long term effects on neurological behavioral adjustment. Severing, as well as preventing, the development of affective bonds also increases the risk for behavioral and emotional disturbance (Bowlby, 1960). Children raised in orphanages or foundling homes, where opportunities for nurturing relationships are limited, exhibit more emotional disturbances and are more susceptible to disease than children reared in a nuclear family. A deviant parental rearing style (Kearsley, 1979) can produce an "iatrogenic retardation" in the child characterized by poor development of adaptive behaviors. Abuse, neglect, poverty, overcrowding, and psychopathology in family members are additional factors that increase the risk for an unfavorable outcome. In addition, coping style can influence later outcome. Learned helplessness, for example, is a behavioral and cognitive characteristic of depression (Seligman, 1975). Other dispositional coping styles, such as turning against others, turning against self, and avoidance of others (Phillips, 1968) are also related to behavioral disturbance. Such biological and psychosocial factors influence postnatal development and long term prognosis.

How

The assessment process should ideally comprise a comprehensive prospective case study of every child in society. Persons deemed to be at risk, as detected from a standardized screening, would be the recipients of therapeutic intervention either before or soon after the prodromal stages of a disorder. Genetic counseling could comprise the first stage of the evaluation, to be followed by monitoring of the fetus and neonate during the pregnancy and perinatal period. Continuing support services during postnatal development would be devoted to maintaining optimal medical care, nutrition, and psychological health. Although such an approach may appear unrealistic, if not outright utopian, it is apparent that this type of integrated health care delivery, involving routine periodic assessment and early intervention, is cost effective for society.

Little headway has been made, however, in quantitatively evaluating children at high psychiatric risk. Anthony (1974) developed a six point scale that codifies seven variables from which a total risk score is obtained. Vulnerability is evaluated in the context of perceptual-motor, intellectual, and personality characteristics. In addition, ratings of coping capacity, ego defenses, controls, aggressivity, reality testing, identity conflicts, anxiety, cognitive concreteness, and logicality are obtained. This approach constitutes a major advance in developing an objective and quantitative instrument to evaluate children who are at risk for becoming psychotic. Although Anthony has utilized this instrument as part of an ongoing research program, the variables are, nonetheless, organized into clinically meaningful categories that can serve as a useful guide in clinical assessment.

Crow (1978) developed a 450 item scale to measure risk. A summary score, the *Early Identification Index,* purportedly estimates the probability of an unfavorable outcome. The child is rated on severity of cognitive and perceptual disturbances, sensory deficits, social maladjustment, physical disorders, psychosomatic distress, and family difficulties. In addition, neurotic complaints and emotional disturbances are recorded. Each symptom is subsumed into one of five problem areas: physical/organic, emotional, social, environmental, and academic. Although the construct and predictive validity of this instrument have not been established, it does, nonetheless, afford an opportunity for the clinician or teacher to obtain a profile on the child in multiple areas of functioning.

In summary, there are presently no available standardized and validated instruments that can be routinely employed to assess vulnerability and quantitatively ascertain risk. Therefore, clinical judgment is usually the basis of the decision whether to initiate prevention and early intervention in high risk children. It is hoped, as more is learned about the quantitative relationships between vulnerability and outcome variables, that greater objectivity and validity in assessment and prediction will evolve.

Outcome prediction

Because of the effort and expense involved in the assessment process, it is essential that a commitment be made to monitor the child's social, emotional, and academic progress during the course of development. With a longitudinal approach, outcome can be charted as a process, rather than as an event, such as hospitalization or imprisonment. Unfortunately, there is no formal organizational structure in society to facilitate a long term involvement with the child who shows signs of future maladjustment.

Four possible associations between vulnerability and outcome can be described on a 2 × 2 grid. Children of high or low vulnerability are at risk for either a favorable or an unfavorable outcome. A favorable outcome is implied by the individual's capacity to meet diverse environmental demands without adverse somatic and emotional consequences. Such persons can be said to have mastered their environment. Of particular interest are those individuals who, despite a vulnerability, can somehow make a successful social and emotional adjustment. Little is known, however, of the factors that compensate for a vulnerability, although a supportive home environment has been found to militate against the effects of perinatal injury (Werner & Smith, 1977) or of physical and psychological abuse (Kadushin, 1970).

To date, studies of outcome have considered only unfavorable or negative consequences. Apart from the effort of Jahoda (1958), in which positive aspects of mental health and personal growth were emphasized, little research has been directed to elucidating the factors that determine healthy outcome. At the macrosystem level of health care policy and delivery, progress has been made by legislation that regulates environmental quality, housing standards, and distribution of drugs, alcohol, and tobacco. The purpose of this type of legislation is to promote lifestyles that increase work productivity, attenuate the risk for disease, and augment opportunities for pleasurable and healthy leisure activities. In effect, such legislation is a form of primary prevention directed to an entire population, taking into consideration the interaction of human biology, life-style, and environmental quality (Lalonde, 1974).

The harbingers of an unfavorable outcome, on the other hand, have been studied to some extent. Morris and his colleagues (Morris, Soroker & Burvass, 1954) followed 54 fearful, anxious, introverted children and found that only two of them had significant coping problems as adults, although 15 subjects admitted to some persisting social and vocational problems. Waldron (1976) found that outcome evaluated at 22 years of age did not distinguish neurotic and phobic children. After combining the neurotic and phobic subjects into one group and comparing them to a normal group, it was observed that 15% of the normal group reported mild disturbances in comparison to 75% of the neurotic-phobic group. Of the neurotic-phobic group, 12% suffered severe disturbances, of which the most frequent diagnoses were personality disorder and psychosis. No control subjects exhibited a severe psychiatric or behavioral disturbance. Gardner (1967) noted a sex difference in the outcome of neurotic disorders. High remission rates were observed in females, but male children were at risk for developing schizophrenia. Coolidge, Brodie, and Feeney (1964) conducted a 10-year follow-up of phobic children and found that 34 of the 47 children who could be located had some form of adjustment difficulty. Of those exhibiting severe difficulties, ten had a character disorder, three were borderline psychotic, and one was overtly psychotic.

These investigations indicate that a neurotic or phobic diagnosis in childhood may be ameliorated or, alternatively, may evolve into a more severe type of disorder in adulthood. The diagnosis of sociopathy, on the other hand, tends to remain stable over time (Robins, 1966). Morris, Escoll, and Wexler (1956) found that about two-thirds of their sample of aggressive children were still poorly adjusted at 18 years of age. Glueck and Glueck (1948) examined criminal behavior in 9- to 17-year-old boys and noted that 34% of them were arrested at least once a year between the ages of 17 and 25. They also found that 19% were arrested at least once a year between the ages of 23 and 31 years, confirming that antisocial conditions are more likely to persist and remain diagnostically constant.

The factors responsible for a change in diagnostic status are poorly understood. Discontinuity, or a change in diagnostic status, was found in almost one-half of 200 child guidance cases (Cass & Thomas, 1979). Those most likely to change were the least disturbed; the most disturbed children were the least prone to change. The loss of a parent before age six and a broken home were more frequent occurrences in the most disturbed group. Impulsiveness, poor relationships with adults, accident proneness, and resistiveness were also more prevalent in the most disturbed group. Not surprisingly, persistence of the initial diagnosis was found mainly in the psychotic and antisocial conditions, whereas in the neurotic disturbances the diagnosis changed.

With respect to continuity, three general conclusions can be tentatively drawn. First, antisocial behavior in childhood places a youngster at high risk for a similar disorder in adulthood. Second, the prognosis for the neurotic disorders is fairly good, but a small proportion of children develop more severe disturbances in adulthood. Third, schizophrenia may have both continuous and discontinuous characteristics. Asarnow (Chapter 7) has observed certain "micropsychotic" features in high risk children, whereas others report only relatively benign features such as depression, dependency, and submissiveness (Bower & Skillhammer, 1960) or traits such as negativism, defiance and irritability (Watt, 1974).

Subsequent chapters will systematically address the major psychiatric disorders. As will be seen, a rapidly evolving literature indicates that the predisposition to these disorders is rather specific. It will also be observed that very little is known about the factors that could militate against a negative outcome in vulnerable individuals. Once an understanding of the relationship between vulnerability and outcome is obtained, an empirical basis for prevention and intervention could then be practical.

References

Anthony, E. A risk-vulnerability intervention model of children of psychotic parents. In E. J. Anthony & C. Koupernik (Eds.), *The child in his family: Children at psychiatric risk* (Vol. 3), New York: Wiley, 1974.

Bower, E. & Skillhammer, T. School characteristics of male adolescents who later become schizophrenic. *American Journal of Orthopsychiatry*, 1960, *30*, 712–729.

Bowlby, J. Separation anxiety. *International Journal of Psychoanalysis*, 1960, *41*, 89–113.

Buchsbaum, M., Coursey, R., & Murphy, D. The biochemical-high risk paradigm: Behavioral and familial correlates of low platelet monoamine oxidase activity. *Science*, 1976, *194*, 339–341.

Buss, A., Plomin, R., & Willerman, L. The inheritance of temperament. *Journal of Personality*, 1973, *41*, 513–524.

Cantwell, D. Familial-genetic research with hyperactive children. In D. Cantwell (Ed.), *The hyperactive child: Diagnosis, management, current research*. New York: Spectrum Publications, 1975.

Cantwell, D. & Mattison, R. The prevalence of psychiatric disorder in children with speech and language disorder. *Journal of the American Academy of Child Psychiatry*, 1979, *18*, 459–461.

Cass, L. & Thomas, C. *Childhood pathology and later adjustment: The question of prediction*. New York: Wiley, 1979.

Clark, M. *Reading difficulties in schools*. London: Pergamon Press, 1970.

Coolidge, J., Brodie, R., & Feeney, B. A ten-year follow-up study of sixty six school phobic children. *American Journal of Orthopsychiatry,* 1964, *34,* 675–689.

Costello, A. Deprivation and family structure with particular reference to twins. In E. J. Anthony, C. Koupernik, & C. Chiland (Eds.), *The child in his family* (Vol. 4), New York: Wiley, 1978.

Cowen, E., Pederson, A., Babigian, H., Izzo, L., & Trost, A. Long term follow-up of early detected vulnerable children. *Journal of Consulting and Clinical Psychology,* 1973, *41,* 438–446.

Crow, G. *Children at risk.* New York: Schocken Books, 1978.

Crowe, R. An adoption study of antisocial personality. *Archives of General Psychiatry,* 1974, *31,* 785–791.

Dales, R. Motor and language development of twins during the first three years. *Journal of Genetic Psychology,* 1969, *114,* 263–271.

Ferinder, W. & Jacobson, S. Early identification of learning disabilities. *Journal of Learning Disabilities,* 1970, *3,* 589–593.

Floderus-Myrhed, B., Pederson, N., & Rasmuson, J. Assessment of heritability for personality based on a short form of the Eysenck Personality Inventory: A study of 12,898 twin pairs. *Behavior Genetics,* 1980, *10,* 153–162.

Fries, M. & Woolf, P. The influence of constitutional complex on developmental phases. In J. McDevitt & C. Saltlage (Eds.), *Separation-individuation.* New York: International Universities Press, 1971.

Fulker, D. The genetic and environmental architecture of psycheticism, extraversion and neuroticism. In H. Eysenck (Ed.), *A model for personality.* New York: Springer, 1980.

Gardner, G. The relationship between childhood neurotic symptomatology and later schizophrenia in males and females. *Journal of Nervous and Mental Diseases,* 1967, *144,* 97–100.

Glueck, S. & Glueck, E. *Juvenile delinquents grown up.* New York: The Commonwealth Fund, 1948.

Goodwin, D. *Is alcoholism hereditary?* New York: Oxford University Press, 1976.

Heineman, O., Slone, D., & Shapiro, S. *Birth defects and drugs in pregnancy.* Acton, MA: Publishing Sciences Group, 1977.

Jahoda, M. *Current concepts of positive mental health.* New York: Basic Books, 1958.

Kadushin, A. *Adopting older children.* New York: Columbia University Press, 1970.

Kearsley, R. Iatrogenic retardation: A syndrome of learned incompetence. In R. Kearsley & I. Sigel (Eds.), *Infants at risk: Assessment of cognitive functioning.* Hillsdale, NJ: Lawrence Erlbaum Associates, 1979.

Lalonde, M. *A new perspective on the health of Canadians: A working document.* Ottawa: Government of Canada, 1974.

Mathey, A., Dolan, A., & Wilson, R. Twins with academic learning problems: Antecedent characteristics. *American Journal of Orthopsychiatry,* 1976, *46,* 464–469.

Mellsop, G. Psychiatric patients seen as children and adults: Childhood predictors of adult illness. *Journal of Child Psychology and Psychiatry*, 1972, *13*, 91–101.

Morris, H., Escoll, P., & Wexler, R. Aggressive behavior disorders of childhood: A follow-up study. *American Journal of Psychiatry*, 1956, *112*, 991–997.

Morris, D., Soroker, E., & Burvass, G. Follow-up studies of shy, withdrawn children. I. Evaluation of later adjustment. *American Journal of Orthopsychiatry*, 1954, *24*, 743–754.

Mulligan, G., Douglas, J., Hamond, W., & Tizard, J. Delinquency and symptoms of maladjustment: The findings of a longitudinal study. *Proceedings of the Royal Society of Medicine*, 1963, *56*, 1089–1096.

Niswander, K. & Gordon, M. *The collaborative perinatal study of the National Institute of Neurological Diseases and Stroke: The women and their pregnancies*. Philadelphia: Saunders, 1972.

Omolulu, A. Nutritional factors in the vulnerability of the African child. In E. J. Anthony & C. Koupernik (Eds.), *The child in his family: Children at psychiatric risk* (Vol. 3), New York: Wiley, 1974.

Parnell, R. Physique and mental breakdown in young adults. *British Medical Journal*, 1957, *1*, 1485–1490.

Pasamanick, B. & Knoblock, H. Epidemiological studies on the complications of pregnancy and the birth process. In G. Caplan (Ed.), *Prevention of mental disorders in children*. New York: Basic Books, 1961.

Phillips, L. *Human adaptation and its failure*. New York: Academic Press, 1968.

Plomin, R. & Rowe, D. Genetic and environmental etiology of social behavior in infancy. *Developmental Psychology*, 1979, *15*, 62–72.

Ricks, D. & Berry, J. Family and symptom patterns that precede schizophrenia. In M. Roff & D. Ricks (Eds.), *Life history and research in psychopathology* (Vol. 1), Minneapolis, MN: University of Minnesota Press, 1970.

Robins, L. *Deviant children grown up*. Baltimore: Williams & Wilkins, 1966.

Rutter, M., Tizard, J., & Whitmore, K. *Education, health and behavior*. London: Longman Group Limited, 1970.

Schuckit, M. & Rayes, V. Ethanol ingestion: Differences in blood acetaldehyde concentrations in relatives of alcoholics and controls. *Science*, 1979, *203*, 54–55.

Seligman, M. *Helplessness*. San Francisco: Freeman, 1975.

Serwer, B., Shapiro, B., & Shapiro, P. Achievement prediction of "high risk" children. *Perceptual and Motor Skills*, 1972, *35*, 347–354.

Skaberne, B., Blejec, M., Skalar, V., & Voopivec, K. Criminal prevention and elementary school children. *Revue de Criminologie*, 1965, *16*, 8–14.

Streissguth, A., Landesmann-Dwyer, S., Martin, J., & Smith, D. Teratogenic effects of alcohol in humans and laboratory animals. *Science*, 1980, *209*, 353–361.

Thomas, A., Chess, S., & Birch, H. *Temperament and behavior disorders in children*. New York: New York University Press, 1968.

Ullman, C. Teachers, peers and tests as predictors of adjustment. *Journal of Educational Psychology*, 1957, *48*, 257–267.

Waldron, S. The significance of childhood neurosis for adult mental health. *American Journal of Psychiatry*, 1976, *133*, 532–538.

Walker, R. Body build and behavior in young children. *Monographs of the Society for Research in Child Development*, 1962, 27, 1–94.

Watt, N. Childhood and adolescent routes to schizophrenia. In D. Ricks & A. Thomas (Eds.), *Life history research in psychopathology* (Vol. 3), Minneapolis, MN: University of Minnesota Press, 1974.

Weintraub, S., Liebert, D., & Neale, J. Teacher ratings of children vulnerable to psychopathology. In E. J. Anthony, C. Kupernik, & C. Chiland (Eds.), *The child in his family* (Vol. 4), New York: Wiley, 1978.

Werner, E. & Smith, R. Kauai's children come of age. Honolulu, HI: University of Hawaii Press, 1977.

Winokur, G., Cadoret, R., Dorzab, J., & Baker, M. Depressive disease: A genetic study. *Archives of General Psychiatry*, 1971, *24*, 135–144.

2. Methodology of high risk research: Genetic approaches[1]

Brian Suarez, John Rice, and Theodore Reich

The elucidation and evaluation of risk factors are important aspects of genetic research. Indeed, much contemporary research in genetic epidemiology is directly concerned with identifying groups of individuals at high risk for specific diseases and, additionally, with identifying biological and environmental variables that increase risk. Familiar examples abound. For instance, Ashkenazi Jews are at high risk for Tay-Sachs disease, whereas Africans are at high risk for sickle-cell anemia. Individuals homozygous for the alpha-1-antitrypsin-deficient allele, Pi^z, are at high risk for emphysema, whereas persons carrying the *HLA B-27* allele are at high risk for ankylosing spondylitis. As regards environmental risk factors, the association between exposure to asbestos or tobacco smoke and lung cancer is a familiar example.

From a genetic perspective, the notion of "risk" has two sometimes ambiguous meanings. First, it may refer to the demonstration that a disorder is familial and heritable in the sense that it is transmitted via the gametes. But it is also possible that transmission, although familial, is entirely cultural. Second, it may refer to factors in an epidemiological sense. Here we have in mind statements like "Risk factor X is necessary (or sufficient) for disease state Y" or "Risk factor X is associated with illness Z, although it is neither sufficient nor necessary." These two no-

[1] This work has been supported, in part, by USPHS grants GM 28067, MH 14677, MH 31302, MH 25430, and AA 03539.

15

tions of "risk" are not mutually exclusive and, indeed, their intersection may be the most interesting genetic aspect of a disorder.

General risk paradigm

Before proceeding to a discussion of current methods used to detect the presence of a genetic component in any particular disorder, it is appropriate to develop a general paradigm that can be used to assess relative risk.

In the usual case, an investigator is presented with two classes of individuals—those affected with the disorder and those not affected with it. There are any number of independent variables that could be important in predisposing to (or even directly causing) the disorder, and it is the investigator's responsibility to ferret out those that are important among those that are unimportant or related to the disease only spuriously.

Here D denotes the presence of the disease and ~D its absence and, similarly, "+" the presence of the putative risk factor and "−" its absence, and the data are usually displayed in a 2 × 2 table as follows.

		Disease Status	
		D	~D
Hypothesized risk factor	+	a	b
	−	c	d

The cell entries can be either the actual sample sizes (i.e., $a + b + c + d = N$) or percentages ($a + b + c + d = 1$). The relative risk (RR) is defined as

$$RR = \frac{P(D|+)}{P(D|-)} = \frac{a/(a+b)}{c/(c+d)}$$

That is, RR is the conditional probability of having the disease, given the presence of the risk factor, divided by the conditional probability of having the disease, given the absence of the risk factor.

Another important measure of association is the odds ratio (or cross product ratio defined by

$$\alpha = \frac{a/b}{c/d} = \frac{ad}{bc}$$

Thus, α is the odds in favor of D when the risk factor is present divided by the odds in favor of D when the risk factor is absent, so that α will be 1 if there is no relationship between the disease and the alleged risk factor. Note that

$$\alpha = RR \times \frac{[1 + (a/b)]}{[1 + (c/d)]}$$

so that $\alpha = RR$ if the disease has a low frequency whether the risk factor is present or absent. Moreover, α has the property of being independent of the marginal frequencies and so is invariant under alternative sampling schemes.

Often, risk studies will be carried out using either a prospective or a retrospective design. In a prospective study, two samples are selected on the basis of the presence or absence of the risk factor and then followed up to establish the incidence of the disease in each group (i.e., the row marginals are fixed in the above table). Both RR and α may be computed in this design, although measures such as the phi coefficient are inappropriate due to the fixed marginal frequencies. Prospective studies have the disadvantages that large samples are necessary if the disease is rare and that the length of time required for the study can be excessive if there is a long period between exposure to the risk factor and manifestation of the disease. These difficulties may be avoided by using a retrospective design, in which the samples are selected on the basis of the presence or absence of the disease (i.e., the column marginals are fixed in the above table), and the presence or absence of the (antecedent) risk factor is determined. However, RR cannot be estimated without additional knowledge about the disease incidence, although α may be estimated. In both types of designs, other characteristics are often matched to control for extraneous factors, as in a case-control study. The reader is referred to Fleiss (1973) and Susser (1978) for a more thorough statistical treatment of risk from an epidemiological viewpoint.

From a genetic point of view, the putative risk factor in the relative risk paradigm can be some measurement on the patient's family. Indeed, a consistent finding in studies of many complex developmental traits is that more of the patient's relatives than expected have similar traits. Consequently, a positive family history can be the best predictor of risk, even when premorbid characteristics of an individual are considered. A familiar example is that the risk for developing schizophrenia jumps from under 1% in the general population to about 10% when one parent is affected and to about 44% when both parents are affected (Slater & Cowie, 1971).

In general, however, the quantitative models used in genetics may be used to predict the risk for a family member, so that such association measures as RR or α are not as commonly used as in epidemiological studies.

The use of family studies

From a genetic–epidemiological point of view, psychiatric disorders can be thought of as the tip of an iceberg—the exposed peak is the observable phenotype. Beneath, however, lies the bulk of iceberg's mass, and it is this region about which we wish to make inferences (Figure 2-1). With respect to the observable phenotypes, geneticists have somewhat arbitrarily distinguished two categories—phenotypes that are discrete (Figure 2-1a) or appear discrete, depending on one's perception (Figure 2-1b), and phenotypes that are continuously distributed (Figure 2-1c). The argument can be advanced that most behavioral disorders are of the latter variety, that is, persons differ by degree not kind, but because of distributional features nosologists find it convenient to classify the disorder as either present or absent. At any rate the classification of traits into the categories discrete versus continuous has a long-standing tradition, historically spawned, no doubt, by two competing schools of thought (Provine, 1971; Froggatt & Nevin, 1971).

An individual's phenotype represents the end product of a complex sequence of events, which, for many disorders, ultimately depends on a person's genotype and the environment in which the genotype grows. It is the province of genetic epidemiology to sort out the risk factors that lead to disease. It is worth stressing from the outset, however, that genes and their products do not operate in a vacuum and that for even the simplest Mendelian diseases non-genetic factors may play an important role, as illustrated, for instance, by the fact that phenylketonuria homozygotes can be spared the consequences of their genotype if their diet is free of phenylalanine.

Correct diagnosis is the first step in any investigation of risk. And, although this statement seems self-evident, it is often difficult in practice to obtain a correct diagnosis. Even when the phenotype of interest is clinically uniform in its appearance, there is no assurance that it is homogeneous in its etiology. Indeed, the problem of heterogeneity for the com-

GENETIC ICEBERGS

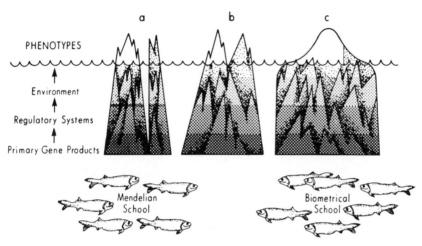

Fig. 2–1. In the early years of this century, an intense battle raged between two schools of geneticists. It centered on the evolutionary significance each school attached to the importance of heritable discrete variation versus heritable continuous variation. The two schools were eventually reunited by Sir Ronald Fisher's synthesis, here illustrated, that human disease (the stippled region above the waterline) can be due to a single gene that results in an aberrant gene product (a) or due to the compound effect of many genes that give rise to a deviant phenotype (c). The clinical perception of many disease states, however, strongly depends on environmental circumstances as can be seen in panel (b) by raising or lowering the water level.

mon diseases is one of the most troublesome problems in clinical genetics. That heterogeneity can be important is obvious from a consideration of mental subnormality in which separate autosomal genes are known to be operative in some cases (e.g., phenylketonuria and Tay-Sachs disease), X-linked genes in others (e.g., hypoxanthineguanine phosphoribosyltransferase in Lesch-Nyhan syndrome), chromosomal aberrations in others (e.g., Down's syndrome and cri-du-chat syndrome), and environmental factors in still others (e.g., brain damage from anoxia). From a consideration of family patterns, it is clear that there are probably other X-linked forms and an even larger reservoir of undifferentiated polygenically caused cases.

A "family pattern" has been used to detect heterogeneity in a number of disorders. For instance, the finding that retinitis pigmentosa can be caused by an autosomal gene in some, by an autosomal recessive in others, and by an X-linked gene in still others was demonstrated not by distinguishing subtle differences in the phenotype, but rather by observing that heterogeneity is present in the transmission pattern. Of course, there is a certain danger in relying solely on transmission pattern to detect heterogeneity, since for most non-Mendelian disorders—regardless of their mode of inheritance—it is usually possible to select families that appear to be segregating a dominant gene or a recessive gene or even an X-linked gene by judiciously choosing an appropriate ascertainment rule. Once homogeneous subgroups are selected (with respect to familial transmission pattern), it becomes very difficult to test the heterogeneity hypothesis without ancillary information.

Genetic strategies

We will somewhat arbitrarily consider two classes of diseases: those that are discrete and those that are continuously distributed, since the methodology used depends, to a certain extent, on the distribution of the character. We will consider two classes of observational units: family units, both nuclear and extended, and smaller, more restrictive units—which include monozygotic and dizygotic twins and sib-pairs. Figure 2-2 schematically shows this cross-classification layered according to the purpose of the investigation. One can envision the natural course of events proceeding from the top layer down. One first wants to establish whether the disorder is familial. Once the disorder is shown to be familial, it is necessary to determine if the transmission of the disorder is genetic or cultural (or perhaps both). Adoption and cross-fostering studies are necessary to be confident that transmission is genetic rather than cultural for all but the simplest Mendelian disorders. If adoption studies reveal a genetic component, then linkage analysis may be used to map the relevant genes. If adoption studies indicate that transmission is largely cultural, then it is appropriate to look for environmental risk factors to which the proband's affected relatives have been exposed. We hasten to point out that with respect to any given methodology these layers are not always mutually exclusive. In what follows we will illustrate the various methodologies that are represented by the layered cross-classification of Figure 2-2.

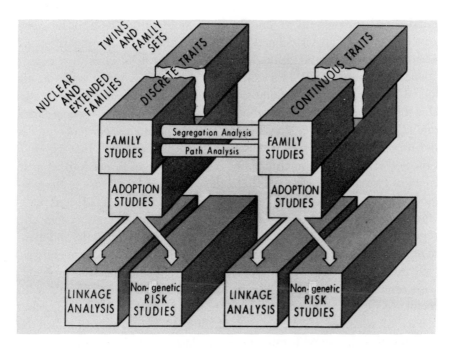

Fig. 2–2. Representation of steps necessary to establish a genetic component for human diseases. Segregation analysis and path analysis can be employed with discrete and continuously distributed phenotypes.

Twin studies

Undoubtedly, the favorite unit—which is more restrictive than the nuclear family—for genetic analysis is twins. Ever since Sir Francis Galton (1876) suggested using twins as "a criterion of the relative powers of nature and nurture," their study has grown. Since monozygotic (MZ) twins are genetically identical and dizygotic (DZ) twins share, on average, only one-half of their genes, it seemed almost self-evident that their comparisons would yield a simple technique to determine if a given disorder is heritable. Indeed, since DZ twins are contemporaries (*in utero,* and subsequently), the allure of the comparison appears all the more forceful. Accordingly, for discrete disorders, MZ and DZ twins have been compared by calculating a concordance rate (Allen & Hrubec, 1979).

A number of different methods are used to compute concordance rates, and it is important to specify which method is used if confusion is to be avoided (Allen, Harvald, & Shields, 1967; Smith, 1970, 1974). The *case-wise* concordance rate is defined as the proportion of *cases* (regardless of whether they are found through a register or in field work as a consequence of being sought as a co-twin of a registered twin) with an affected co-twin. If C is the number of cases with an affected co-twin and D is the number with unaffected co-twins, then the casewise concordance rate (C_c) is $C/(C + D)$. The corresponding *pairwise* concordance rate is the proportion of *pairs* in which both twins are affected, that is, $\frac{1}{2}C/(\frac{1}{2}C + D)$. These two measures are related, since each concordant pair contains two affected cases. Perhaps the most useful measure is the *probandwise* concordance rate, defined as the proportion of affected individuals among the co-twins of previously ascertained (i.e., specifically registered) probands. If C^* is the number of concordant *pairs* independently ascertained through both affected twins, then the probandwise concordance rate (C_p) is $(C + C^*)/(C + C^* + D)$. Since the probandwise concordance rate is a rate in co-twins, it may be compared with incidence rates in the general population and those derived from other classes of relatives (Gottesman & Shields, 1972). In short, it can be thought of as a casewise rate corrected downwards for mode of ascertainment. The usual finding in a twin study of a genetically conditioned trait, regardless of the method used, is that the concordance rate in MZ twins is greater than that in DZ twins. This finding must always be interpreted with caution, however, since the environmental similarity for MZ pairs is surely greater than for DZ pairs. Identical twins reared apart and adoption strategies can sometimes be used to resolve this problem.

When continuously distributed traits are studied, an index of similarity is computed, and, as with measures of concordance rates, a number of different indices have been proposed. Osborne and DeGeorge (1959) suggest a comparison of the intrapair variance with the interpair variance. If X_1 and X_2 are the values for the first and second members of a twin pair, respectively, then the intrapair variance is

$$V_W = \Sigma \frac{(X_1 - X_2)^2}{2N} \quad df = N$$

and the interpair variance is

$$V_B = \frac{1}{(N-1)} \frac{\Sigma (X_1 - X_2)^2}{2} - \frac{[\Sigma(X_1 - X_2)^2]}{2N} \quad df = N - 1$$

For each type of variance, MZ twins can be compared to DZ twins. Additionally, these variance components can be used to calculate the intraclass correlation coefficient (r), defined as

$$r = \frac{V_B - V_W}{V_B + V_W}$$

This is a convenient statistic, since it is related to the heritability (h^2) as $h^2 = r/R$, where R is the coefficient of genetic relationship; R is unity for MZ's and one-half for DZ's. Other estimates of h^2 are available that allow for environmental contributions to the phenotypic similiarities. For instance, $2(r_{MZ}\text{-}r_{DZ})$ estimates the broad sense heritability as long as there is not appreciable dominance variance.

Another statistic in general use is the so-called coefficient of genetic determination (H) defined as

$$H = \frac{V_{DZ} - V_{MZ}}{V_{DZ}}$$

where V_{DZ} and V_{MZ} are the means of the squares of the differences between members of DZ pairs and MZ twin pairs, respectively.

That neither simple concordance rates, nor the H statistic, is necessarily an adequate measure of the role of heredity is clear from a consideration of the assumptions underlying the twin approach. To the extent that the environmental influences on the two types of twins are not equivalent and to the extent that genotype-environment interactions are present, both simple concordance rates and the H statistic can grossly overestimate the importance of genetic factors. In short, comparison of MZ twins and DZ twins is an efficient way to determine quickly if there are familial factors—be they genetic or environmental—but without ancillary information and, in particular, without adoption studies, the comparison may be misleading.

Single major locus models

These models are used to determine if the observed population variation in some trait and its distribution within families is due, principally or entirely, to allelic variation at a single major locus. Although these models are usually applied to traits with a discrete distribution, they may be just as applicable to continuously distributed traits.

PHENOTYPES

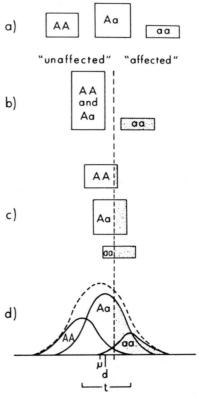

Fig. 2–3. The two allele autosomal locus model. (a) Co-dominant phenotypes, (b) Mendelian recessive transmission, and (c and d) two formulations of the incompletely penetrant single locus model. The quantities μ, d, and t are parameters from the formulation of Morton et al., 1971 (see text for description).

For ease of exposition we will only consider diallelic loci with alleles, A and a, that have respective population frequencies of p and $q = (1 - p)$. The simplest case occurs when the probability of a particular phenotype given a particular genotype is either one or zero (Figure 2-3a). With just two alleles, the above relationship can maximally give rise to three distinct phenotypes, each corresponding to a fixed genotype. Classic Mendelian transmission occurs when two of the genotypes (AA and Aa or aa and Aa) give rise to identical phenotypes (Figure 2-3b). In this setting, the population consists of two phenotypes, affected and unaffected, and the disorder is considered dominant or recessive depending on whether or not the heterozygote is affected. When an investigator suspects that a disorder is transmitted in this fashion, then simple segregation analysis should be used.

In this Mendelian case, the recurrence risk among families (the so-called "segregation" frequency) is assumed to be constant. The validity of the model is verified by demonstrating that the recurrence risk is three-quarters or one-quarter for intercross matings (i.e., $Aa \times Aa$) and one-half for backcross matings (i.e., $Aa \times aa$) depending on whether the dis-order is transmitted as a dominant or a recessive.

To the extent that there is a variable age of onset in the expression of the phenotype as in, for instance, Huntington's chorea, empirical recur-rence risks are apt to be less than their Mendelian expectations and an appropriate correction needs to be made.

Another important complication is the bias introduced by ascertaining a family through an affected individual. Ascertainment refers to the method used to gather families for genetic analysis. And although it is most important in testing segregation ratios, it can have important impli-cations for epidemiological studies as well. To illustrate the potential con-founding effect that ascertainment bias can exert, consider a disorder that is inherited as a simple rare recessive. The simplest design is to study all affected persons in a given population. This sampling strategy is called "complete" in the sense that no affected individual is missed. What will be missed, however, are intercross families that could segregate affected offspring, but, by chance, have not. A sample of sibships will be ascer-tained in which unaffected but otherwise at risk sibships will not be rep-resented. In other words, among all sibships from intercross matings, the ascertained sample will be truncated by virtue of the fact that only sib-ships containing *at least* one affected sib will be included. Were we to compute the segregation ratio from our biased sample, we would obtain an estimate larger than the theoretically expected value of one-quarter. A number of correction procedures have been developed when ascertain-ment is complete; these are the *a priori* (direct) method (Hogben, 1931), the maximum likelihood method (Haldane, 1938), and the so-called "sin-gles" method (Li & Mantel, 1968).

Studies in which ascertainment is close to complete are the exception rather than the rule. When only a fraction of a population's affected mem-bers are sampled in such a way that each sibship contains one and only one proband, then ascertainment is said to be "incomplete." When the proportion of sampled affecteds is small compared to the total number of all affected members in the population, then ascertainment is said to be "single." Consequently, the probability of ascertaining a given family will be proportional to the number of affected individuals in the family. Fisher (1934) devised the so-called "sib" method to correct for the bias introduced by single incomplete ascertainment. This correction, however, often underestimates the true segregation parameter (Li, 1961).

The usual situation is when ascertainment is somewhere between complete and single incomplete. Then ascertainment is said to be multiple incomplete; interestingly, this was the first situation dealt with in a rigorous way (Weinberg, 1912). Refinements for the method of multiple incomplete ascertainment can be found in Fisher's (1934) "probability of ascertainment" parameter and in Bailey (1951) and Morton (1959).

It is often the case that an investigator may not know the precise mode of ascertainment or, for that matter, which affected family members are probands and which are secondary cases. This is especially true when families are culled from the literature, and when many of the families originally appeared as case reports because they were unusual. In this situation, the segregation ratio can be computed first under the assumption that ascertainment is complete and then under the assumption that it is single incomplete. The true value should be somewhere between these two estimates.

The simple two-allele model can be generalized to include those cases where the probability of the phenotype, conditional on the genotype, is neither one nor zero. Two formulations of this more general model are shown in Figure 2-3. In Figure 2-3c, each genotype has a fixed probability of giving rise to an affected phenotype. No assumptions concerning the distribution of liability within a genotype are made (Suarez et al., 1976). This general model is defined by four parameters—the gene frequency (q) and the three penetrances (f_1, f_2, and f_3). That this model is indeterminant when only frequency data are available is readily seen by defining three useful quantities, the population prevalence (K) of the disorder

$$K = p^2 f_1 + 2pq f_2 + q^2 f_3$$

the loci's additive variance (V_A)

$$V_A = 2pq[q(f_3 - f_2) + p(f_2 - f_1)]^2$$

and the loci's dominance variance (V_D)

$$V_D = p^2 q^2 (f_1 - 2f_2 + f_3)^2$$

James (1971) showed that the frequency of the disorder in the jth class of relatives (K_{R_j}) can always be expressed as

$$K_{R_j} = K + \frac{u_j V_A + v_j V_D}{K}$$

where u_j and v_j are constants determined by the class of relatives (see Table 2-1). Accordingly, an infinite number of parameter sets (q, f_1, f_2, f_3) can lead to the same frequencies in relatives. This indeterminancy of the model can be overcome when two or more thresholds are discernible (Reich, James, & Morris, 1972).

A slightly different formulation of the single major locus model—and one that is easily generalized to continuous traits—posits a separate continuous distribution for each of the three genotypes. Each distribution is assumed to be normal and homoscedastic (Figure 2-3d). The model is defined by four parameters: the overall mean of the continuous distribution (μ); the gene frequency; the distance between the mean of the heterozygote distribution and the overall mean (d); and the distance between the means of the two homozygote distributions (t). In the version of this model formulated by Morton and his colleagues, this last parameter is expressed in phenotypic standard deviations, not in terms of the standard deviation within each of the major locus genotypes as in some other formulations. The model can be used for dichotomous traits by imposing one threshold, graded traits (multiple thresholds), or continuous traits (no thresholds). Moreover, the model can be used with complex

Table 2-1. Coefficients of V_A and V_D for various classes of relatives.

Relationship	u	v
Monozygotic twins	1	1
Dizygotic twins, full sibs	1/2	1/4
Parent-child	1/2	0
Double first cousins, quadruple half first cousins	1/4	1/16
Half-sibs, grandparent-grandchild aunt(uncle)-niece(nephew)	1/4	0
First cousins	1/8	0
Double second cousins	1/16	1/64
Spouse, stepchild	0	0

segregation analysis to allow for the possibility that recurrence risks are variable among families. This is desirable since segregation analysis can be inverted to give recurrence risks in kindred with a particular structure, thereby allowing the recurrence risk to be predicted from the full weight of the analyzed kindred rather than the usually less specific empirical risk (Morton, Yee, & Lew, 1971; Lalouel, 1978).

Complex segregation analysis can, at least in principle, be extended to large multiple generation pedigrees. With respect to any particular disorder, a single large pedigree is probably more likely to be homogeneous than a collection of nuclear families. Elston and Stewart (1971) developed a general method of expressing the unconditional likelihood of any arbitrarily large pedigree that can allow for such modifications as nonrandom ascertainment and consanguineous matings (Elston, 1973; Elston & Yelverton, 1975; Elston et al., 1975; Lange & Elston, 1975).

The detection of a major single locus has profound implications for genetic counseling. This is especially true for recessively inherited disorders, since, once this mode of transmission has been established, it is reasonable to attempt to develop a diagnostic test capable of detecting heterozygous carriers. For a growing number of Mendelian diseases, carriers can now be distinguished from normal homozygotes (e.g., the lysosome storage diseases and the mucopolysaccharidoses), although not always with 100% accuracy (Table 2-2).

When carriers can be unambiguously diagnosed, the calculation of the recurrence risk is straightforward. In the absence of enough information, or when the distribution of carriers overlaps the distribution of normal homozygotes, every effort should be made to base the estimate of the re-

Table 2-2. Some important diseases in which carriers can be detected.

Disorder	Method of carrier detection
Lesch-Nyhan syndrome	Hypoxanthine-guanine phosphoribosyl-transferase assay
Duchenne-type muscular dystrophy	Creatine phosphokinase assay
Hemophilia A	Anti-hemophilic globulin (Factor VIII)
Galactosemia	α-D-Galactose-1-phosphate-uridyl transferase
Sickle cell anemia	Hemoglobin electrophoresis
Tay-Sachs disease	Hexosaminidase A assay
B-thalassemia	Hemoglobin A-2 assay and erythrocyte morphology
Familial hypercholesterolemia	Receptor assay
Type III hyperlipoproteinemia	VLDL Apo E

currence risk on as much information as the pedigree can provide. The preferred approach is to use Bayes' theorem. In general we wish to estimate the probability of some event E, given some observation O, that is, $P(E|O)$. We usually know the prior probability of E and its complement not E ($\sim$E), as well as the probability of the observation given the event, that is, $P(O|E)$ and its conditional complement $P(O|\sim E)$. Using elementary probability theory and recalling that the joint probability $P(O, E)$ can be expressed as $P(O) \, P(E|O)$, we find the posterior probability as

$$P(E|O) = \frac{P(E) \, P(O|E)}{P(E) \, P(O|E) + P(\sim E) \, P(O|\sim E)}$$

In the usual counseling setting, the event E is the probability that a child will be affected, whereas O may be any observation on the affectational status of the pedigree or ancillary information concerning the parents' score on a test that only imperfectly detects heterozygosity.

To illustrate the use of the Baysian approach, consider the family shown in Figure 2-4. The consultand's brothers (II-1 and II-4) have Du-

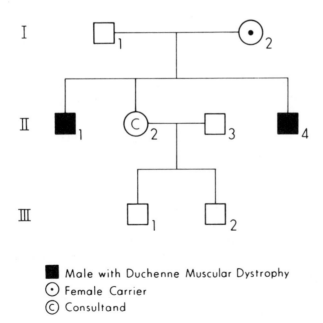

Male with Duchenne Muscular Dystrophy
Female Carrier
Consultand

Fig. 2–4. Pedigree segregating Duchenne muscular dystrophy, an X-linked recessive.

Table 2-3. Bayesian calculation for the pedigree shown in Figure 2-4. The family is segregating Duchenne muscular dystrophy, an X-linked recessive.

	Assuming consultand is	
	Carrier	Not a carrier
A		
Prior probability	1/2	1/2
Conditional probability	1/4	1
Joint probability	1/8	1/2
Posterior probability	$\dfrac{1/8}{1/2 + 1/8} = .2$	$\dfrac{1/2}{1/2 + 1/8} = .8$
B		
Prior probability	.2	.8
Conditional probability	1/3	19/20
Joint probability	.067	.76
Posterior probability	$\dfrac{.067}{.067 + .76} = .08$	$\dfrac{.76}{.067 + .76} = .92$

chenne-type muscular dystrophy. This is an X-linked recessive disorder that is fully penetrant in hemizygous males. Had the consultand not had any sons, her probability of being a carrier would be one-half, *a priori*. Taking into account the fact she has already produced two normal boys, the posterior probability that she is a carrier is one-fifth (Table 2-3a). We can complicate this example slightly by assuming that the consultand had a biochemical test to determine her serum level of the enzyme creatine phosphokinase (CPK) and that it is found to be below the 95th percentile of the normal distribution. Emery (1965) has shown that two-thirds of all obligate heterozygotes have values of CPK higher than the 95th percentile. This information can be incorporated into the risk analysis (Table 2-3b). We build on the results obtained from the earlier analysis by taking as our estimate of the prior probability that the consultand is a carrier, the old posterior value of 0.2. Now, conditioning on the results obtained from the biochemical assay, we see that the new posterior probability that she is a carrier is only 8%. The analysis can be made even more sophisticated by incorporating the probability that the muscular dystrophy of the consultand's brothers resulted from two *de novo* mutations. Since both brothers are affected, however, this probability is too small to alter the conclusions materially.

Genetic counseling is a burgeoning field and much work remains to be done, not only on how counseling might alter the gene pool of our species, but also on the psychological correlates for those seeking consultation and their families. A good account of calculation methods for counseling can be found in Murphy and Mutalik (1969) and Murphy and Chase (1975). For a discussion of the psychological aspects of making a reproductive choice after counseling, the interested reader should consult Lippman-Hand and Fraser (1979a, b).

It is important to note that in the search for a major gene—whether pursued in large extended pedigrees or in observations on small nuclear families—segregation analysis is quite sensitive to distributional assumptions. Continuously varying phenotypes skewness, for instance, can simulate a major gene when none exists; its removal, however, via an appropriate transformation, can attenuate the evidence when a major locus is present (MacLean, Morton, & Lew, 1975; MacLean, Morton, Elston, & Yee, 1976).

The multifactorial model

Traits such as blood pressure, height, IQ, and total cholesterol level show continuous variation, in contrast to the natural discontinuities observed in such Mendelian traits as albinism or blood groups. Since quantitative traits exhibit a continuous range of variation with individuals differing in degree rather than type, the genes involved are distinguished by the relative magnitudes of their effects. Thus, PKU is a recessive disease in which there is an inability to convert phenylalanine to tyrosine, which leads to mental retardation. Even though PKU is a Mendelian character, within the distributions of phenylalanine blood levels for normals and homozygous recessives there is quantitative variation (resulting, no doubt, from environmental factors and genes of small effect), but these distributions are separated by 13 standard deviations so that the clinically relevant variation is determined by the major locus (Cavalli-Sforza & Bodmer, 1971).

Conversely, continuous traits often have Mendelian subforms. For example, achondroplasia (a type of dwarfism) is a Mendelian dominant disorder that affects height. However, since it is rare (about 1/10,000 births), it would not be important in a study of height in the general population, and knowledge gained about "normal" height does not contribute insight into the understanding of achondroplasia.

Thus, the distinction between a Mendelian trait and a continuous trait is not always clear cut and depends upon both the focus of investigation and the population studied. Some current approaches simultaneously allow for a major locus with a heritable background (Morton & MacLean, 1974) and are appropriate when both types of variation are important.

Multifactorial inheritance and heritability

The study of continuous (or metric) traits requires the statistical models of quantitative or biometrical genetics (Falconer, 1960; Kempthorne, 1957). Since the segregation of individual genes is not discernible, the continuous trait P, which is measured, is called the phenotype, and it is assumed that P may be partitioned as

$$P = G + E$$

where G is the genetic value of the individual and E is the environmental deviation from his genetic value. In the multifactorial model, it is further assumed that the genes that contribute to the development of P are each of small effect and act additively, so that the statistical distribution of P is Gaussian in the population. The genetic value itself may be partitioned into a part that is additive (A) and the deviation from additivity (D), referred to as dominance, so that (1) becomes

$$P = A + D + E$$

The narrow heritability h^2 and the dominance variance d^2 are the proportion of the variability of P that is due to A and D, respectively, so that

$$h^2 = V_A/V_P \tag{2}$$

and

$$d^2 = V_D/V_P \tag{3}$$

The broad heritability is defined as V_G/V_P and, in the absence of interaction effects, is equal to $h^2 + d^2$. The parent-offspring correlation r_{po} and the full sibling correlation r_{oo} are given by

$$r_{po} = \tfrac{1}{2}\, h^2 \tag{4}$$

and

$$r_{oo} = \tfrac{1}{2}\, h^2 + \tfrac{1}{4}\, d^2 \tag{5}$$

Consequently, parent-offspring and sibling observations are sufficient to estimate h^2 and d^2, if we assume, of course, that the genetic model chosen is correct.

The techniques of quantitative genetics have been very successful in the area of animal and plant breeding where h^2 measures the response to selection (since d^2 is not involved in r_{po}, it does not influence the response when selecting parents). However, the usefulness of the concept of heritability for human traits has been seriously questioned (Feldman & Lewontin, 1975; Kempthorne, 1978) for two reasons. The first involves the interpretation of h^2. From equation (2) we see that h^2 is defined as a variance component, which applies to a population with those specific G and E distributions, and does not directly address how environmental changes would affect the mean of P. For example, suppose a group of children receive a uniformly poor diet, the trait P is adult weight, and h^2 may be large due to the lack of environmental variability. Even though the trait is "genetic" in the sense of high h^2, the mean of P may be increased simply by better nutrition.

Again, in the model described above, it is assumed that the environmental components between a parent and offspring and between two siblings are uncorrelated. The term E above may be partitioned as $E = E_c + E_w$ (see Falconer, 1960), where E_c is that portion common to a sibship so that r_{oo} is augmented by V_{E_c}/V_P. The consideration of parent–offspring environmental similarity will be discussed below. Since it is not possible to randomize environments in human studies experimentally, investigators have relied on the compatibility of parameters for nuclear families with those of adoptive, half-sib, or twin families in order to estimate h^2.

Nonetheless, the observed high degree of family resemblance for many developmental and behavioral phenotypes, coupled with the likelihood that many factors, both genetic and environmental, contribute to an individual's phenotype, make the multifactorial model a plausible model for examining such phenotypes. However, in human studies the final goal is not to estimate h^2, but rather to provide a theoretical framework for more rigorous analysis.

Multifactorial inheritance for quasi-continuous traits

A quasi-continuous trait is one for which there is an underlying continuous variable for which phenotypic effects can be measured only within

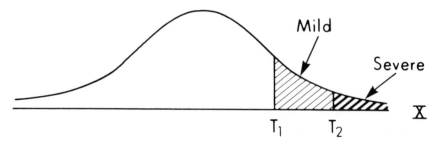

Fig. 2–5. The multifactorial model assumes a normally distributed liability scale, shown here truncated at two points and giving rise to three apparently discrete phenotypes (normal, mildly affected, and severely affected).

certain ranges. Such a trait may arise when there is an underlying continuous process, but individuals can be classified only as "affected" or "unaffected," or they may be graded as "mild" or "severe." The underlying variable is termed the *liability scale* and is assumed Gaussian with one or more threshold values as in Figure 2-5.

In Figure 2-5, the liability scale X has two threshold values, T_1 and T_2, and an individual with score x is (a) unaffected if $x < T_1$, (b) mildly affected if $T_1 < x < T_2$, and (c) severely affected if $x > T_2$. If the prevalences of the subforms of the disorder are known for the general populations, then the threshold values may be directly estimated using tables of normal deviates (e.g., if the prevalence of severe illness were 2.5%, then T_2 would equal 1.96). This model has been described (Carter, 1965; Falconer, 1965, 1967; Reich, James, & Morris, 1972; Reich, Cloninger, & Guze, 1975; Curnow & Smith, 1975). Kidd et al. (1973) have allowed for different liability distributions for males and females, and Reich, Cloninger, Wette, & James (1979) have allowed for correlated liability distributions to resolve phenotypic heterogeneity. A mathematically equivalent formulation may be obtained by replacing the concept of the abrupt threshold T by a Gaussian statistical distribution with mean T.

Similarity between relatives is quantified by the correlations in liability between family members, and the concept of heritability above may be applied to the liability distribution. These correlations may be estimated using the tetrachoric correlation coefficient (Kendall & Stuart, 1973) from the affectional status of relatives.

Accordingly, approaches such as the path analytic models described below for quantitative traits are applicable also to qualitative threshold traits by simply including the thresholds as additional parameters.

Path analysis

Path analysis is a technique introduced by Wright (1921) as a method to explain the interrelationship among variables by analyzing their correlational structure. The relationships among the variables of a model are depicted by a path diagram as in Figure 2-6, where each variable is assumed to be standardized with mean 0 and variance 1. Single-headed arrows indicate the direct influence of one variable (an independent variable) on another (the dependent variable). In addition, curved double-headed arrows may be used to indicate correlations between independent variables. Path coefficients are standardized partial regression coefficients and are associated with each single-headed arrow, thereby measuring the change in the dependent variable per unit change in that independent variable when all other independent variables are held constant. The correlation between any two variables in the diagram may be easily obtained by tracing all paths between the variables that do not pass through the same variable twice, that do not contain adjacent arrow heads (e.g., $\leftarrow$A$\rightarrow$), and that do not contain two double-headed arrows as described by Li (1975).

Figure 2-6 depicts the resemblance between a father (F), a mother

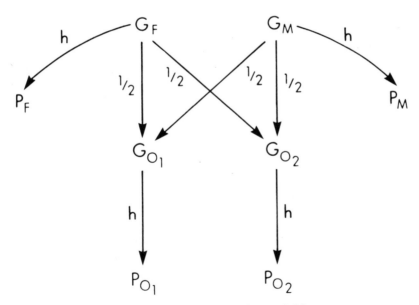

Fig. 2–6. Path diagram of a nuclear family with two children.

(M), and two offspring (O_1 and O_2) for the multifactorial model without dominance deviation. The path coefficients between the genetic values of parental offspring are one-half and the path coefficient between G and P is h (the square root of heritability). The corresponding path equations are

$$P = hG + \sqrt{1 - h^2}\, E \qquad (6)$$

and

$$P_{Oi} = \tfrac{1}{2}G_F + \tfrac{1}{2}G_M + \tfrac{1}{2}\sqrt{2}S \qquad (7)$$

where the residual S is segregation from midparent genetic value. For convenience, the residual terms E and S are omitted from the diagram, since they do not contribute to family resemblance. Using the rules of path analysis, we have $r_{po} = r_{oo} = \tfrac{1}{2}h^2$, in agreement with equations (4) and (5), since we are assuming here that $d^2 = 0$.

Path models of cultural inheritance

Over the past decade, much work has been done in modeling cultural transmission, i.e., the vertical transmission of environmental factors between parent and offspring. Such transmission may be effected by social learning and modeling or by parents teaching their offspring certain customs and preferences. This work includes that of Cavalli-Sforza and Feldman (Cavalli-Sforza & Feldman, 1973, 1978; Feldman & Cavalli-Sforza, 1977, 1979), Morton (1974), Rao, Morton, & Yee (1974, 1975), Cloninger, Rice, & Reich (1979a, b), and Rice, Cloninger, & Reich (1978, 1980, 1981). These models provide a rigorous framework for examining familial resemblance without *a priori* excluding either genetic or cultural transmission. Path analysis has proven a useful tool in formulating these models and in providing a statistical methodology for data applications.

One approach has been the generalization of equation (6) to the form

$$P = hG + bB + eE$$

where B denotes environmental factors transmissible from parent to offspring according to the path equation

$$B_O = \beta_M B_M + \beta_F B_F + rR$$

The path coefficients β_M and β_F measure the influences of the mother's $B(B_M)$ and the father's $B(B_F)$ on the B of the offspring (B_O). In addition, the models allow for the nontransmissible environments of siblings reared together to be correlated and, moreover, they allow for phenotypic assortative mating. (See Cloninger et al., 1979a, b; Rice et al., 1980; Cavalli-Sforza & Feldman, 1978.) Cavalli-Sforza and Feldman (1978) also allow for direct paths between the phenotypes of parents and offspring.

Another approach has been not to explicitly separate genetic and cultural factors, but rather to consider them combined into a single variable (Rice et al., 1978). When individuals are reared in intact nuclear families, there can be a complete confounding of genetic and transmissible environmental factors so that the proportion of each type of variation cannot be estimated without separation or adoption data. Rice et al. (1980) and Karlin (1979a, b, c, d) have described models in which transmission from parent to offspring depends upon the sex of the parent and upon the sex of the offspring. Transmission from parents to an offspring of sex i may be described by

$$T_{0i} = \tau_{1i}T_1 + \tau_{2i}T_2 + r_iR_i$$

where T_{0i}, T_1, and T_2 denote the transmissible factors of an offspring of sex i, the father, and the mother, respectively. Rice et al. (1980) describe the following submodels: (a) the Maternal Effects Model given by $\tau_{11} = \tau_{12}$, $\tau_{21} = \tau_{22}$; (b) the Daughter Effects Model given by $\tau_{11} = \tau_{21}$, $\tau_{12} = \tau_{22}$; (c) the Cross Effects Model given by $\tau_{11} = \tau_{22}$, $\tau_{12} = \tau_{21}$, and (d) the Environmental Model given by $\tau_{11} = \tau_{12} = \tau_{21} = \tau_{22}$. This approach allows the testing of specific cultural mechanisms and provides a model for investigating the sex differences observed in many behavioral traits.

Rao et al. (1974, 1976) have advocated the simultaneous use of environmental indices along with family phenotypic data. With this approach, it may be possible to create and validate environmental or other relevant types of indices that measure specific components of a given phenotype. Such goals may prove to be the most important ones in applying quantitative genetic models to human data, with the estimation of such parameters as heritability only a necessary intermediate step.

Adoption and half-sib studies

The nature–nurture controversy has been a major concern of psychiatrists and psychologists since the turn of the century. At that time, the rediscovery of Mendelism resulted in an enthusiastic wave of family studies that purported to illustrate a genetic etiology for psychiatric illness. This point of view was further bolstered by many extensive twin studies that showed that with respect to the major psychiatric disorders, MZ twins were more often concordant than DZ twins (Slater & Cowie, 1971). Opponents of this "genetic" view claimed that the increased MZ twin concordance might be the consequence of shared environmental factors and often ignored this large body of data and the support it offered for a genetic interpretation.

Since the mid-1960's, a series of exciting studies have offered renewed support for the view that genetic factors are important in the etiology of many of the major psychiatric disturbances. These studies have tested the hypothesis that the familial aggregation of psychiatric disorders does not disappear if a parent and an offspring are separated, by adoption, at birth. Adoption studies have been conducted for schizophrenia (Heston & Denney, 1968; Kety, Rosenthal, Wender, & Schulsinger, 1968), alcoholism (Goodwin, Schulsinger, Hermansen, Guze, & Winokur, 1973; Bohman, 1978), bipolar affective disorder (Mendelwicz & Rainer, 1977), antisocial personality (Crowe, 1975), and criminality (Hutchings & Mednick, 1977). In each case, the biological parents were apparently able to transmit their own specific psychiatric disturbance to their adopted-away offspring. In most cases, this was independent of the presence or absence of psychiatric illness in the foster parents.

The separation strategy

A typical adoption study begins with the selection of a sample of individuals who suffer a psychiatric disturbance (biological parents) and whose children have been given up for adoption at an early age. The offspring are then followed up after they have become adults, and the foster parents are also studied. The frequency of illness in the offspring is contrasted with a matched control group made up of the adopted-away offspring of parents who are not psychiatrically ill. If the affected biological parents are able to transmit the disorder to their adopted-away offspring, then the inference is drawn that genetic transmission has occurred. It is crucial that the foster parents of both groups be closely matched, since they are required to show persuasively that the adoption process itself does not increase the risk for psychopathology. If postnatal social or psychological factors are responsible for the transmission of a psychiatric disturbance, then the adopted-away offspring will more closely resemble their foster parents than their biological parents.

Most adoption studies have shown that adopted-away offspring of psychiatrically ill biological parents are significantly more often affected by the same psychiatric disturbance as their parents when compared with a control sample of adoptees and, moreover, that genetic factors are important in transmission of the disorder. Rarely is an attempt made to measure the relative influence of the genetic factors. Although this type of study does not "prove" that environmental factors are not important, it highlights the fact that genetic factors must be operating.

The number of hpyotheses that can be tested in an adoption study may be extended by contrasting the degree of familial aggregation of the illness in the adopted families with its degree in nuclear families. For example, the hypothesis that affected parents can transmit a psychiatric disturbance to offspring equally well, whether or not the affected individual rears the child, can be tested. If the hypothesis is proven, then the inference is that transmission is entirely the consequence of genetic factors and not the social or psychological consequence of the particular form of the psychopathology manifested in the ill parents.

As noted above, the question of whether the process of being adopted away can cause an increase in psychiatric illness can be tested by comparing the frequency of psychiatric illness in the adopted-away offspring of healthy parents with the frequency of illness in non-adopted offspring of healthy parents. Adoption by itself has not been shown to cause psychiatric illness.

The hypothesis that a biological defect and defective parenting are both required for the transmission of a psychiatric illness can be tested by examining the adopted-away offspring of psychiatrically ill biological parents reared in homes in which the adoptive parents have the same illness.

It should be noted that hypotheses tested by the adoption strategy pertain to the transmission of specific psychiatric disorders rather than a general tendency for the transmission of amorphous psychological disturbances. Schizophrenic parents, for instance, tend to have a large proportion of schizophrenic offspring regardless of whether or not they are reared in non-schizophrenic foster homes (Heston & Denny, 1968).

Separation experiments can be also used to test hypotheses about the non-genetic transmission of psychiatric disturbances. For example, the frequency of illness in offspring who have been given up for adoption at birth may be contrasted with the frequency of illness in offspring who are older at adoption. Using this strategy, it has been shown that being reared for 6 or 12 months by an antisocial or alcoholic parent enhances the transmission of these disorders, even when the children are later adopted into non-antisocial or non-alcoholic homes (Crowe, 1975; Cloninger et al., 1981). The implication here is that some additional tendency to develop these disorders is transmitted from mother to child in the first year of life. By contrast, no such environmental factor has been discovered for schizophrenia (Gottesman & Shields, 1976).

The experimental design of adoption studies is variable in that affected individuals who had been adopted away early in life may be chosen as probands. If they are, the study requires that the biological and the adoptive parents be examined to determine whether biological or non-biological transmission has occurred. Alternately, full and half sibs of psychiatrically ill, adopted-away individuals may be studied to determine whether a parental biological factor is responsible for the familial aggregation of the disorder.

The possibility that transmission of a psychiatric disorder from parent to offspring is the consequence of an abnormal uterine environment or maternal cytoplasmic factors, rather than genetic factors, has been tested by comparing the biological, adopted-away offspring of ill fathers with those of ill mothers. No support for these hypotheses has yet been found. Indeed, a genetic interpretation has been strengthened in an adoption study of schizophrenia that compared the frequency of illness in the half sibs of adopted-away offspring of schizophrenic probands. Transmission could be observed whether or not the affected biological parent was male or female (Kety, Rosenthal, Wender, Schulsinger, & Jacobsen, 1975).

Sources of bias in adoption studies

Psychiatrically ill individuals who give their offspring up for adoption are not representative of all psychiatrically ill individuals. It is likely that they are younger and more severely ill.

Another potential source of bias is selective placement. Agencies may attempt to match adoptive and biological parents in order to provide a "natural" environment for the offspring. In general, however, adoption agencies attempt to avoid psychopathology in the adoptive parents, and so severe psychopathology in this group is rare.

Perhaps the most important source of uncertainty in adoption studies is their small size. Since the adoption study requires some sort of psychiatric registry and the availability of accessible records for cross-indexing affected individuals and adoptees, the sample is often severely restricted. Accordingly, only a limited range of hypotheses can be tested.

Future directions of adoption studies

An important advance in adoption methodology has recently been reported by Cloninger, Bohman, & Sigvardsson (1981), who analyzed a large sample of parents and offspring placed with non-relatives at an early age. Factors relevant to the familial transmission of alcohol abuse were studied using discriminant analysis. They showed that

multiple genetic and environment factors made additive contributions to risk. Assortative placement and gene-environment correlation had a minor effect. Classification of alcohol abuse according to severity defined clinically overlapping but distinct subgroups. These groups were distinguished by severity and age of onset of alcohol abuse, criminality in the biological parents, and by unstable placements during the first year of life.

Confirmation of the importance of these factors in the transmission of alcohol abuse in non-adoptive nuclear families awaits the study of a comparable non-adoptive population.

The study of half-sibs

The widespread use of contraception and abortion has greatly reduced the population of adopted individuals. However, the increasing frequency of divorce offers a much larger population of subjects who may serve in studying gene-environment interaction. The population of individuals who are half-sibs is increasing and should enable separation studies to continue. Specifically, half-sibs share one biological parent, but it is usually the mother who is responsible for their rearing. Accordingly, some psychiatrically ill individuals may be the offspring of an ill father and a healthy mother, and be reared by a healthy stepfather and their biological mother. A study of these families can determine whether the presence or absence of a psychiatrically ill biological parent is important in the concordance of half-sibs. Of course, the role of assortative mating needs to be closely scrutinized in this setting.

There are many permutations of the half-sib strategy in which the affected individual may be an absent biological parent, a common biological parent, or a foster or stepparent. These combinations offer an excellent opportunity for testing both qualitative and quantitative hypotheses about the relative importance of genetic and non-genetic factors and their interaction in mental illness.

Shuckit, Goodwin, and Winokur (1972) used the half-sib strategy to test the hypothesis that alcoholism might be the consequence of a genetic factor as well as environmental factors. They showed the development of alcoholism in a son of an alcoholic biological parent, although he was reared in a home with no alcoholic parents. The presence of a genetic factor was suggested.

A great deal of work needs to be done before the quantitative analysis of the "half-sib family" is fully understood. There are many potential sources of bias, such as assortative mating, complex and unstable rearing patterns, and maternal effects.

Adoption and half-sib studies have greatly enhanced our understanding of the etiology of many psychiatric disorders. Specific transmission of psychiatric illnesses has been observed, and genetic factors have been identified. Experimental designs for the testing of more specific hypotheses about genetic factors, environmental factors, and gene-environment interaction are being developed and show great promise.

Linkage analysis

Once a disorder has been shown to have a substantial genetic component (top two layers of Figure 2-2), it is appropriate to try to map the responsible gene(s), if not to a particular chromosomal region, then to an unassigned linkage group. There is some disagreement over whether linkage analysis, per se, is useful in *identifying* genetic components (compare, for instance, Elston & Rao, 1978, or Botstein, White, Skolnick, & Davis, 1980, to Morton, 1962). Although it is clear that, for purely environmental reasons, segregation of certain traits can appear Mendelian (Lilienfeld, 1959), it is unlikely that environmental factors could mimic linkage. Nonetheless, it is probably the case that unless the character is determined by at least one locus of major effect, linkage analysis will prove less than profitable.

From a risk point of view, the importance of establishing linkage is obvious, as therein lies the prospect of early identification and, under appropriate circumstances, clinical intervention. If Huntington's chorea, for instance, is found to be tightly linked to a polymorphic marker, then knowledge of the marker phenotype of an "at risk" person, e.g., the offspring of a Huntington's chorea patient, could allow their identification prior to the disorder's onset. Such pre-morbid detection can occur pre-natally with amniocentesis, as has been done for myotonic dystrophy because of its linkage to the secretor locus (Schrott, Karp, & Omenn, 1973). In addition to its potential for identifying persons who are at risk, linkage analysis can reveal genetic heterogeneity. The demonstration by Morton (1956), for instance, that dominantly inherited elliptocytosis can be caused by either of two loci, only one of which is linked to the Rh blood groups, is a notable example.

A large number of linkage methodologies differ depending on the nature of the disorder (discrete vs. continuous) and the type of family units required (sib-pairs vs. nuclear and extended families).

Sib-pairs

The notion that sib-pairs can be used to detect linkage is due to Penrose (1935), and despite the relatively low power of this approach as com-pared, for instance, with maximum likelihood approaches in pedigrees, it is noteworthy that the first autosomal linkage detected in man—the Lutheran blood group-secretor linkage group—was discovered using Penrose's sib-pair method (Mohr, 1951). This method is based on the striking realization that evidence of linkage can be obtained from data on just one generation without reference to parental mating types. With respect to two dichotomous traits, pairs of sibs are arrayed into a 2×2 table according to whether they are like or unlike.

	First Trait Locus	
Second Trait Locus	like	unlike
like	a	b
unlike	c	d

In practice, one of the trait loci is usually a marker that shows Mendelian inheritance. If the two traits are determined by linked loci, then there should be an excess of sib-pairs in cells *a* and *d*. The simplicity of this approach is purchased at the expense of including many sib-pairs from families that cannot segregate, and their inclusion weakens the evidence for linkage. Unfortunately, since parents are not studied, sib-pairs from non-segregating families cannot be removed from the analysis.

In an attempt to increase the power of sib-pair analysis, a number of new approaches have been proposed. These have in common the use of sib-pairs that are ascertained because both are affected with the disorder under study (Day & Simons, 1976; Suarez, 1978; Fishman et al., 1978).

The affected sib-pair method uses perturbations in the distribution of identity by descent (IBD) scores at a marker locus to detect the presence of a linked disease susceptibility locus. In the absence of linkage, the probability that two sibs share neither, one, or both marker alleles identical by descent is independent of their disease phenotypes. Consequently, if pairs of sibs are studied because they are both affected, the distribution of their IBD scores will be ¼, ½, and ¼ for IBD = 0, 1, and 2, respectively. This is easily seen in the toy Punnett square of Figure 2-7 where, for the sake of simplicity, it is assumed that the disorder under investigation is transmitted as a Mendelian recessive (i.e., $Pr[\text{affected}|\text{genotype}$ is $A_1A_1] = 1$ and 0 otherwise). In an intercross mating (both parents heterozygotes), an affected child will come from one of the four cells labeled "*d*" and his genotype at the marker locus will be M1M3, M1M4, M2M3, or M2M4, each with a probability of one-quarter. If this individual has an affected sib, then that person necessarily also comes from cell "*d*," but with respect to the marker locus could have any one of the four marker genotypes. There are altogether 16 combinations for the affected sib-pair and each combination has an equal probability of occurring. Of such sib-pairs, 25% will share both marker alleles *IBD*, 50% will share one allele *IBD*, and the remaining 25% will share neither marker *IBD*. In other words, the fact that the sibs were chosen because they are both affected has not altered the *IBD* distribution at the marker locus in the absence of linkage.

By contrast, the situation shown in the lower Punnett square of Figure 2-7 (where, for simplicity, linkage is assumed to be complete) is quite different, since, by virtue of their affectational status, both sibs must be M2M4 at the marker and thus have an *IBD* score of 2. In other words, the ascertainment procedure (i.e., selecting sibs both of whom are affected) has altered their *IBD* distribution at the marker locus as the

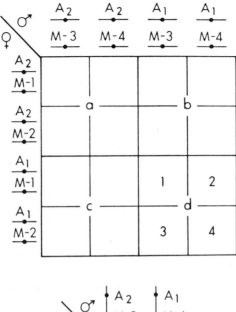

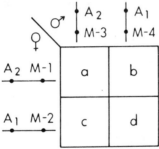

Fig. 2–7. Top, when a trait locus (A_1, A_2) is unlinked to a marker locus ($M1$-4), selection of sib-pairs because of their phenotype at the former locus will not alter their *IBD* distribution at the latter locus. Bottom, when the two loci are linked, ascertainment of affected sib-pairs will result in a marked shift in the number of marker alleles inherited identical by descent.

two loci are linked. The mating type shown in Figure 2-7 for the two-allele disease susceptibility locus is only one of the six possible, and some of these are uninformative for linkage (e.g., $A_2A_2 \times A_2A_2$). The size of the deviation depends on the heritability of the disorder under study and the tightness of the linkage (Suarez et al., 1978). This approach is especially useful for HLA-linked disorders. When the A, B, C, D, and

Dr specifications are all typed, the extensive HLA polymorphism almost always guarantees complete *IBD* information without typing parents. For diseases like insulin-dependent diabetes mellitus, young unaffected sibs who happen to share both HLA haplotypes in common with one or more affected sibs are at especially high risk and should be followed closely (Suarez et al., 1979).

Penrose (1938) suggested that his sib-pair method could be used when the trait (and the marker, for that matter) is continuously distributed, but relatively few applications have been made to human data (Kloepfer, 1946; Brues, 1950; Howells & Slowey, 1956). Haseman and Elston (1972) developed a different approach that also uses sib-pairs. They allow multiple alleles at the marker locus, but assume that the quantitative trait is determined by only two alleles. Their approach has enjoyed only limited application (see, for instance, Pakstis, Scarr-Salapatek, Elston, & Siervogel, 1972), perhaps because a large sample of sib-pairs is required (Robertson, 1973). In an attempt to obtain greater power to detect loci contributing to a continuous trait, Hill (1975) developed an analysis of variance design that uses information from larger sibships. Other sibship approaches include Jayakar's (1970) and Smith's (1975) nonparametric test.

Modern approaches

We have considered approaches to the detection of linkage that rely on units smaller than the nuclear family. For nuclear families and larger extended families, the method of choice is clearly maximum likelihood. Haldane and Smith (1947), modifying a proposal by Bell and Haldane (1937), employed a probability ratio approach. Essentially, the method consists of determining the amount of information available in a collection of data on two loci and comparing the probability of obtaining such a family if the two loci are linked with a given recombination fraction, $\hat{\theta}$, to the probability if they are not (i.e., $\theta = \frac{1}{2}$). The maximum likelihood approach was considerably improved when Morton (1955), using the sequential probability ratio test of Wald (1947), devised a system of lod scores (i.e., log of the odds). This sequential approach was shown to require, on average, fewer observations than the backward odds approach.

An efficient computer program (Ott, 1974) implementing the algorithm of Elston and Stewart (1971) has been developed for linkage analysis and is now in general use. The program has recently undergone important refinements, which allow, for instance, incorporation of an age of onset correction (Hodge, Morton, Tideman, Kidd, & Spence, 1979). Although the LIPED computer program has enjoyed greatest use with discrete traits (Human Gene Mapping, 4, 1977), it can be used for continuously distributed traits assumed to result from a single major locus. Simulation studies have shown, however, that unless the differences between the mean values of the two homozygotes is greater than about twice the standard deviation of the total phenotype, linkage will seldom be detected (Lange, Spence, & Frank, 1976).

References

Allen, G. & Hrubec, Z. Twin concordance: A more general model. *Acta Geneticae Medicae et Gemellologiae*, 1979, *28*, 3–13.

Allen, G., Harvald, B., & Shields, J. Measures of twin concordance. *Acta Geneticae Medicae et Gemellologiae*, 1967, *17*, 475–481.

Bailey, N. The estimation of the frequencies of recessives with incomplete multiple selection. *Annals of Eugenics*, 1951, *16*, 215–222.

Bell, J. & Haldane, J. The linkage between the genes for colour-blindness and hemophilia in man. *Proceedings of the Royal Society, London, Series B*, 1937, *123*, 119–150.

Bergsman, D. (Ed.). *Winnipeg Conference, 4th International Workshop on Human Gene Mapping*, Winnipeg, August, 1977.

Bohman, M. Some genetic aspects of alcoholism and criminality: A population of adoptees. *Archives of General Psychiatry*, 1978, *35*, 269–276.

Botstein, D., White, R., Skolnick, M., & Davis, D. Construction of a genetic linkage map in man using restriction fragment length polymorphisms. *American Journal of Human Genetics*, 1980, *32*, 314–331.

Brues, A. Linkage of body build with sex, eye color, and freckling. *American Journal of Human Genetics*, 1950, *2*, 215–239.

Carter, C. The inheritance of common congenital malformations. *Progress in Medical Genetics*, 1965, *4*, 59–84.

Cavalli-Sforza, L. & Bodmer, W. *The genetics of human populations*. San Francisco: W. H. Freeman, 1971.

Cavalli-Sforza, L. & Feldman, M. Models for cultural inheritance. I. Group mean and within group variation. *Theoretical Population Biology*, 1973, *4*, 42–55.

Cavalli-Sforza, L. & Feldman, M. The evolution of continuous variation. III. Joint transmission of genotypic phenotype and environment. *Genetics*, 1978, *90*, 391–425.

Cloninger, C., Bohman, M., & Sigvardsson, S. Inheritance of alcoholism: Cross fostering analysis of adopted men. *Archives of General Psychiatry*, 1981, *38*, 864–868.

Cloninger, C., Rice, J., & Reich, T. Multifactorial inheritance with cultural transmission and assortative mating. II. A general model of combined polygenic and cultural inheritance. *American Journal of Human Genetics*, 1979a, *31*, 176–198.

Cloninger, C., Rice, J., & Reich, T. Multifactorial inheritance with cultural transmission and assortative mating. III. *Family structure and the analysis* of separation experiments. *American Journal of Human Genetics*, 1979b, *31*, 366–388.

Crowe, R. Adoption studies in psychiatry. *Biological Psychiatry*, 1975, *10*, 353–371.

Curnow, R. & Smith, C. Multifactorial models for familial diseases in man. *Journal of the Royal Statistical Society*, 1975, *138*, 131–169.

Day, N. & Simons, M. Disease susceptibility genes—their identification by multiple case family studies. *Tissue Antigens*, 1976, 8, 109–11.

Elston, R. Ascertainment and age of onset in pedigree analysis. *Human Heredity*, 1973, *23*, 105–112.

Elston, R. & Stewart, J. A general model for the genetic analysis of pedigree data. *Human Heredity*, 1971, *21*, 523–542.

Elston, R. & Rao, D. Statistical modeling and analysis in human genetics. *Annual Review of Biophysics and Bioengineering*, 1978, 7, 253–286.

Elston, R. & Yelverton, K. General models for segregation analysis. *American Journal of Human Genetics*, 1975, 27, 31–45.

Elston, R., Namboodiri, K., Glueck, C., Fallat, R., Tsang, R., & Leuba, V. Study of the genetic transmission of hypercholesterolemia and hypertriglyceridemia in a 195 member kindred. *Annals of Human Genetics*, 1975, *39*, 67–87.

Emery, A. Carrier detection in sex-linked muscular dystrophy. *Journal de Genetique Humaine*, 1965, *14*, 318–329.

Falconer, D. *Introduction to Quantitative Genetics*. New York: Ronald Press, 1960.

Falconer, D. The inheritance of liability to certain diseases, estimated from the incidence among relatives. *Annals of Human Genetics*, 1965, *29*, 51–76.

Falconer, D. The inheritance of liability to disease with variable age of onset, with particular reference to diabetes mellitus. *Annals of Human Genetics*, 1967, *31*, 1–20.

Feldman, M. & Cavalli-Sforza, L. The evolution of continuous variation. II. Complex transmission and assortative mating. *Theoretical Population Biology*, 1977, *11*, 161–181.

Feldman, M. & Cavalli-Sforza, L. Aspects of variance and covariance analysis with cultural inheritance. *Theoretical Population Biology*, 1979, *19*, 276–307.

Feldman, M. & Lewontin, R. The heritability hang-up. *Science*, 1975, *190*, 1163–1168.

Fisher, R. The effect of method of ascertainment upon the estimation of frequencies. *Annals of Eugenics*, 1934, *6*, 13–25.

Fishman, P., Suarez, B., Hodge, S., & Reich, T. A robust method for the detection of linkage in familial diseases. *American Journal of Human Genetics,* 1978, *30*, 308–321.

Fleiss, J. *Statistical methods for rates and proportions.* New York: Wiley, 1973.

Froggatt, P. & Nevin, N. C. The 'law of ancestral heredity' and the Mendelian-ancestrian controversy in England, 1889–1906. *Journal of Medical Genetice,* 1971, *8*, 1–36.

Galton, F. The history of twins as a criterion of the relative powers of nature and nurture. *Royal Anthropological Institute of Great Britain and Ireland,* 1876, *6*, 391–406.

Goodwin, D., Schulsinger, F., Hermansen, L., Guze, S., & Winokur, G. Alcohol problems in adoptees raised apart from alcoholic biological parents. *Archives of General Psychiatry,* 1973, *28*, 238–243.

Gottesman, I. & Shields, J. *Schizophrenia and genetics. A twin study vantage point.* New York: Academic Press, 1972.

Gottesman, I. & Shields, J. A critical review of recent adoption, twin and family studies of schizophrenia: Behavioral genetics perspectives. *Schizophrenia Bulletin,* 1976, *2*, 360–398.

Haldane, J. The estimation of the frequencies of recessive conditions in man. *Annals of Eugenics,* 1938, *8*, 255–262.

Haldane, J. & Smith, C. A new estimate of the linkage between the genes for colour-blindness and haemophilia in man. *Annals of Eugenics,* 1947, *14*, 10–31.

Haseman, J. & Elston, R. The investigation of linkage between a quantitative trait and a marker locus. *Behavior Genetics,* 1972, *2*, 3–19.

Heston, L. & Denney, D. Between early life experience and biological factors in schizophrenia. *Journal of Psychiatric Research* (Suppl. 1), 1968, 363–376.

Hill, A. Quantitative linkage: A statistical procedure for its detection and estimation. *Annals of Human Genetics,* 1975, *38*, 439–449.

Hodge, S., Morton, L., Tideman, S., Kidd, K., & Spence, M. Age-of-onset correction available for linkage analysis (LIPED). *American Journal of Human Genetics,* 1979, *31*, 761, 762.

Hogben, L. The genetic analysis of familial traits. I. Single gene substitutions. *Journal of Genetics,* 1931, *25*, 97–112.

Howells, W. & Slowey, A. "Linkage studies" in morphological traits. *American Journal of Human Genetics,* 1956, *8*, 154–161.

Hutchings, B. & Mednick, S. Criminality in adoptees and their adoptive and biological parents: A pilot study. In S. A. Mednick & K. O. Christiansen (Eds.), *Biosocial basis of criminal behavior.* New York: Gardner Press, 1977.

James, J. W. Frequency in relatives for an all-or-none trait. *Annals of Human Genetics,* 1971, *35*, 47–49.

Jayakar, S. On the detection and estimation of linkage between a locus influencing a quantitative character and a marker locus. *Biometrics,* 1970, *26*, 451–464.

Karlin, S. Models of multifactorial inheritance: I, Multivariate formulations and basic convergence results. *Theoretical Population Biology*, 1979a, *15*, 308–355.

Karlin, S. Models of multifactorial inheritance: II, The covariance structure for a scalar phenotype under selective assortative mating and sex-dependent symmetric parental-transmission. *Theoretical Population Biology*, 1979b, *15*, 356–393.

Karlin, S. Models of multifactorial inheritance: III, Calculation of covariance of relatives under selective assortative mating. *Theoretical Population Biology*, 1979c, *15*, 394–423.

Karlin, S. Models of multifactorial inheritance: IV, Asymmetric transmission of a scaler phenotype. *Theoretical Population Biology*, 1979d, *15*, 424–438.

Kempthorne, O. *An Introduction to genetic statistics.* Ames, Iowa: The Iowa State University Press, 1957.

Kempthorne, O. Logical, epistemological and statistical aspects of nature-nurture data interpretation. *Biometrics*, 1978, *34*, 1–23.

Kendall, M. & Stuart, A. *The advanced theory of statistics: Inference and relationship* (Vol. 2). New York: Hafner Publishing, 1973.

Kety, S., Rosenthal, D., Wender, P., & Schulsinger, F. The types and prevalence of mental illness in the biological and adoptive families of adopted schizophrenics. In D. Rosenthal & S. Kety (Eds.), *The transmission of schizophrenia.* Oxford: Pergamon, 1968.

Kety, S., Rosenthal, D., Wender, P., Schulsinger, F., & Jacobsen, B. Mental illness in the biological and adoptive families of adopted individuals who have become schizophrenic: A preliminary report based upon psychiatric reviews. In R. Fieve, D. Rosenthal, & H. Brill (Eds.), *Genetic research in psychiatry.* Baltimore: Johns Hopkins Press, 1975.

Kidd, K., Reich, T., & Kessler, S. The use of sex effect to discriminate between different genetic models. Presented at the Thirteenth International Conference of Genetics, Berkeley, California, 1973.

Kloepfer, H. An investigation of 171 possible linkage relationships in man. *Annals of Eugenics*, 1946, *13*, 35–71.

Lalouel, J. Recurrence risks on an outcome of segregation analysis. In N. E. Morton & S. S. Chung (Eds.). *Genetic Epidemiology.* New York: Academic Press, 1978.

Lange, K. & Elston, R. Extensions to pedigree analysis. I. Likelihood calculations for simple and complex pedigrees. *Human Heredity*, 1975, *25*, 95–105.

Lange, K., Spence, M., & Frank, M. Application of the lod method to the detection of linkage between a quantitative trait and a qualitative marker: A simulation experiment. *American Journal of Human Genetics*, 1976, *28*, 167–173.

Li, C. *Human genetics.* New York: McGraw-Hill, 1961.

Li, C. *Path analysis: A primer.* Pacific Grove, California: Boxwood Press, 1975.

Li, C. & Mantel, N. A simple method of estimating the segregation ratio under complete ascertainment. *American Journal of Human Genetics*, 1968, *20*, 61–81.

Lilienfeld, A. A methodological problem in testing a recessive genetic hypothesis in human disease. *American Journal of Public Health,* 1959, *49,* 199–204.

Lippman-Hand, A. & Fraser, F. Genetic counseling: Parent's responses to uncertainty. In D. Bergsma (Ed.), *Birth Defects, Original Article Series,* 1979a, *15,* 325–339.

Lippman-Hand, A. & Fraser, F. Genetic counseling—the postcounseling period: II. Making reproductive choices. *American Journal of Medical Genetics,* 1979b, *4,* 73–87.

MacLean, C., Morton, N., & Lew, R. Analysis of family resemblance. IV. Operational characteristics of segregation analysis. *American Journal of Human Genetics,* 1975, *27,* 365–384.

MacLean, C., Morton, N., Elston, R., & Yee, S. Skewness in commingled distributions. *Biometrics,* 1976, *32,* 695–699.

Mendelwicz, J. & Rainer, J. Adoption study supporting genetic transmission in manic-depression illness. *Nature,* 1977, *258,* 326–329.

Mohr, J. A search for linkage between the Lutheran blood groups and other hereditary characters. *Acta Pathologica et Microbiologica Scandinavica,* 1951, *28,* 207–210.

Morton, N. Sequential test for the detection of linkage. *American Journal of Human Genetics,* 1955, *7,* 277–318.

Morton, N. The detection and estimation of linkage between the genes for elliptocytosis and the Rh blood type. *American Journal of Human Genetics,* 1956, *8,* 80–96.

Morton, N. Genetic tests under incomplete ascertainment. *American Journal of Human Genetics,* 1959, *11,* 1–16.

Morton, N. Segregation and linkage. In W. J. Burdette (Ed.), *Methodology in human genetics.* San Francisco: Holden Day, 1962.

Morton, N. Analysis of family resemblance. I. Introduction. *American Journal of Human Genetics,* 1974, *26,* 318–330.

Morton, N. & MacLean, C. Analysis of family resemblance. III. Complex segregation of quantitative traits. *American Journal of Human Genetics,* 1974, *26,* 489–503.

Morton, N., Yee, S., & Lew, R. Complex segregation analysis. *American Journal of Human Genetics,* 1971, *23,* 602–611.

Murphy, E. & Chase, G. *Principles of genetic counseling.* Chicago: Year Book Medical Publishers, 1975.

Murphy, E. & Mutalik, G. The application of Bayesian methods in genetic counseling. *Human Heredity,* 1969, *19,* 126–151.

Osborne, R. & DeGeorge, F. *Genetic basis of morphological variation.* Cambridge: Harvard University Press, 1959.

Ott, J. Estimation of the recombination fraction in human pedigrees: Efficient computation of the likelihood for human linkage studies. *American Journal of Human Genetics,* 1974, *26,* 588–597.

Pakstis, A., Scarr-Salapatek, S., Elston, R., & Siervogel, R. Genetic contributions to morphological and behavioral similarities among sibs and dizygotic twins: Linkages and allelic differences. *Social Biology*, 1972, *19*, 185–192.

Penrose, L. The detection of autosomal linkage in data which consists of pairs of brothers and sisters of unspecified parentage. *Annals of Eugenics*, 1935, *6*, 133–138.

Penrose, L. Genetic linkage in graded human characters. *Annals of Eugenics*, 1938, *8*, 133–138.

Provine, W. B. *The Origins of theoretical population genetics*. Chicago: University of Chicago Press, 1971.

Rao, D., Morton, N., & Yee, S. Analysis of family resemblance. II. A linear model for familial correlation. *American Journal of Human Genetics*, 1974, *26*, 331–359.

Rao, D., Morton, N., & Yee, S. Resolution of cultural and biological inheritance by path analysis. *American Journal of Human Genetics*, 1976, *28*, 228–242.

Reich, T., James, J., & Morris, C. The use of multiple thresholds in determining the mode of transmission of semi-continuous traits. *Annals of Human Genetics*, 1972, *36*, 163–184.

Reich, T., Cloninger, C., & Guze, S. The multifactorial model of disease transmission. I. Description of the model and its use in psychiatry. *British Journal of Psychiatry*, 1975, *127*, 1–10.

Reich, T., Rice, J., Cloninger, C., Wette, R., & James, J. The use of multiple thresholds and segregation analysis in analyzing the phenotypic heterogeneity of multifactorial traits. *Annals of Human Genetics*, 1979, *42*, 371–390.

Rice, J., Cloninger, C., & Reich, T. Multifactorial inheritance with cultural transmission and assortative mating. I. Description and basic properties of the unitary models. *American Journal of Human Genetics*, 1978, *31*, 618–643.

Rice, J., Cloninger, C., & Reich, T. Analysis of behavioral traits in the presence of cultural transmission and assortative mating: Application to IQ and SES. *Behavior Genetics*, 1980, *10*, 73–92.

Rice, J., Cloninger, C., & Reich, T. General causal models for sex differences in the familial transmission of multifactorial traits: An application to human spatial visualizing ability. *Social Biology*, 1980, *27*, 36–47.

Robertson, A. Linkage between marker loci and those affecting a quantitative trait. *Behavior Genetics*, 1973, *3*, 389–391.

Schrott, H., Karp, L., & Omenn, G. Prenatal prediction in myotonic dystrophy: Guidelines for genetic counseling. *Clinical Genetics*, 1973, *4*, 38–45.

Shuckit, M., Goodwin, D., & Winokur, G. A study of alcoholism in half siblings. *American Journal of Psychiatry*, 1972, *123*, 1132–1136.

Slater, E. & Cowie, V. *The genetics of mental disorders*. London: Oxford University Press, 1971.

Smith, C. Heritability of liability and concordance in monozygous twins. *Annals of Human Genetics*, 1970, *34*, 85–91.

Smith, C. Concordance in twins: Methods and interpretation. *American Journal of Human Genetics*, 1974, *26*, 454–466.

Smith, C. A non-parametric test for linkage with a quantitative character. *Annals of Human Genetics*, 1975, *38*, 451–460.

Suarez, B. The affected sib pair IBD distribution for HLA-linked disease susceptibility genes. *Tissue Antigens*, 1978, *12*, 87–93.

Suarez, B., Reich, T., & Trost, J. Limits of the general two-allele single locus model with incomplete penetrance. *Annals of Human Genetics*, 1976, *40*, 231–244.

Suarez, B., Rice, J., & Reich, T. The generalized sib pair IBD distribution: Its use in the detection of linkage. *Annals of Human Genetics*, 1978, *42*, 87–94.

Suarez, B., Hodge, S., & Reich, T. Is juvenile diabetes determined by a single gene closely linked to HLA? *Diabetes*, 1979, *28*, 527–532.

Susser, M. *Causal thinking in the health sciences: Concepts and strategies in epidemiology.* New York: Oxford University Press, 1978.

Wald, A. *Sequential analysis.* New York: Wiley, 1947.

Weinberg, W. Weitere Beitrage zur Theorie der Verebung. 4. Uber Method und Fehlerquellen der Untersuchung suf Mendelsche Zahlen beim Menschen. Arch, 1912.

Wright, S. Correlation and causation. *Journal of Agriculture Research*, 1921, *20*, 557–585.

3. Methodology of high risk research: Longitudinal approaches

Terrie E. Moffitt, Sarnoff A. Mednick, and Robert Cudeck

Introduction

Any intervention program aimed at the primary prevention of mental illness will very likely be restricted to those at high risk for developing such disorders. Thus, a first step in intervention research is to devise assessment procedures that will efficiently identify individuals (probably children) who are in great danger of some day becoming psychiatric patients, alcoholics, or criminals. The high risk study design can thus contribute to the development of methods for the early identification of such individuals.

The high risk method involves the prospective study of individuals who have characteristics that are empirically predictive of eventual psychological or social deviance. For example, the characteristic most commonly used to identify children at risk for schizophrenia has been parental schizophrenia.

Figure 3-1 illustrates a hypothetical study using a high risk sample of 200 children with schizophrenic mothers and 100 low risk control subjects. The design can be conceptualized as developing at three levels.

At the first level, we can compare the distinguishing characteristics of children with schizophrenic mothers (high risk subjects) with the characteristics of children with no familial psychiatric history (low risk subjects). At the second level, we can estimate that about 50% of the

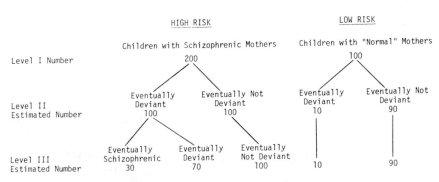

Fig. 3–1. A high risk paradigm investigating schizophrenia.

high risk children will become seriously socially or psychologically deviant. A good control group for these deviants are the children who do not become deviant, but who have schizophrenic mothers. At the third level, we can estimate that 20 or 30 of the 100 high risk deviants will be diagnosed schizophrenic. The remaining 70 high risk deviants are one group of controls for these 30 schizophrenics, in addition to the non-deviant high risk children and the low risk children.

Such a study may not be readily, or at least easily, replicated. Others using even the same design may not use the same variables. Thus, a form of replication can be built into the design. At Level II, the 100 eventually deviant individuals may be conceived of as suffering breakdown in five waves of 20 subjects each. Thus, there are four potential replications of the first data analysis. (The precision of the replication might be attenuated if the waves differ in age at breakdown or in diagnosis.) At level III, the 30 schizophrenics may be conceived of as suffering breakdown in two waves of 15 subjects each.

It should be emphasized that the *risk* model is used only because of its efficiency. A superior research design would assess and follow an entire unselected cohort. However, in view of the fact that only 1% of such a population would become schizophrenic, it would be necessary to survey 3,000 subjects to yield 30 schizophrenics for a study of schizo-
The critical predisposing factors we hope to ascertain with this only be detected by time-consuming, intensive individual cohorts with higher yields of schizophrenics are the reason we turn to children with chronically When the risk of schizophrenia is between 10%

and 16%, we need sample only 300 subjects to yield 30 schizophrenics. These same efficiency considerations, of course, explain the use of the risk design in other fields. (A level II benefit is the special understanding that may be obtained of the lives of children with deviant parents.)

After the high risk subjects are identified and intensively assessed (typically along with controls), they are followed for an appropriate period of time until some level of decompensation is observed in some of the subjects. The life data and individual characteristics of the decompensated subjects are then examined to find characteristics that distinguish them from their more fortunate cohorts. If the distinguishing characteristics result in efficient and reliable discrimination (and if generalization is feasible from high risk subjects to the general population), then we will have devised an assessment battery that can be administered to an unselected population of children to identify a target group for intervention research. These distinguishing characteristics might also help us provide hypotheses concerning the causes of the disorder.

Advantages of high risk research

Most risk research projects follow a prospective longitudinal model. This approach has certain advantages.

Cost efficiency. As mentioned above, the high risk method offers the advantage of increasing the probability that a sufficient number of subjects will eventually evidence symptoms of disturbance. Relatively small samples can be studied with intensive measures, thereby making high risk projects more feasible. Thus, less time need be invested in order to yield a sufficient number of pathological subjects.

Premorbid assessment. The high risk subjects, at the time of initial examination, are not yet mentally or socially ill; thus, because they have not experienced the epiphenomena of the illness, their performance on tests are not heavily colored by these clinical epiphenomena. The behavior of schizophrenics and many other deviant groups is unquestionably markedly altered as a consequence of their illness. The schizophrenic experiences educational, economic, and social failure; pre-hospital, hospital, and post-hospital drug regimens; and, often long-term institutionalization as part of a chronic illness. Consequently, in cross-sectional comparison of controls and schizophrenics, it is often difficult to judge what por' of the reported differences has unique relevance to the etiology of schizophrenia and what portion is a function of the consequences of the illness. For example, Silverman (1964) demonstrated critical differences between acute and chronic schizophrenics on a perceptual task. Subsequently, Silverman, Berg, and Kantor (1966) repeated the same tasks with long-term and short-term non-psychiatric *prisoners*. They found that the differences observed on these tasks among the normals and the "acute" and "chronic" prison inmates were almost precisely the same as those observed among the normals and the acute and chronic schizophrenics. The actual scores for the imprisoned and the hospitalized were quite similar for equal lengths of institutionalization. Thus, the original differences observed between the schizophrenics were interpreted as due to institutionalization. This study points out that schizophrenics may be so affected by the consequences of their illness, or other related factors, that they are not suitable subjects for research into etiology. A similar conclusion can be drawn with respect to conditions of social deviance and other mental illnesses.

Because high risk subjects are usually children or adolescents, any manifest characteristics observed in these individuals are only minimally affected, if they are affected at all, by the consequences of the abnormality in question. For example, young children of alcoholics, who are themselves at risk for alcoholism (Goodwin, Schulsinger, Knopp, Mednick, & Guze, 1977), have not suffered the physiological damage associated with heavy drinking. When some of these children first succumb to alcoholism, the characteristics that distinguish them from those who do not cannot be attributed to the effects of heavy alcohol consumption. Elucidating the characteristics of the pre-alcoholic will be helpful in determining the etiology of alcoholism, as well as identifying future alcoholics.

Reduced bias. Researchers and relatives do not know that the subject will become socially deviant or mentally ill, nor does the subject, himself; consequently, their reports and assessments are less biased. The bias is certainly not greater for future deviant subjects than for other high risk subjects who do not succumb.

Current data. In the longitudinal high risk method, the information gathered is current, not retrospective. This ensures a greater accuracy than is otherwise attainable from retrospective reports, especially when such reports derive from descriptions by parents of the early behavior of their children (Garmezy, 1971).

Uniform data. Another advantage of prospective data collection in longitudinal risk research is that the data are uniformly and systematically obtained, in contrast to retrospective studies, which use childhood and school records concerning adults who are socially deviant or mentally ill.

Limitations of the longitudinal high risk approach

The longitudinal study of a relatively large sample at risk for social or mental deviance does present certain problems and limitations. These include the following.

Financial and administrative problems. Perhaps the most common criticism of longitudinal risk studies has been the long-term financial commitment that must be made by a granting agency. In addition, administrative continuity of the projects is very often difficult to maintain. Typically, these two problems are not independent.

Although the allegation regarding high costs for longitudinal projects has been very freely and frequently made, to our knowledge no one has actually cost-accounted this factor. Typically, the largest cost in a longitudinal high risk project is the initial assessment of the subjects. If expensive apparatus is to be used, it will be purchased at this initial stage. The initial assessment will also typically encompass the largest number of individuals in the sample. Furthermore, it will require the longest and most expensive training period for the staff. In the simplest form of high risk projects, assessment of final outcome (mental illness, criminality, school performance, socioeconomic level, personality characteristics, etc.) is the only required additional step. If only the initial and outcome assessments are made, annual costs can be very modest. More frequently, however, assessments of the subjects are undertaken at intermediate stages of the research.

Although not directly relevant to high risk research, there is a method that can provide "instant" longitudinal projects at tremendous savings of time and resources. We refer to the re-analysis of older existing longitudinal projects. Some potential European projects have been identified by Mednick and Baert (1980), and some potential United States projects are described by Mednick and Harway (in press). As an example, Harway, Mednick, and Satz are planning to return to a ten-year-old longitudinal study by Satz and Ross (1970). These latter investigators conducted a thorough, multifaceted assessment of learning disability starting with an examination of all kindergarten children in a school system. By ascertaining the delinquency of this population, an "instant" ten-year prospective longitudinal study can be completed on the relationship between learning disability and delinquency.

Obsolescence. One serious criticism of longitudinal research is that the measures and the theories that are important at the inception of the project may be dated 20 years later. It is important, therefore, that the researcher beginning a longitudinal risk project avoid strong theoretical biases, and select measures that are fairly eclectic. The researcher is wise if he records raw data from his subjects. That is to say, he should record actual verbalizations rather than just code attitudes and opinions; he should record raw physiological data on magnetic tape rather than only complex derivations. Such basic raw data can be rescored by new techniques 20 years hence.

Sleeper effects. In a study by Atkins, Cherry, Douglas, Kierdan, and Wadsworth (1980), it was reported that children up to two years of age who were exposed to polluted air did not suffer significantly more coughing or bronchitis in adolescence. At age 25, however, those so exposed *did* evidence significantly more coughing and bronchitis (personal communication). This study demonstrates the impact of sleeper effects; an antecedent factor that does not manifest itself until a later period of life. Conclusions regarding the influence of a childhood factor in a longitudinal high risk study should not be made in an absolute manner. The Atkins study (1980) teaches us that conclusions should be restricted to their age-specific period. As another example, there is reason to suspect that delinquency may not have the same origins as adult criminality. It is possible, therefore, that factors that relate to delinquency may be different from those that relate to adult criminality. Thus, if an antecedent factor is not associated with an increase in the probability of delinquency, this does not mean that it will be unrelated to adult criminality in the same population.

Subject loss. When there are large amounts of emigration or the absence of population registers, the investigator could find it difficult to locate his subjects after a period of time. Sending birthday and Christmas cards will help determine when the subjects change residence. Obtaining the addresses and telephone numbers of relatives and friends of the subject will also help locate the subject in the case of residence change.

Publication. One frequently mentioned problem in longitudinal research projects pertains to the difficulty or delay in publishing the findings. The reason for this is fairly clear. The exciting payoff for most such projects comes only after the subjects have reached adult age, have failed to reach certain life goals, or have manifested deviance. This sometimes requires a long wait by the investigator.

In order to minimize such difficulties, the researcher should explore the possibility of achieving short-term goals in the course of the project. For example, if the sample is at risk for criminality, the researcher might set as a short-term goal the study of delinquency. If the sample is at risk for a mental illness, he could set school adjustment as a short-term goal. These strategies would allow more continuous involvement in the project, as well as offer the opportunity to investigate related problems.

Repeated measurements. In some high risk projects, the same measurements are repeatedly administered to the subjects. This, of course, entails the danger of the measurement itself changing the subject. Typically, however, this danger is minimal. To illustrate, long-term psychological interventions with schizophrenics, criminals, and alcoholics usually have minimal effect. Therefore, it seems unlikely that several interviews during a lifetime would have any effect on the subject population. Of course, under certain circumstances, and under some special testing conditions, the repeated measurement effect could be important. Then, it would be possible to assess the effect of repeated measurements by adding a control group that is assessed less frequently.

Choices in research design

Age of subjects

Age of subjects at the time of data collection, as well as age at the time of planned follow-up, are important factors to consider in the choice of variables to be included in a longitudinal high risk research project. The degree to which a given variable can successfully predict short- and long-term outcome is greatly influenced by the age of the subject (Mednick,

Griffith, & Mednick, 1981). A rather high degree of predictability can be expected from cognitive and personality measurements in adolescence to similar measurements in adulthood. Measurements obtained on younger children have considerably less relationship with later measurements (Thomas, Chess, & Birch, 1968; McCall, Appelbaum, & Hogarty, 1973). Long term prediction is poorest when measurements have been obtained during infancy and the early preschool years (Sameroff, 1979).

Control groups

In the planning of a high risk project, one consideration is whether to include a control group. Under some circumstances, a "low risk" group is not necessary, since etiological inferences can be made by comparing the high risk subjects who did not develop the deviance or illness at the time of follow-up with those who did. In addition, the high risk subjects who develop the deviance or illness can be compared with high risk subjects who develop other deviances. The comparison will elucidate which antecedent factors are specifically predictive of the "target" disorder.

Dispensing with a control group when designing a high risk project will certainly yield savings in funds and examination time. Initial savings, however, must be weighted against limited opportunities for later multipurpose use of the sample. Generalization of results may also be a problem in the absence of control subjects. Do factors that predict a particular illness among high risk subjects also predict the same illness in children who do not have the risk-defining characteristics? For example, it is possible that the variables found to predict schizophrenic breakdown in children with schizophrenic mothers may not predict schizophrenia in children with non-schizophrenic parents.

Finally, McNeil and Kaij (1979) point out that comparisons between high risk and low risk groups often reflect the characteristics, correlates, and/or consequences of the risk criterion. From such a comparison, a better understanding can be obtained of the role of the risk criterion for a child at psychiatric risk.

If the decision is made to assess a group of low risk control subjects, the researcher should be aware that selecting an unbiased control group is difficult. In the typical contrasted group design, the researcher generally recognizes that his research design involves some biased selection of deviant cases. An attempt is often made to overcome this bias by observing control groups matched for "relevant" factors. But do we really know what factors are relevant? We must face the fact that almost any control group we select will be biased in some respects. For example, for a valid generalization, the number of patients and controls in the study should be in proportion to their numbers in the population. Otherwise, generalization is likely to be fallacious. This often-repeated fallacy in research design is well known in epidemiological research; it is called Berkson's fallacy. To quote Berkson (1955): "If the subpopulation . . . of a group X and its control not-X is not representative in the ratio of the marginal totals of X and not-X . . . in the general population, then association will appear even if it does not exist in the general population from which the study population is drawn." We might add that associations in the parent population may be masked by control groups not representative of the not-X population. This means that another investigator, studying the same population in the same manner, may select a sample that is biased in some other way. This problem is very likely at the root of some failures to replicate research results in the fields of mental illness and antisocial behavior (Mednick, 1978).

One final issue concerning the use of control groups in the special case of experimental manipulative high risk research merits discussion. In some discussions of intervention research, it has been suggested that all identified risk children should receive preventive treatment. It is implied that using a control group is immoral and unethical, since "optimal" treatment of some selected subgroups would be withheld. To follow such a dictum would simply mean that no useful high risk research would be conducted. In this context, we should keep in mind the report of Ricks (1967). His follow-up study revealed that some therapists seemed to "immunize" clinic children from later hospitalization for schizophrenia. Other therapists seemed to inexorably push numbers of clinic children into schizophrenia. In this situation, the children or their parents sought out the clinic service. We will be seeking out subjects for intervention. How many of us are completely certain that our staffs do not include examples of these latter therapists? Since we are far from certain that our interventions will be of benefit, we can hardly consider it immoral to withhold them from some subjects.

Method of selection of risk subjects

We study children at risk in an attempt to identify predisposing factors and to help us determine the causes of some specific form of adolescent or adult deviance. Decisions regarding methods of selection of subjects for study will depend, in part, on the type of deviance we are investigating. However, some subject-selection decisions are independent of the type of disorder studied. For example, if we are investigating the origins of delinquency, we might examine subjects with both parents having a history of antisocial behavior. Children with such parents are at high risk for antisocial behavior. On the other hand, if we have a theory involving physiological or personal characteristics of children that predisposes them to delinquent behavior, we might test a population of children, and select as our risk subjects those children who are at the extremes on this personality or physiological dimension.

Methods of selection may thus be usefully sorted into two categories: selection based on characteristics of the child's family or environment and selection based on the characteristics of the child.

Family or environmental characteristics. One type disorder most frequently studied by the high risk method is schizophrenia. The first major project was begun in 1962 in Copenhagen. Mednick and Schulsinger (1968) studied children whose mothers were chronic schizophrenics. This method of subject selection has been shown to be appropriate, since the number of children who have become schizophrenic to date is about what was anticipated (Mednick, Schulsinger, & Schulsinger, 1975). Differentiating characteristics of these children have been described in several reports (Mednick & Schulsinger, 1968; Griffith, Mednick, Schulsinger, & Diderichsen, 1980; Talovic, Mednick, Schulsinger, & Falloon, 1980).

The objective of this project was to understand the development of schizophrenia in the general population. However, it should be recognized that this sample of children with schizophrenic parents, who have subsequently become schizophrenic themselves, may not be representative of all schizophrenics, since only a small proportion of schizophrenics have schizophrenic mothers. Therefore, it is possible that schizophrenic offspring with schizophrenic mothers are disproportionately influenced by genetic or disruptive family factors and may comprise a particular subset within the disorder.

Venables and colleagues (Venables, Mednick, Schulsinger, Raman, Bell, Dalais, & Fletcher, 1978) then examined a more representative population of children in order to evaluate the influence of autonomic reactivity, one of the factors that was found to be related to schizophrenia. Another method for assessing the degree to which the findings from a sample are representative of all individuals with the disorder is to compare the results of a high risk investigation with findings from research on already affected schizophrenics. If the distinguishing characteristics of high risk children who become schizophrenic agree with the findings in the literature concerning unselected schizophrenic patients, then this can be interpreted as providing additional indirect support for the generalizability of findings.

One advantage of using parental characteristics for selection of high risk subjects is the good predictability of the yield of specific forms of deviance. This expected yield is based upon family studies that specify the likelihood of the outcome. If such a family study is not available in the literature, one must be conducted before initiating the high risk project. Another advantage lies in the fact that since the parents' characteristics determine subject selection, the high risk subjects can be chosen at almost any age. Thus, for example, in 1978 McNeil and Kaij began to study the offspring of Swedish psychotic women. They observe their high risk subjects at the time of delivery. But when one selects on the basis of subject characteristics (rather than parental characteristics), one must wait for the child to reach an age at which the relevant examination procedures can be undertaken. It is difficult to assess IQ reliably before two years of age, so if we intend to examine children with high and low IQs, we could not reliably do so at birth. But we could compare children of mentally defective parents and children of highly intelligent parents at birth.

For some forms of deviance, selection of high risk subjects by parental characteristics is an especially efficient method because of the high rates of expressed deviance in the children. A good example of this is alcoholism, since 25% of sons of severe alcoholics succumb to alcoholism (Goodwin et al., 1977).

Selection based on physiological or personal characteristics of the child. If the hypothesis to be tested is that monoamine oxidase inhibitors (MAO) are somehow involved in the etiology of psychological deviance, the MAO levels of a population at one point in time can be obtained, and those persons who are extreme in MAO characteristics can be observed to determine if they subsequently develop the disorder studied. Buchsbaum (1976) conducted such a high risk study.

In another investigation, results from the Copenhagen high risk schizophrenia project suggested that deviant autonomic nervous system (ANS) functioning predisposed children to psychological disorder (Mednick & Schulsinger, 1968). These investigators, in collaboration with Peter Venables, assessed the developmental significance of ANS functioning. They tested a population ($N=1,800$) of three-year-olds in Mauritius and identified subjects at risk on the basis of extreme ANS scores. It was hypothesized that those subjects with extreme scores would have a higher incidence of psychological and social disorders (including schizophrenia and antisocial behavior). Other investigators have chosen infants with perinatal problems, early childhood deprivation, sex chromosome deviation, or psychological test score deviance as characteristics predictive of future deviance.

The use of selection criteria based on characteristics of subjects is an ideal strategy for primary prevention studies. Intervention techniques can be tested on a subset of the identified risk subjects, and the outcomes compared with the untreated risk subjects. For example, in the Mauritius project, some of the ANS-defined high risk children were treated in especially established nursery schools. Their outcomes are currently (at age 10–11) being evaluated in the context of a summer educational camp program, which almost all of the original 1,800 will attend.

Thus, this method of selecting high risk subjects can yield important information about the long-term association between outcome and the criterion measurement. If the variable is an effective predictor of outcome, it may be of importance in intervention planning. Another advantage of this research is that it is open-ended; that is, in addition to the hypothesized outcomes (e.g., schizophrenia), other unexpected forms of mental illness and social deviance might appear in the population and also prove to be related to the selection criterion.

Issues in the analysis of data from longitudinal projects

Measurement issues

Categorical diagnoses in high risk research. Whatever the behavioral or mental disorder under inquiry, the issue of diagnosis and diagnostic accuracy is a recurring problem. If subjects are selected on the basis of parental deviance, the project begins by diagnosing the parents. During the course of longitudinal follow up, the children will also be diagnosed. Invariably, these diagnoses are categorical; that is, the subject either suffers the disorder or he does not. Categorical diagnoses have certain serious limitations. For example, it is difficult to justify some multivariate methods when a dichotomous classification is the dependent variable. Simple categorical diagnosis does not convey the richness of the symptoms, nor does it describe the duration or severity of the symptom pattern. Moreover, differences among individuals with the same diagnosis are not taken into account.

Concepts of diagnosis in mental health research have traditionally been strongly tied to clinical practice. In the clinical setting, individual practitioners make a diagnosis on the basis of their patients' presenting problems and history. This is a subjective enterprise, which, in the research setting, can be a source of severe bias. In an effort to standardize techniques and increase reliability, recent efforts have resorted to computer-scored interview schedules (Wing, Cooper, & Sartorius, 1974). This makes diagnosis more objective, even though some form of categorical clinical diagnosis is necessary. Certain fundamental weaknesses exist in all techniques of diagnostic formulation.

For example, consider the diagnosis of schizophrenia. The value of dividing schizophrenia into paranoid, hebephrenic, catatonic, and simple types has been seriously questioned. Carpenter, Bartko, Carpenter, and Strauss (1976) found very little symptomatic discrimination among these traditional subtypes in the International Pilot Study of Schizophrenia. Other researchers have also expressed dissatisfaction with the schizophrenia subtypes (Katz, Cole, & Lowery, 1964; Brill & Glass, 1965). Moreover, as Stephens (1978) has pointed out, the diagnosis of schizophrenia has no invariate predictive value. Nor is their any evidence that a narrow Scandinavian diagnosis is a better predictor of outcome than the broader Bleulerian-American diagnosis of schizophrenia (Hawk, Carpenter, & Strauss, 1975).

Most diagnostic systems are basically Kraepelian or Bleulerian. Individuals are shoehorned into categories, despite the general recognition that differences between the mildest schizophrenic and the most severely ill borderline patients may not be meaningful. Nevertheless, our research instruments are expected to differentiate between these individuals, when there may be, in fact, little realistic basis for this differentiation.

Dimensional models of diagnosis. It has been suggested that an attempt should be made to systematically describe disorders in terms of continuously distributed variables (Strauss & Carpenter, 1978). To do so would involve detecting the variables that characterize measurable aspects of the illness, such as age of onset, work history, history of social functioning, and duration of symptoms. It seems reasonable that specific combinations of variables would constitute categorizations of mental illness in terms of relatively independent dimensions. Since the dimensions are continuous, the interaction of these variables will, in theory, produce an infinite number of subtypes. An individual's "diagnosis" would then be defined by an intersection of the relevant dimensions.

In the Copenhagen high risk project, we attempted to define schizophrenia by means of "longitudinal syndromes." We have found that autonomic nervous system variables are only descriptive of men who are characterized by the more withdrawn, schizoid form of schizophrenia (Mednick, Schulsinger, Teasdale, Schulsinger, Venables, & Rock, 1978). Analyses have revealed that a pattern of high scores in children on schizoid, anhedonic, inexpressive, and passive dimensions is related to "dull affect" in their schizophrenic mothers. In addition, separation from the parents, which resulted in institutionalization of the high risk boys, was related to later symptoms of thought disorder (Walker, Cudeck, Mednick, & Schulsinger, 1981). The latter study indicates that an important approach in the study of schizophrenia involves investigating current expressions of pathology in the context of early life events.

DATA REDUCTION

High risk studies generate extensive amounts of data. A common problem, therefore, is to reduce the data into a few meaningful scores that represent cogent features of the subjects' characteristics and experiences. For example, a detailed interview of high risk subjects could yield 500 items and, thus, would present a serious difficulty for the investigator who intends to relate this information to another variable, for example, early family experience. In the context of our schizophrenia project, we have recently dealt with this problem and have resolved it so usable data are obtained.

The approach involves coding the data obtained from an interview conducted in 1972 (Schulsinger, 1976). The interview consisted of the Present State Examination (Wing et al., 1974), Current and Past Psychopathology Scales (Endicott & Spitzer, 1972), and a series of supplementary items describing coping methods and mental status. The total interview resulted in over 700 coded items. Before beginning the analysis, the sample was randomly split into two parts, one containing two-thirds of the subjects (A), the other one-third (B). The initial analyses were conducted on Sample A and then cross-validated with Sample B.

Next, several scales were devised, on a rational basis, from the large item pool. We then subjected each scale to an item analysis to maximize coefficient alpha (Cronbach, 1951), by emphasizing biserial correlations between items and scale totals. This method is related to other approaches aimed at aggregating items into scales, such as factor analysis (Henrysson, 1962), but produces generally superior results (Hase & Goldberg, 1967; Nunnally, 1967). This analysis, thus, enabled us to drop items from the scales that did not maximize coefficient alpha. Several raters checked to ensure that the remaining items in each scale were homogeneous in context.

The scales were then scored for each subject, and the principal components of the entire set of scale scores were calculated. The method of principal components was chosen because a reduced set of scores for each subject was desired. Components describe the variance among a set of variables better than such other alternatives as common factor analysis.

Discriminant analysis. As a result of the original clinical interview (Schulsinger, 1976), a consensus diagnosis was made for each subject. If the factor scores could distinguish between diagnostic groups, this would then indicate that the factors could explain variations in the sample in a manner that agreed with another criterion. The factors that resulted from the principal components analysis were used in a discriminant function analysis (Cooley & Lohnes, 1971; Tatsouka, 1971) to distinguish between subjects who belonged to different diagnostic groups. The results of this analysis were quite encouraging.

Cross-validation. As indicated above, the item analysis, principal components analysis, and the discriminant analyses were first conducted on Sample A. To test the generalizability of the results, the entire process was repeated using Sample B. This step was crucial to this study in which many items and relatively few subjects were used. Relationships found in Sample A, but not in Sample B, were viewed with suspicion. The cross-validation revealed excellent generalizability.

Products of analysis. This series of analyses resulted in 35 scales measuring characteristics ranging from "obsessive compulsive" to "thought disorder." These 35 scales were grouped by the principal components analysis into seven factors designated Major Mental Illness; Interpersonal Communication Disorder; Psychopathy, Inadequate Personality; Aggression; Severe Depression; Hypersensitive, Avoidant; Neurosis.

We have now embarked on a series of analyses to relate differentially early life experiences and characteristics to the clinical outcomes represented by these scales and factors. A great advantage of these scales and factors is that they lend themselves to powerful multivariate analysis techniques, since they are continuous and reasonably well distributed and have an adequate range.

Statistical issues

Complexity of relationships. One objective of risk research is to relate early life events and characteristics to later outcomes. These life events often influence outcome in a complex, interactive manner. For example, in the Copenhagen project, it was necessary to consider variables that span the lifetime of the individual. We begin with the seriousness of the schizophrenia of the mother and then examine perinatal factors and the characteristics of the home. These are considered in the light of socioeconomic status during rearing, the functioning of the autonomic nervous systems, and sex. We know that many of these independent variables are intercorrelated. For example, the earlier the onset of illness of the mother, the more separation from the mother the child experiences. Other, less obvious, intercorrelations also exist in these data. Therefore, multiple analyses of individual independent variables in relationship to the dependent variable schizophrenia run the risk of emphasizing a few common findings.

It is clear that by stressing a few of these relationships, our study ignores the fact that there is a wider fabric of interdependencies that should be explored. Thus, one difficulty with exploratory, longitudinal studies is that the number of interrelated facets of behavior is quite large. Examining these factors two or three at a time is simply not an effective or satisfactory research strategy.

Problems with single variable use. At the same time, it is well known that individual measurements of any given phenomenon, such as intelligence or psychopathy, are limited. They are limited for two reasons, both of which have serious consequences for the validity of analyses from longitudinal studies. The first reason is simply that psychological and behavioral variables cannot be measured without error. Indeed, the cornerstone of psychometric theory is that measurement error is inherent in *every* test score (Lord & Novick, 1968; Nunnally, 1967). It is an interesting sociocultural phenomenon that researchers laboring in a certain substantive field frequently retain a healthy skepticism about their own measurements, but covet those in fields that they suppose are more reliable. Witness, for example, the frequent, almost uncritical use of biological measures by psychologists who would normally demand the most rigorous proof of the reliability of a psychological variable. The point is not that one type of variable is "better" than another, but rather that error occurs in both and that they should be treated accordingly (Cliff, in press).

The second limitation of single measuremnts of a phenomenon has to do with the problem of validity. As a general rule, since we cannot be completely confident that our pet measurement of aggressiveness captures the essence of that construct, a minimum condition for the validity of a measurement is that it correlates with other variables purporting to measure the same thing (Campbell & Fiske, 1959). For example, the reason the Stanford-Binet IQ is often accepted as a measure of intelligence is because it correlates with school performance, success on the job, and other types of behavior believed to be related to intelligence. Again, an interesting sociocultural commentary on research in the behavioral sciences is that we frequently demand that most strenuous standards of convergent validity for variables in some areas (e.g., the measurement of intelligence), but accept with an almost cavalier attitude the variables in others (e.g., diagnoses of psychopathology based on a single interview). The standard should be, rather, that we require the evidence of convergence between independently obtained measurements before we are satisfied that the construct has been adequately assessed.

Analysis of covariance structures. Obviously, the ideal method of analyzing data from a longitudinal project would somehow include several measurements of each variable. Then, the unreliability of any individual variable would be minimized, and, in addition, one could have confidence that the psychological constructs of interest are accurately depicted. Furthermore, one would include in the analysis as many aspects of the phenomenon as are potentially involved. Of course, no statistical technique could ever manage such an analysis if it were carried to the extreme. Recent developments in statistical methods, however, have made it possible to achieve this goal to a limited extent.

The general method of performing such an analysis has come to be called the *analysis of covariance structures.* Joreskog (1978) is generally credited with the most important contributions in this area, although several others have played major roles in the development of this method. The name is derived from the fact that the method seeks to analyze the correlation or covariance among a group of variables and obtain a more fundamental structure. Special cases of this general model are multiple regression, path analysis, and factor analysis. The strength of the method stems from the fact that mixtures of these distinct approaches are now available together. That is, because our interest is in longitudinal designs, regression-type models are clearly important. Since we seek to describe complex relationships among a number of variables that may directly or indirectly influence an outcome, elements of path analysis may be desirable. And, since we desire to minimize individual variables and emphasize convergent validity among several measures, many aspects of factor analysis theory are relevant. Inasmuch as the statistics are still in their infancy and can be complicated, there are presently no completely satisfactory introductions to the technique. However, the recent work of Bentler (1980), Kenny (1979), Maruyama and McGarvey (1980), and Nesselroade and Baltes (1979) provide a good beginning. Examples of the use of this method in the context of high risk research may be found in Beuhring, Cudeck, Mednick, Walker, and Schulsinger (in press), and in Walker et al. (1981).

The advantages of using the analysis of covariance structures approach is only briefly discussed here. Suffice it to say, this method is the first step in analyzing data from high risk studies that seek to operationalize many of the ideals of multiple-measurement research. The primary strength of the method is its emphasis on the statistical relations among latent variables, rather than on measured variables. *Measured variables* are the typical bill of fare of all research work and may consist of test scores, rating scales, or behavioral measurements. *Latent variables,* on the other hand, are composites of measurements. For example, a latent variable for socioeconomic status might be constructed to use several measured variables, such as income, amount of education, vocational status, and a rating of neighborhood quality. Any one of these four variables is too limited a measurement of the more global construct of socioeconomic status, but, considering the four variables together, the composite they form may comprise a very effective measurement system.

In multiple regression analysis, which is perhaps the principal statistical model used in longitudinal research, relationships between measured variables are examined. As we have seen, the success of such an analysis depends upon the reliability and validity of the variables used. Even the the best variables, however, can be criticized on these grounds. By contrast, in the analysis of covariance structures, one studies the relationships between latent variables. Therefore, the problems inherent in any one variable can be minimized. For this, and other reasons, this method is an extremely useful tool in the analysis of data from high risk projects.

Future directions: The experimental-manipulative method

A source of difficulty for the researcher interested in studying the causes of mental illness or social deviance is the unavailability of the experimental-manipulative approach. *This is because we cannot, for research purposes, impose conditions on children that might contribute to social or psychological deviance.* How, then, can we develop a strategy for research into the etiology of social and mental illness? The high risk group method can help, but it is not sufficient; it does not involve experimental manipulation. We can point to maternal, physiological, and perinatal variables that markedly distinguish the premorbid status of a group that later suffers breakdown, but we cannot be sure that any of these variables are etiological or are closely related to primary causal agents. Correcting all, or any, of these premorbid variables in deviant subjects may not circumvent eventual deviance if the deviance springs directly from biochemical anomalies that remain unaffected by our corrections. The maternal, physiological, and perinatal variables may only be correlates of a very early undetected stage of deviance or illness. Again, we must face the fact that research that does not involve experimental manipulation is correlational in nature and, thus, conclusions about causation cannot be drawn from such research.

The high risk method does suggest areas worth exploring. A key to the exploitation of these suggestive leads lies in the italicized sentence above. The same moral code that bars scientists from attempting to manipulate experimentally the lives of humans so as to cause them to become deviant, also encourages and supports reasonable attempts at experimental manipulations that are aimed at reducing the incidence of deviance. Positive results in such research would certainly warrant drawing conclusions on the causes of a reduction in incidence of social deviance and mental illness. These results, however, would not by themselves warrant conclusions on the etiology of mental illness. (We thus may be able to pinpoint the administration of penicillin as a cure for an illness without detailed and specific knowledge of the cause of the illness.) If, however, preventive research reveals that the administration of a given drug or a given mothering experience (or a combination of the two) materially reduces the incidence of mental illness, we can begin to deduce the causes of mental illness with more precision and undertake more focused and discriminating preventive research that could eventually lead to more firmly based conclusions about etiology.

The great conceptual problem facing the prospective research worker in the area of prevention is "What justification can be found for the mode of intervention?" The high risk group method can make its contribution in this area.

It is in order to provide data necessary for the development of etiological hypotheses, intervention tools, and early detection techniques that longitudinal risk research projects are conducted as part of a primary prevention program. When the data from the initial assessment of a group of high risk subjects are analyzed, after some significant portion of the subjects evidence deviance, characteristics may be found that, in retrospect, reliably distinguished the eventual deviants. Such distinguishing characteristics may be useful in early detection programs and may also provide hypotheses regarding intervention techniques. The prospective longitudinal method is central to this approach.

Then, an experimental-manipulative high risk project may be initiated, using those distinguishing characteristics suggested by the earlier high risk project as criteria for subject selection. Intervention techniques suggested by results of the earlier risk project may also be carefully implemented. If, at follow-up of these risk subjects, significantly fewer subjects evidence deviance than expected, the intervention techniques used in the project may suggest etiological hypotheses. In addition, the results may be useful for evaluating the efficacy of the intervention techniques attempted during the project.

The Mauritius study: An example of experimental-manipulative high risk research

In 1968, a follow-up of subjects at risk for schizophrenia in Copenhagen, Denmark, suggested that the rate of recovery of skin conductance was an important possible premorbid indicant of later pathology. Mednick, as part of a World Health Organization (WHO) panel, reported this finding, and also described the high risk research method. It was then proposed that the Copenhagen high risk study be repeated. Since Dr. A. C. Raman, Chief Psychiatrist of Mauritius, had requested WHO to initiate a program of mental health research in his country, this island nation was selected as the research site. Inspection of the island revealed that the necessary infrastructure existed to make the project feasible.

Sample and procedure

A sample of 1,800 children 3 to 3¼ years of age was examined. These children comprised nearly the entire population of three-year-olds residing in two Mauritian communities that were representative of the islands' population. The assessment consisted of parent interview, social behavior laboratory observation, psychological-cognitive assessment, psychophysiological reactivity (skin conductance, skin potential, and electrocardiogram), obstetric information, pediatric examination, and EEG examination (for a subset of the sample).

Selection for nursery school

The project established two nursery schools, each with 50 children. On the basis of the psychophysiological screening of the 1,800 three-year-olds, 54 children with an extremely fast autonomic recovery and 32 with an average autonomic recovery were selected. In light of results obtained by Venables et al. (1978), 14 children who were "non-responders" in skin conductance were also included. These three types of children were then divided evenly between the two nursery schools. Thus, in each nursery school, two-thirds of the class psychophysiologically defined high risk children. For each of the 100 children in the nursery schools, a control, matched for skin conductance characteristics and area of residence, was selected. These community controls were simply identified and permitted to remain undisturbed in the community.

Initial results

Of the 200 children, 108 exhibited fast autonomic recovery (54 nursery school children and 54 community controls) and 64 were average in their recovery speed. Group comparisons revealed that the fast recoverers cried more during the testing and evidenced more fear and anxiety. They also caused more disturbances and were more aggressive in the nursery school. These findings corresponded to observations made on fast recoverers in the Danish high risk project.

Since the opening of the nursery school, the children have been observed in accordance with a system devised by Bell, Weller, and Waldrop (1971), which times rates and counts instances of specific behaviors. The factor structure of the observations and ratings on the Mauritian children has been found to closely resemble that reported by Bell for American nursery school children.

When the children first entered the nursery schools, an abnormally large number were terribly frightened and had to be held most of the time. This continued for the first month. The mothers of many of the children urged that a sibling be substituted for the selected child. They protested that the selected child would be hopeless, since he or she spent most of the day in the closet, under a table, or in hiding. This parental report and nursery school behavior were interesting in view of the theoretical interpretation of the significance of fast autonomic recovery (Mednick, 1970).

A notable change in the behavior of most of the children occurred during the course of the nursery school experience. The children played spontaneously and greeted strangers with lively interest and curiosity. At home they were described by their parents as having become more like normal and happy children.

The positive effect may have been related to any one, or a combination of, the following:

1. Good, protein-rich nursery school diet
2. Placement in a group with a high density of other autonomically sensitive children
3. A group of enthusiastic young nursery school teachers
4. The special atmosphere created by the Danish nursery school experts who ran the schools and trained the teachers
5. Separation from their home environments for part of the day
6. Selection for this special experience

First follow-up. The nursery school experience was evaluated objectively by comparing the nursery school children with their community controls just before the children entered primary school. Results indicated that the nursery school experience had a positive effect. More importantly, the effect varied as a function of the autonomic nervous system the child had brought to the experience (Mednick, Schulsinger, & Venables, 1979).

Second follow-up. Follow-up examinations of the subjects of this study
are being conducted in the context of summer camps established for
this purpose. The educational camp setting provides an "environmental
studies" course. Each child will attend the camp for one week. Teachers
and teaching facilities will be provided by the Mauritian Institute of
Education. It is estimated that 1,620 of the original 1,800 children first
seen in 1972 will attend the camp. Prior to camp attendance, a social
worker will obtain parental ratings of the children. At the camp, observational techniques are being used to measure aggressiveness, hyperactivity,
withdrawal, schizoid tendencies, and sociability/social competence. Psychophysiological changes to stimuli presented from a standard auditory
tape allow the orienting response to be assessed. Event-related cortical
potentials elicited by visual stimuli allow processing of sensory input to
be measured. Additionally, assessment of smooth pursuit eye tracking is
being conducted. All these mesaures have been shown to be predictive
of, or related to, schizophrenic breakdown.

The total project is expected to last until 1995 or beyond. Methods of
maintaining contact with the sample and gaining information about any
breakdowns or disturbances of behavior are being developed. In the
meantime, the data will provide important insights into the relation
between present psychophysiological status and behavior and will allow
estimates to be made of the extent to which data collected at age three
is predictive of behavior and status at age eleven.

References

Atkins, E., Cherry, N., Douglas, J., Kiernan, K., & Wadsworth, M. The 1946
    British birth cohort: An account of the origins, progress, and results of the
    National Survey of Health Development. In S. Mednick & A. Baert (Eds.).
    Prospective longitudinal research. New York: Oxford University Press,
    1980.
Bell, R., Weller, S., & Waldrop, M. Newborn and preschooler: Organization and
    behaviour and relations between periods. *Monographs of the Society for
    Research in Child Development,* 1971, 36, 1–145.
Bentler, P. Multivariate analysis with latent variables: Causal modeling. *Annual
    Review of Psychology,* 1980, 31, 419–456.
Berkson, J. The statistical study of association between smoking and lung can-
    cer. *Proceedings of Staff Meetings of the Mayo Clinic,* 1955, 30, 319–348.
Beuhring, T., Cudeck, R., Mednick, S., Walker, E., & Schulsinger, F. Suscepti-
    bility to environmental stress: High risk research in the development of
    schizophrenia. In R. W. J. Neufeld (Ed.), *Psychological stress and psy-
    chopathology.* New York: McGraw-Hill, in press.

Brill, N. & Glass, J. Hebephrenic schizophrenic reactions. *Archives of General Psychiatry*, 1965, *12*, 545–551.

Buchsbaum, M. The biochemical high risk paradigm: Behavioral and familial correlates of low platelet monoamine oxidase activity. *Science*, 1976, *194*, 339–341.

Campbell, D. & Fiske, D. Convergent and discriminate validation by the multi-trait-multimethod matrix. *Psychological Bulletin*, 1959, *56*, 81–105.

Carpenter, W., Bartko, J., Carpenter, C., & Strauss, J. Another view of schizophrenia subtypes. *Archives of General Psychiatry*, 1976, *33*, 508–516.

Cliff, N. What is and isn't measurement? In G. Keren (Ed.), *Issues in quantitative psychology*. New York: Erlbaum, in press.

Cooley, W. & Lohnes, P. *Multivariate data analysis*. New York: Wiley, 1971.

Cronbach, L. Coefficient alpha and the internal structure of tests. *Psykometrika*, 1951, *16*, 297–334.

Endicott, J. & Spitzer, R. Current and past psychopathology scales (CAPPS). *Archives of General Psychiatry*, 1972, *27*, 678–687.

Garmezy, N. Vulnerability research and the issue of primary prevention. *American Journal of Orthopsychiatry*, 1971, *41*, 101–116.

Goodwin, D., Schulsinger, F., Knopp, J., Mednick, S., & Guze, S. Psychopathology in adopted and nonadopted daughters of alcoholics. *Archives of General Psychiatry*, 1977, *34*, 1005–1009.

Griffith, J., Mednick, S., Schulsinger, F., & Diderichsen, B. Verbal associative disturbances in children at high risk for schizophrenia. *Journal of Abnormal Psychology*, 1980, *89*, 125–131.

Hase, H. & Goldberg, L. Comparative validity of different strategies of constructing personality inventory scales. *Psychological Bulletin*, 1967, *67*, 231–248.

Hawk, A., Carpenter, T., & Strauss, J. Diagnostic criteria and five-year outcome in schizophrenia. *Archives of General Psychiatry*, 1975, *32*, 343–347.

Henrysson, S. The relation between factor loadings and biserial correlations in factor analysis. *Psychometrika*, 1962, *27*, 419–442.

Joreskog, K. Structural analysis of covariance and correlation matrices. *Psychometrika*, 1978, *43*, 443–477.

Katz, M., Cole, J., & Lowery, H. Non-specificity of diagnosis of paranoid schizophrenia. *Archives of General Psychiatry*, 1964, *11*, 197–202.

Kenny, D. *Correlation and causality*. New York: Wiley, 1979.

Lord, F. & Novick, M. *Statistical theories of mental test scores*. Reading, MA: Addison-Wesley, 1968.

Maruyama, G. & McGarvey, B. Evaluating causal models: An application of maximum-likelihood analysis of structural equations. *Psychological Bulletin*, 1980, *87*, 502–512.

McCall, R., Appelbaum M., & Hogarty, P. Developmental changes in mental performance. *Monograph of the Society for Research in Child Development*, 1973, *38*, 1–84.

McNeil, T. & Kaij, L. Obstetric factors in the development of schizophrenia. In L. Wynne, R. Cromwell, & S. Matthysse (Eds.), *The nature of schizo-*

phrenia: New approaches to research and treatment. New York: Wiley, 1978.

McNeil, T. & Kaij, L. Etiological relevance of comparisons of high-risk and low-risk groups. *Acta Psychiatrica Scandanavica,* 1979, 59, 545–560.

Mednick, S. Breakdown in individuals at high risk for schizophrenia: Possible predispositional perinatal factors. *Mental Hygiene,* 1970, 54, 50–63.

Mednick, S. Berkson's fallacy and high-risk research. In L. Wynne, R. Cromwell, & S. Mattysse (Eds.), *The nature of schizophrenia: New Approaches to research and treatment.* New York: Wiley, 1978.

Mednick, S. & Baert, A. *Prospective longitudinal research.* New York: Oxford University Press, 1980.

Mednick, S. & Harway, M. (Eds.), *Longitudinal research in the United States.* Hingham, Ma.: Martinus Nijhoff, in press.

Mednick, S. & Schulsinger, F. Some premorbid characteristics related to breakdown in children with schizophrenic mothers. *Journal of Psychiatric Research,* 1968, 6, 267–291.

Mednick, B., Griffith, J., & Mednick, S. Some recommendations for the design and conduct of longitudinal investigations. In F. Schulsinger, S. Mednick, & J. Knop (Eds.), *Longitudinal research: Methods and uses in behavioral science.* London: Martinus Nijhoff, 1981.

Mednick, S., Schulsinger, F., & Schulsinger, H. Schizophrenia in children of schizophrenic mothers. In A. Davids (Ed.), *Childhood personality and psychopathology: Current topics* (Vol. 2). New York: Wiley, 1975.

Mednick, S., Schulsinger, F., Teasdale, T., Schulsinger, H., Venables, P., & Rock, D. Schizophrenia in high-risk children: Sex differences in predisposing factors. In G. Serban (Ed.), *Cognitive defects in the development of mental illness.* New York: Brunner/Mazel, 1978.

Mednick, S., Schulsinger, F., & Venables, P. Risk research and primary prevention of mental illness. *International Journal of Mental Health,* 1979, 7, 150–164.

Nesselroade, J. & Baltes, P. (Eds.), *Longitudinal research in the study of behavior and development.* New York: Academic Press, 1979.

Nunnally, J. *Psychometric theory.* New York: McGraw-Hill, 1967.

Ricks, D. Discussion: Early differentiation of psychopathological life patterns. Paper presented at the meeting of the American Psychological Association, Washington, D.C., September, 1967.

Sameroff, A. The etiology of cognitive competence: A systems perspective. In R. Kearsley & L. Sigel (Eds.), *Infants at risk: Assessment of cognitive functioning.* Hillsdale, NJ: Wiley, 1979.

Satz, P. & Ross, J. (Eds.), *Specific reading disability: Advances in theory and method.* Rotterdam, The Netherlands: University of Rotterdam Press, 1970.

Schulsinger, H. A ten-year follow-up of children of schizophrenic mothers: Clinical assessment. *Acta Psychiatrika Scandanavica,* 1976, 53, 371–386.

Silverman, J. Scanning-control mechanism and cognitive functioning in paranoid and non-paranoid schizophrenia. *Journal of Consulting Psychology,* 1964, 28, 385–393.

Silverman, J., Berg, P., & Kantor, R. Some perceptual correlates of institutionalization. *Journal of Nervous and Mental Disease*, 1966, *141*, 651–657.

Stephens, J. Long-term prognosis and follow-up in schizophrenia. *Schizophrenia Bulletin*, 1978, *4*, 25–47.

Strauss, J. & Carpenter, W., Jr. The prognosis of schizophrenia: Rationale for a multidimensional concept. *Schizophrenia Bulletin*, 1978, *4*, 56–67.

Talovic, S., Mednick, S., Schulsinger, F., & Falloon, I. Schizophrenia in high-risk subjects: Prognostic maternal characteristics. *Journal of Abnormal Psychology*, 1980, *89*, 501–504.

Tatsouka, M. Multidimensional representation of similarity structures. In M. Katz, J. Cole, & W. Barton (Eds.), *The role and methodology of classification in psychiatry and psychopathology*. Washington: U.S. Public Health Service (No. 1584), 1971.

Thomas, A., Chess, S., & Birch, H. *Temperament and behavior disorders in children*. New York: New York University Press, 1968.

Venables, P., Mednick, S., Schulsinger, F., Raman, A., Bell, B., Dalais, J., & Fletcher, R. Screening for risk of mental illness. In G. Servan (Ed.), *Cognitive defects in the development of mental illness*. New York: Brunner/ Mazel, 1978.

Walker, E., Cudeck, R., Mednick, S., & Schulsinger, F. Effects of parental absence and institutionalization on the development of clinical symptoms in high risk children. *Acta Psychiatrika Scandinavica*, 1981, *63*, 95–109.

Wing, J., Cooper, J., & Sartorius, N. *The measurement and classification of psychiatric symptoms*. New York: Cambridge University Press, 1974.

4. Hyperactivity and minimal brain dysfunction: Epidemiological perspectives on questions of cause and classification[1]

Michael Rutter, Oliver Chadwick, and Russell Schachar

Introduction

The term minimal brain dysfunction (MBD) has come to be used very widely by both child psychiatrists and pediatricians. In some centers, the diagnosis is thought to refer to a specific disease entity with a specific etiology and a specific response to treatment (Wender, 1971). This is a bold view that implies a level of knowledge considerably greater than that available for most disorders in child psychiatry. If this view is true, it would be essential that all concerned know this supposed truth with its promise of effective therapeutic action. But is it true? And what does it mean? These are the questions we want to consider in this chapter. The topic is a large one and the issues may be approached through a variety of research strategies. We will make passing mention of some of these strategies, but our main focus will be on the perspectives provided by an epidemiological approach.

[1] This paper was prepared while Michael Rutter was a Fellow at the Center for Advanced Study in the Behavioral Sciences. Thanks are expressed to the Grant Foundation, the Foundation for Child Development, the Spencer Foundation, and the National Science Foundation (BNS 7825671) for financial support. Paper originally presented at the Nineteenth Carrier Foundation Symposium, October 3, 1979.

Concepts of minimal brain dysfunction and
the hyperkinetic syndrome

Let us begin by attempting to define MBD, that is, how do we recognize this hypothesized syndrome? Our difficulties begin immediately, as it is all too obvious that there is no general agreement on diagnostic criteria. Most people would regard attentional deficits and/or hyperactivity as usual, if not essential, features. Indeed, many workers would prefer to use the terms hyperkinetic syndrome or attentional deficit syndrome. However, it should not be supposed that the two categories MBD and hyperkinetic syndrome are synonymous. Indeed, Wender (1971) has explicitly argued that the concept of MBD goes wider than the phenomena of overactivity and poor attention.

It is important to realize that several rather different clinical and research issues are involved. First, there is the hypothesis that the hyperkinetic syndrome constitutes a valid, meaningful, and clinically useful diagnostic entity that differs from other forms of psychiatric disorder. Second, there is the hypothesis that brain damage of a minimal kind not only causes psychiatric disorder, but also that it leads to a distinctive behavioral syndrome that is recognizably different from other psychiatric conditions. Third, there is the hypothesis that organic brain dysfunction due to genetic or metabolic factors, rather than trauma, leads to a clinical syndrome that is meaningfully different from other syndromes.

It is apparent that all three hypotheses revolve around the question of *differences,* a point to which we will return repeatedly in this chapter, as it is fundamental to all matters of diagnosis and classification. By calling an animal a sheep you are necessarily implying, thereby, that it is not a goat, and the validity of the notion of a sheep is heavily dependent on the evidence that a sheep posseses sheep-like qualities that are *not* shared by goats, or, for that matter by dogs, cats, or any other kind of furry animal. The same questions of validity apply equally to psychiatric classification (Rutter, 1978). The concept of an MBD, or a hyperkinetic syndrome, depends upon the facts that there are also psychiatric conditions that are *not* MBD or the hyperkinetic syndrome and that the presence of MBD-like qualities serves to differentiate the syndrome from all other psychiatric disorders. The basic premise seems elementary and obvious, and indeed it is, but it has been widely disregarded in most research on this topic.

What, then, are the implications of this basic premise? Two stand out as crucial. First, there is the essential criterion that for any diagnostic category to have scientific meaning it must be shown to differ in terms of etiology, course, response to treatment, or some variable *other than the symptoms that define it* (Rutter, 1978). The last clause, of course, is vital. It is of no use to say that what differentiates the hyperkinetic syndrome from other disorders is the presence of hyperactivity. It must also be demonstrated that this behavioral feature predicts to something else. The second point is that the differentiation must be from *other psychiatric disorders* and not from normality. Many studies show that hyperactive children or children with MBD differ from youngsters in the general population, but that merely shows that there is something wrong with them, which is not particularly helpful, since that was the starting point. The key question is whether children with this hypothesized syndrome differ from children with *other* psychiatric disorders. In other words, does MBD differ from conduct disorders, depression, schizophrenia, sociopathy, etc., or is it merely a fancy name that incorporates nearly all behavioral disturbances without any differentiation?

The effects of brain damage in childhood

So much for the concepts. Let us now turn to the factual evidence with respect to each of the three basic issues already mentioned, starting with the hypotheses on the effects of brain damage (Rutter, 1981a). These constitute not one question, but several, and it is important that they be clearly differentiated. The most basic of these is whether the presence of brain damage in childhood increases the risk that the child will develop some form of psychiatric disorder.

Brain damage and the risk of psychiatric disorder

Several epidemiological studies have clearly demonstrated that the rate of psychiatric disorder in children with a known brain injury is much increased. Figures 4-1 and 4-2 provide a summary of the findings from the Isle of Wight studies of school-age children (Rutter, Graham, & Yule, 1970). As assessed on a teacher's questionnaire and on a clinical psychiatric interview, brain-damaged children of normal intelligence were twice as likely as children with other physical handicaps (such as asthma, diabetes, or heart disease) to show behavioral deviance or disorder. The difference between the groups suggested that brain injury specifically increased the psychiatric risk. However, this remained an uncertain infer-

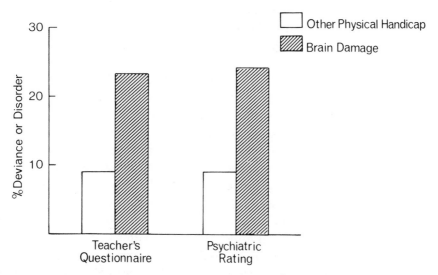

Fig. 4–1. Brain damage and psychiatric disorders, compared with other physical handicaps, in children with an IQ of 86 or more. (Rutter, Graham, and Yule, 1970.)

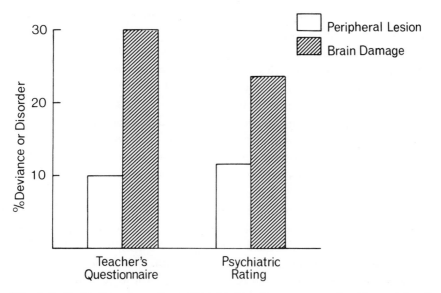

Fig. 4–2. Brain damage and psychiatric disorders, compared with peripheral lesions, in children. (Seidel et al., 1975.)

ence in that the other physical handicaps were less likely to be accompanied by visible crippling. Circumstantial evidence suggested that it was the brain damage rather than the crippling which was crucial, but doubt necessarily remained.

This doubt was resolved by means of a study carried out in North London (Seidel, Chadwick & Rutter, 1975). Thirty-three school-age children of normal intelligence, but with cerebral disorders, were compared with 42 children with handicapping disorders due to lesions below the brain stem (polio, muscular dystrophy, etc.). Although the groups were comparable in terms of visible crippling, psychiatric disorder was found to be much more frequent in the group whose handicap was attributable to brain damage. The inference of a *causal* relationship was strong in that the two groups were well matched in other respects. However, inferences on cause from cross-sectional associations (no matter how good the statistical controls) are inevitably based on circumstantial evidence. Longitudinal data showing *changes* in behavior following brain injury would provide a more convincing and powerful demonstration of a causal effect.

Such data are available from a recently completed prospective study (Brown, Chadwick, Shaffer, Rutter, & Traub, 1981; Chadwick, Brown, Rutter, Shaffer, & Traub, 1981; Rutter & Chadwick, 1980; Rutter, Chadwick, Shaffer, & Brown, 1980), in which a sample of children with head injuries that resulted in a posttraumatic amnesia (PTA) of at least one week were compared with an individually matched control group of children with orthopedic injuries that involved no damage to the head and no loss of consciousness. A third group of children with mild head injuries, involving a PTA of more than one hour, but less than a week, were also studied. All the parents were interviewed as soon as possible after the injury to obtain an assessment of the child's behavior *before* the accident. As the interviews were undertaken before it could be known how the child would be affected by the accident, the data on pre-injury behavior were likely to be as accurate and unbiased as data of this kind can be. Similar information was obtained from school teachers by means of a standardized questionnaire. All three groups were followed up for 2¼ years with further standardized assessments at 4 months, 1 year, and 2¼ years after the accident. It will be readily appreciated that the question of whether brain damage *causes* psychiatric disorder can be tested by determining whether the groups differed in terms of *changes* in behavior following the injury.

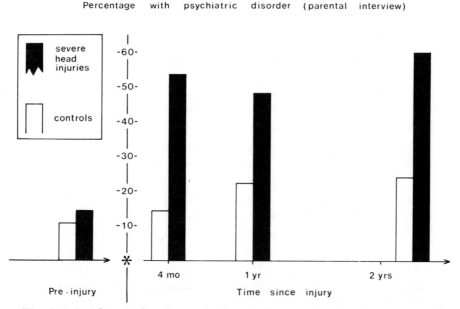

Fig. 4–3. Psychiatric disorder in children with severe head injuries, pre- and postinjury.

The findings for the severe head injury cases and their matched controls are summarized in Figure 4-3. This shows that the rates of psychiatric disorder were closely similar in the two groups *before* the accident, but that by 4 months after the injury, the rate of disorder in the severe head injury group had increased to a level well above that in the control group children who had suffered orthopedic injuries. The rate of disorder in the severe head injury group remained high and well above that in the control group throughout the whole of the 2¼-year follow-up.

It should be noted, however, that the findings for the *mild* head injury group were quite different in two crucial respects. First, children in this group showed an unusually high rate of behavioral disturbances *before* the accident. Thus, on the overall psychiatric assessment utilizing both the parental interview data and the information from schools, one-third of the children with mild head injuries showed a socially handicapping psychiatric disorder in comparison with only one in ten of the controls, a threefold difference. The implication is that the children with mild head injuries (unlike those with severe injuries) were behaviorally different (and more disturbed) *before* they sustained their head injury. Previous studies have produced closely comparable findings (Craft, Shaw, & Cartlidge, 1972). Second, the rate of psychiatric disorder in the mild head injury group showed *no* tendency to increase after the injury. The inference is that the psychiatric problems in the mild head injury group were unrelated to the head injury. It appears that whereas severe head injuries increase the risk of psychiatric disorder, mild head injuries do not.

This conclusion may be examined more closely by studying just those disorders that arose only *after* the injury, in children who were without disorder prior to the accident. A certain number of problems may be expected to arise simply as a consequence of the passage of time and the experience of the stresses that this may involve. In particular, problems may develop as a result of the stresses of the accident and of the subsequent hospital admission. However, these should occur in the controls to roughly the same extent as in the children with head injuries, since all but a few had had a hospital admission as a result of their accident. The *difference* between the head injured children and their matched controls in rates of *new* disorder should represent the disorders *specifically* due to brain injury. An additional methodological check may be achieved by utilizing independent psychiatric assessments made on the basis of interview protocols, from which all identifying data had been deleted, by a rater who was blind to whether the child was a case or a control. The findings are conclusive in showing that substantial psychiatric risk follows severe head injury. The rate of disorders arising *de novo* after the accident, in children without psychiatric disorder before the accident, was about 16 to 17% in the controls, but about 40% in the children who had sustained severe head injuries.

A further way of testing whether this represents a *causal* effect of brain injury is to determine the extent to which the head injury-psychiatric disorder association follows a consistent "dose-response relationship" (Rutter, 1981b). In other words, if it could be shown that the more severe the brain injury the greater the likelihood of psychiatric disorder, it would considerably strengthen the causal inference. This possibility was tested in three separate ways by using a number of different indices of brain injury: (a) the duration of the PTA, (b) neurological abnormalities on a systematic clinical examination by a research neurologist at the 2¼-year follow-up, and (c) the presence of transient or persistent intellectual impairment (which had been found to be a good index of the severity of brain injury). The analyses showed a statistically significant association between the rate of the psychiatric disorder and the duration of the PTA, but weaker and less consistent associations with both of the other indices of brain injury. In short, there was some kind of dose-response relationship, but of only moderate strength and consistency. These analyses give rise to two conclusions: (a) they confirm that there is indeed a truly *causal* effect by which severe head injury much increases the risk of psychiatric disorder; and (b) they suggest that the effect is often indirect rather than direct. Incidentally, this suggests a difference between psychiatric disorder and cognitive impairment with respect to the etiological role of brain injury. The dose-response relationship with cognitive impairment is strong and consistent, indicating a direct causal effect.

A threshold for psychiatric risk following brain injury

The second question with respect to the effects of brain damage in childhood is whether there is a threshold for psychiatric risk. In other words, what degree (or type) of brain injury is needed in order for the psychiatric risk to be increased? This issue may be approached by utilizing the same research strategies as those employed when considering the causal question. That is, we may use either the emergence of new disorders in children psychiatrically normal before the accident or a dose-response relationship as indicators that the psychiatric disorders were due to brain injury. The query, then, is how severe must the head injury be for such disorders to develop? The answer is the same whichever research strategy we use. There is no indication of any increased psychiatric risk with head injuries giving rise to a PTA of less than a week. In other words, in this group, there was no increase over controls in the rate of psychiatric disorders that arose *de novo* after the accident. Moreover, there was no evidence of a dose-response relationship within the PTA range of one hour to one week. That is to say, new psychiatric disorders were just as common in either controls who had no head injury or in the children with the very mildest of head injuries (with a PTA under 24 hours), as in the children with injuries of intermediate severity (involving a PTA of one to seven days). We may conclude that not only is there a threshold for psychiatric risk, but also that the threshold is a fairly high one. For any increase in psychiatric risk to be demonstrable, the head injury must have been sufficiently severe to cause a PTA of at least seven days. The evidence provides *no* support for the notion that very mild brain injury causes psychiatric problems. Brain damage may greatly increase the risk of psychiatric problems; however, it seems that the damage must be severe.

Of course that conclusion does not take into account either the locus or lateralization of the brain injury, which could be crucial modifying factors. The limited evidence available to date, however, provides no good indication that psychiatric risk in brain damage in childhood varies substantially according to the part of the brain damaged. The question was examined, for example, in a study of children with head injuries resulting in a compound depressed fracture, a dural tear, and visible damage to the underlying cortex (Shaffer, Chadwick, & Rutter, 1975). Because the site of the cortical trauma was identified visually at the time of neurosurgery, it was possible to place the locus of injury accurately. No association was found with psychiatric outcome; however, two caveats are necessary. First, because it was a follow-up rather than a prospective study we could not determine which disorders had arisen only after the injury. Without this information it was impossible to identify the psychiatric problems specifically with brain injury. Second, the lesions mainly involved cortical damage and it could be that subcortical lesions might give rise to more differentiated behavioral sequelae. There are too few data for the topic to be regarded as closed. Nevertheless, from research findings now available, behavioral effects did not vary with the locus of brain injury, although clearly it would be premature to conclude that there is no relationship (Rutter, Graham, & Yule, 1970). Accordingly, the conclusion stands that only fairly severe brain lesions substantially increase the risk of psychiatric disorder. The suggestion that minimal lesions may give rise to marked psychiatric sequelae has no sound research support.

Psychiatric sequelae in the absence of neurological signs

The suggestion above, however, does not adequately deal with the concept of "minimal brain dysfunction," in that the behavioral syndromes linked with this diagnostic term are usually said to occur in children who lack a history of brain damage and who do not exhibit unequivocally abnormal signs on a clinical neurological examination (Wender, 1971). As a result, there is no means of judging whether they have suffered minimal damage, maximal damage, or for that matter, any damage to the brain.

Rather, the concept turns on two other questions. First, is it possible for overt and indisputable brain damage to occur and yet for the neurological examination and/or EEG to reveal no abnormalities? The answer to that question is a clear-cut "yes." It is known that children who have had definite neurological abnormalities in infancy may appear normal when examined some years later (Solomon, Holden, & Denhoff, 1963). Similarly, it has been found that the neurological sequelae of encephalitis may disappear completely as the affected children grow older (Meyer & Byers, 1952). Also, in our study of children with gross damage to the brain confirmed at operation, only one-third showed definite neurological signs at follow-up a few years later, and one-third showed no signs whatever of abnormality, dubious or definite (Shaffer, Chadwick, & Rutter, 1975). All these findings indicate that there are some children with definite brain damage who show no abnormalities on clinical neurological examination. That part of the concept of "minimal brain dysfunction" has been supported by research findings (Rutter & Chadwick, 1980).

The second question is whether there is an increased psychiatric risk in children who show definite brain damage, but yet appear normal on clinical neurological examination. To answer that question we need to return to the findings from our prospective study of children with severe head injuries. Only about one-half these children showed neurological abnormalities in spite of the fact that all had experienced a PTA of more than one week. What was the rate of new psychiatric disorders (that is, those arising only *after* the head injury) in children without neurological abnormalities? As shown in Figure 4-4, the rate of disorder in children with severe head injuries was, in fact, still substantially above that in the controls even in the subgroup with a normal neurological examination (although the rate of psychiatric disorder was highest in those with abnormalities on a clinical examination). The finding shows that brain injury (as indicated by a PTA of more than one week) can lead to psychiatric abnormalities even when there are no discernible neurological sequelae.

Of course, it could be argued that the clinical examination is a very crude tool for the detection of brain injury. That is certainly true, but the concept of "minimal brain dysfunction" is based on clinical findings. We may approach the same problem another way by utilizing measurements of intellectual impairment. Psychiatric disorder is not restricted to those brain-damaged children who showed serious cognitive deficits as a result of their head injury, as illustrated by the findings in Figure 4-5. Although the psychiatric risk was indeed greater in those children with persisting intellectual impairment (a subgroup of those with the most

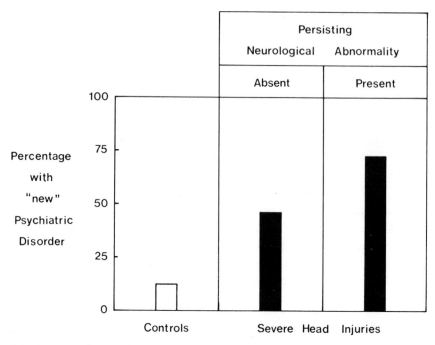

Fig. 4–4. Psychiatric disorder in children with severe head injuries according to the presence or absence of persisting neurological abnormality.

severe injuries), the rate was still well above the control group, even in children with *no* measurable intellectual impairment.

In summary, the research findings show that psychiatric disorders due to brain injury arise in children of normal IQ and with a normal neurological examination. To that limited extent, there is support for the hypothesis of psychiatric disorders due to MBD. But once more, serious caveats have to be added. We must re-emphasize that this conclusion applies only to children who have suffered a *severe* head injury. No such effect was found in children with a PTA of less than one week. It seems that the threshold for psychiatric risk is fairly high. Accordingly, the conclusion cannot be generalized to children with milder head injuries and certainly not to the even wider concept of MBD sometimes held to apply to one-half the child psychiatric clinic population (Wender, 1971). A second caveat is that the concept of MBD includes the notion of a distinctive and diagnosable psychiatric syndrome that differs from other mental disorders of childhood.

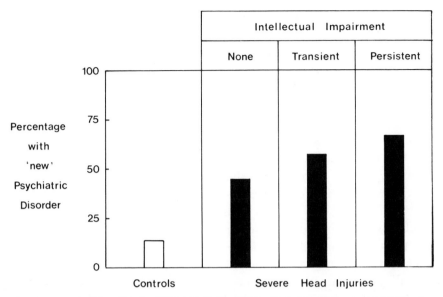

Fig. 4–5. Psychiatric disorder following severe head injuries according to the presence or absence of intellectual impairment.

A characteristic brain dysfunction syndrome?

That brings us to the fourth major question concerning the effects of brain damage in childhood—Is there a type of syndrome that, by its form and characteristics, can be identified as a consequence of brain injury? The question has been considered in a variety of different neurobehavioral studies with largely negative findings (Rutter, 1977, 1981a). Whether subjects have been examined through questionnaires or detailed interview assessments (Rutter, Graham, & Yule, 1970) or by objective measures of molecular detail (Shaffer, McNamara, & Pincus, 1974), the result has always been that brain-damaged children show a heterogeneous range of psychiatric disorders that lack specific features and that appear generally similar to those seen in any other group of children. However, it is possible that this generally negative finding might be a consequence of the fact that much psychiatric disturbance in brain-damaged children arises, at it does in other children, from psychosocial disadvantage and family adversity, rather than directly from the brain injury per se. It is clear that many mechanisms are involved in the genesis of psychiatric disorder (Rutter, 1977). In order to test adequately the hypothesis of behavioral specificity, it is necessary to focus on that subgroup of psychiatric disorders specifically *due* to brain damage. The prospective study of children with severe head injuries helps in this connection. It was possible to choose psychiatric conditions that could reasonably be attributed to brain injury by specifying that three operational criteria be met: (a) that they occurred in children who experienced a head injury of sufficient severity that some form of brain dysfunction or damage could be regarded as likely (namely injuries resulting in at least seven days PTA); (b) that the disorders arose *after* the head injury; and (c) that they occurred in children who did *not* exhibit psychiatric disorder before the injury. These conditions could then be compared with psychiatric disorders known *not* to be due to brain injury because they occurred in control children with orthopedic injuries or because they had been present before the accident in children with head injuries.

These two groups were systematically compared according to psychiatric diagnoses (made by an independent rater who was "blind" to the child's group), detailed parental interview ratings of individual behaviors, observations of the children's behavior during psychological testing, and teacher questionnaire ratings. In brief, with one important exception, all these separate comparisons showed that the emotional and behavioral problems attributable to head injury were closely similar to those known not to be due to head injury. It was especially noteworthy, in view of hypotheses about hyperactivity and MBD, that hyperactivity was *not* particularly linked with brain injury. Indeed, on three of the comparisons, hyperactivity was actually significantly *less* frequent in the disorders attributable to brain injury. This difference was mainly a consequence of the fact that hyperactivity was most frequent of all in the case of disorders present *before* the accident in children with mild head injuries. Clearly, the presence of hyperactivity *cannot* be used as an indicator of brain damage.

The only way in which the disorders attributable to brain injury differed was in terms of the frequency of socially inappropriate or socially disinhibited behavior. There were five cases of disorder in which this constituted the predominant feature; all were in the group of conditions attributable to head injury. These children were markedly outspoken and showed a general lack of regard for social convention. Frequently, they made very personal remarks or asked embarrassing questions, and they sometimes undressed in social situations in which this would ordinarily be regarded as unacceptable behavior. Some of these disinhibited disorders also included forgetfulness, overtalkativeness, carelessness in personal hygiene and dress, and impulsiveness. Clearly, these conditions resemble the frontal lobe syndromes sometimes seen in brain-injured adults. The more detailed measures of individual behaviors merely served to confirm that this group of symptoms was indeed probably a specific consequence of brain injury.

Interestingly, by the time of the 2¼-year follow-up, there were two cases in which this disinhibited state had changed its form and was diagnosed as hyperkinetic syndrome. These constituted only a minority of cases, but there was the slight suggestion that *some* varieties of the hyperkinetic syndrome may be due to brain damage. The numbers are far too small for any firm conclusions, although it seems that it may be worth further exploring the possibility that within the broad group of hyperkinetic conditions there may be a small subgroup in which the etiological process involves brain injury.

Conclusions on the psychiatric effects of brain injury

Let us summarize the results so far. Four main conclusions may be drawn: (a) brain injury definitely increases the risk of psychiatric disorder to a marked degree; (b) this increased vulnerability applies not only to children with cerebral palsy, epilepsy, or some other obvious neurological disorder, but also to those for whom the clinical neurological examination reveals no such abnormality; (c) this increased risk of psychiatric disorder applies only above a rather high threshold to children who have suffered a fairly severe brain injury (it does *not* extend to those with only mild injuries); and (d) with the exception of social disinhibition, there is nothing particularly distinctive about the psychiatric disorders attributable to brain injury, and, in particular, they do *not* usually take the form of hyperkinesis.

The hyperkinetic syndrome

We turn now to the second major hypothesis that specifies that the "hyperkinetic syndrome" constitutes a valid, meaningful, and clinically useful diagnostic category that differs from other forms of psychiatric disorder (Rutter, 1982). In this hypothesis, the postulate that the hyperkinetic syndrome differs from *other* psychiatric syndromes (and not just from normality) is crucial. Together with colleagues we have undertaken several rather different types of study to investigate this issue.

The first study, by Seija Sandberg (Sandberg, Rutter, & Taylor, 1978), was based on primary school boys (aged 5 to 11 years) referred to the Maudsley Hospital. The research design involved the comparison of disorders in which the symptoms of hyperactivity or inattention occurred in marked degree, on the one hand, and, on the other, all other psychiatric disorders. In short, the purpose was to determine if these hyperkinetic symptoms differentiated a distinctive psychiatric group. Various measures were used to determine hyperkinesis, but in line with most other previous investigators in this field, we place particular reliance on the Conners' teacher and parent scales. We also assessed hyperactivity by means of systematic observations of the child during psychological testing. Our dependent variables were chosen on the basis of the features generally supposed to be associated with the hyperkinetic syndrome. Thus, we examined the children for congenital stigmata and neurological abnormalities and obtained data on perinatal complications. We assessed impulsivity by means of the Matching Familiar Figures Test and administered tests of general intelligence and scholastic achievement.

Four main findings stand out from the data analysis. First, different measures of hyperactivity did not correlate well. This result has been evident in all previous investigations. Children who were hyperkinetic on one measure or in one situation quite often were *not* hyperactive on other measures or in other situations. Second, not only did a high proportion of psychiatric disorders involve the symptoms of hyperactivity and poor concentration, but there also was a very substantial overlap between hyperactivity and general disturbances of conduct (aggression and/or antisocial behavior). Third, the presence of hyperkinesis (as defined in terms of a score on the hyperactivity factor of the Conners' scale, which was 1.5 or 2 standard deviations above the general population mean) was of no clinical significance. There were only three significant differences between the hyperactive and the non-hyperactive disorders and these did not fit the MBD hypothesis. That is, hyperactivity was associated with a *slow* reaction time, a *lack* of perinatal complications, and large family size. We are forced to conclude that the differences between hyperactive children and normal children are quite different from those between hyperactive children and children with *other* psychiatric conditions.

All three conclusions run entirely against the hyperkinetic syndrome hypothesis. The fourth conclusion, however, leaves open the possibility

that there may be a meaningful and valid *rarer* subgroup of hyperactive
children. The results summarized in the first three conclusions all refer
to hyperkinesis as assessed on just one measure. What happens if, instead,
hyperactivity is defined in terms of abnormality on *all* measures of hyperactivity. To examine this question, we took only children with abnormal
scores on the teachers' questionnaire *and* the parents' questionnaire *and*
the observational measures. This left us with only seven children—just
10% of the total group of those with psychiatric disorders. These seven
children were both younger and of lower intelligence than the total
group, so we picked out seven normally active controls individually
matched for age and IQ. The findings are summarized in Table 4-1. This
rarer group of children with pervasive hyperactivity differed significantly
in having been hyperactive from preschool years, in showing more errors
on the Matching Familiar Figures Test, and in being more likely to have
neurodevelopmental abnormalities. The findings suggest that this rarer
group of hyperkinetic children might constitute a valid diagnostic entity,
although the numbers were far too small for this conclusion to be anything but tentative and provisional. However, the study provided *no* evidence to support the more usual wider concept of hyperkinetic syndrome.

The above study constituted a one-time examination of a clinic sample,
the hyperkinetic syndrome has also been studied using a different research strategy—the longitudinal study of a general population sample
(Schachar, Rutter, & Smith, 1981). Data from the Isle of Wight survey
were utilized for this purpose. This involved the investigation of *all* ten-

Table 4-1. Summary of test results of previously hyperactive children and
controls matched for age and IQ. (Adapted from Sandberg et al., 1978.)

	Pervasively Hyperactive (n = 7) Mean (S. D.)	Matched Controls (n = 7) Mean (S. D.)
Matching familiar figures		
reaction time (secs)	5.0 (1.5)	4.8 (1.8)
errors	24.4 (6.4)*	16.4 (4.0)
Neurological examination score	12.7 (7.8)*	5.0 (4.0)
Congenital anomalies	3.7 (2.3)	2.7 (1.2)
	Proportion	Proportion
Onset before 5 years	6/7**	1/7

* Significantly different from matched controls $p < 0.05$ (t Test)
** Significantly different from matched controls $p < 0.05$ (Fisher's Exact Test)

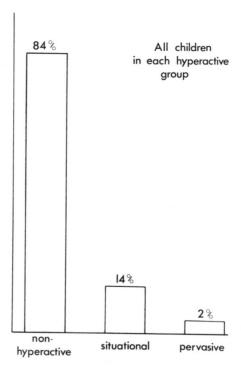

Fig. 4–6. Situational and pervasive hyperactivity in 10-year-old children on the Isle of Wight.

year-olds living on the island, using behavioral questionnaires completed by teachers and by parents and psycho-educational tests taken by the children. The whole population was followed up to age 14 to 15 years and re-investigated, using the same methods. The questionnaire in this case, unlike the previous study, was the Rutter scale. A principal components analysis of the questionnaire in different age groups gave rise to a highly consistent hyperactivity factor; the items in this factor were used to produce a hyperactivity score. These scores were then used to divide the total general population into three non-overlapping groups, as shown in Figure 4-6. First, there were those few children with high scores on *both* the parent *and* the teacher questionnaires; these constituted about 2% of the population and this group was called the "pervasive overactivity" group. Second, there were the children with high scores on one or other of the questionnaires, but not on both; they constituted about 14% of the total population, and it was termed the "situational overactivity"

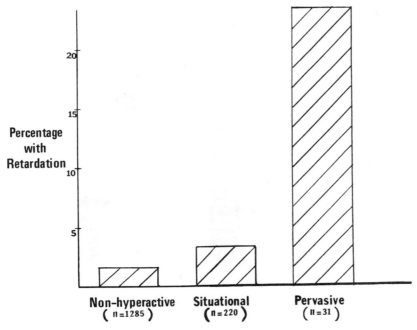

Fig. 4–7. The association between hyperactivity and intellectual retardation as measured on non-verbal tests in 10-year-old children on the Isle of Wight.

group. The third group, involving the majority of the population, was made up of children who were not overactive on either measure. The question, then, is how do these three groups differ, after having controlled for the presence of psychiatric disorder, socioeconomic background, and any other relevant variable?

The first very striking finding was that *pervasive* overactivity was strongly associated with the presence of cognitive deficits, as indicated by Figure 4-7. This association was equally strong whether examined in terms of scores on tests of general intelligence or on tests of scholastic achievement. It is noteworthy, however, that this association did *not* apply to situational hyperactivity. This result provided the first indication that pervasive and situational hyperactivity might reflect rather different types of behavioral disturbance.

The second equally striking finding was that pervasive overactivity

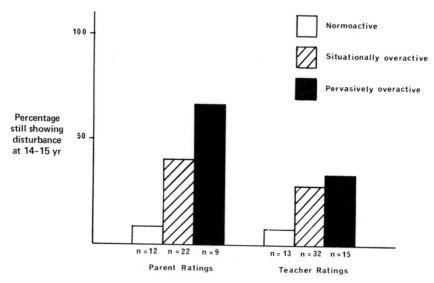

Fig. 4–8. Overactivity and behavioral prognosis in children with behavior disturbance at 10 years.

was strongly associated with the persistence of psychiatric disorder, however this was measured. There was a similar, but less marked, association with situational overactivity as shown in Figure 4-8. These two findings taken in combination suggested that pervasive, but not situational, hyperactivity might constitute a meaningfully different behavioral syndrome that was distinctive both in terms of its association with cognitive impairment and in terms of its chronicity and persistence into adolescence.

A further methodological check was needed before we could conclude that these associations were specific to pervasive hyperactivity. We needed to determine whether comparable results would have been obtained with any other constellation of behaviors. Poor peer relationships have been found to have a strong association with general social and behavioral disturbance and to carry a poor prognosis (Roff, Sells, & Golden, 1972). Accordingly, this behavioral pattern seemed to constitute an appropriate one to compare with hyperactivity. The three items on the parent and teacher scales that reflected poor peer relationships were summed to provide an "unsociability" score comparable to the hyper-

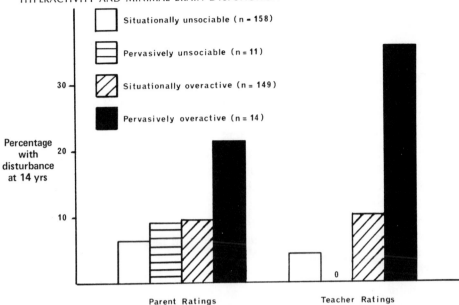

Fig. 4-9. Prediction of behavior disturbance at 14 years, according to the presence of unsociability or overactivity at 10 years.

activity score. Situational and pervasive unsociability were defined in the same way as hyperactivity. As might well be expected, there was a good deal of overlap between hyperactivity and unsociability; these "overlap" children were excluded for the purposes of comparing the two behaviors.

Figure 4-9 shows the findings with respect to the persistence of behavioral problems between 10 and 15 years of age. It is immediately apparent that there were no differences between the situationally unsociable and the situationally overactive children. On the other hand, the pervasively hyperactive children stood out as quite different from all other groups in terms of their worse prognosis. This strong persistence of disorder into adolescence was *not* found with pervasive unsociability.

The cognitive findings also clearly differentiated the pervasive hyperactivity group. This group had a mean non-verbal IQ score of about 80. In contrast, all the other groups had a mean non-verbal score that was about average. We may conclude that the characteristics associated with *situational* hyperactivity were probably nonspecific and, hence, of no particular diagnostic significance. On the other hand, the very small group of children with *pervasive* hyperactivity did seem distinctively different. Evidently this rarer phenomenon may have some clinical significance; the hypothesis of a valid syndrome of pervasive overactivity is worth further exploration. However, there are no findings to support the more common, wider concept of hyperkinesis.

Of course, these results in no way resolve the question of the etiology of hyperkinesis, which requires a quite different form of investigation. The observation that many of the pervasively hyperactive children were also cognitively retarded is consistent with the hypothesis that the syndrome is due to some form of brain damage or dysfunction. However, there was no direct measure of brain function, and other causal explorations are both possible and plausible.

So far, the only etiological possibility considered is organic brain injury. In order to put matters into better perspective we turn briefly to two other different types of influences on child behavior. First, there are the findings from Penny Dixon's (1981) study of the effects of different patterns of upbringing. In brief, she compared the behavior of three groups of infant-school children: one group reared in institutions from the first year of life, one group brought up by foster parents from the first year, and a control group of children reared in the ordinary way by biological parents.

Of all the behavioral differences between these three groups, the most marked concerned overactivity. As shown in Figure 4-10, the institutional boys were very liable to show hyperkinesis, but fewer of the fostered boys exhibited this behavior. These data derive from teacher questionnaire scores, but closely similar findings were obtained from interview ratings

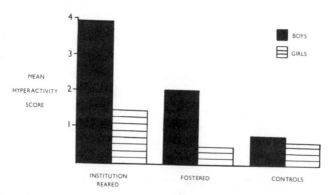

Fig. 4–10. Hyperactivity in institution-reared, fostered, and control children aged 5 to 8 years. (Dixon, 1981.)

and from systematic time-sampled observations in the classroom. Moreover, in an independent study, Tizard and Hodges (1978) found the same pattern of results with overactivity very prevalent among children who had spent their first few years in an institution. Of course, it could be argued that the overactivity derives from genetic predisposition rather than from a particular form of upbringing. That suggestion might apply to the case-control difference, but it seems most unlikely that it could account for the institution-foster family difference. Both groups of children came from a severely disadvantaged background with overt mental illness and serious personality disorders evident in many of the parents. However, an analysis of the family history data (which were rated "blind" to which group the child was in) showed no differences between the institution and foster children in this connection. Accordingly, it seems that the syndrome of hyperactivity, often linked with MBD, may sometimes be due to environmental factors.

A recent comparative study of secondary schools in inner London provides a second example of the role of environmental influences on such behaviors as activity and attention (Rutter, Maughan, Mortimore, & Ouston, 1979). Among other things, the study provided data on possible school influences on children's behavior. The children were studied *before* they entered secondary school as well as during and after their secondary schooling. This made it possible to determine how much variation was due to differences in intake of the schools and how much to experiences while they were at secondary school. Because the characteristics of the schools were studied in great detail over the course of three years, we could relate school characteristics to pupil behavior. Two measures are relevant for present purposes. First, there is what we called "school process," in essence a composite measure of various features of the schools as social institutions. Second, there is our summary measure of "pupil behavior" based on systematic observations in the classroom and self-reports from the pupils. It was *not* designed to pick out hyperkinetic children; nevertheless, the scale focused on the inattentive socially disruptive behavior that involves many elements of the syndrome. As shown in Figure 4-11, we found that these two measures of "school process" and "pupil behavior" were strongly associated. The total pattern of findings enabled us to conclude that it was highly likely that the children's behavior was being strongly influenced by experiences at school. Some of these influences concerned overactive, inattentive, and disruptive behavior—elements of the hypothesized hyperkinetic syndrome.

Fig. 4–11. The association between school characteristics (as reflected in the combined process score) and pupil behavior in school.

Conclusions on the hyperkinetic syndrome

What conclusions, then, can be drawn on the validity of this syndrome? We suggest that there are four. First, hyperactivity and attentional deficits do not constitute a unitary syndrome. There are relatively low correlations between different measures of overactivity and inattention, and both behaviors tend to vary a good deal from situation to situation. Second, there is enormous overlap between the behaviors of overactivity and those of antisocial aggressive activity. The main question here concerns how this very broad group of disorders involving socially disapproved behavior should be subdivided. Third, the symptom of hyperactivity does not have a single cause, and is not necessarily due to brain damage. Fourth, there appear to be crucial differences between situational and pervasive hyperactivity. The more common situational variety seems to be of no particular clinical significance; but the rarer pervasive variety may constitute a meaningfully distinct syndrome; certainly that possibility warrants further investigation.

Minimal brain dysfunction as a genetic or metabolic syndrome

The last hypothesis to be considered is that of MBD as a genetic or meta-bolic syndrome (Wender, 1971). We have shown that brain injury does not give rise to a distinctive behavioral syndrome (with the exception of social disinhibition), and we have found that hyperactivity is not a uni-tary phenomenon and is not necessarily due to brain damage. However, these largely negative findings are not sufficient to discard the concept of MBD. After all, there are many examples in medicine of diseases that show themselves in a variety of ways. This is true, for example, of infec-tions, such as tuberculosis or syphilis, which can affect different organs in a variety of different ways. This also applies to such genetic conditions as dystrophia myotonica, which can affect the eyes without the muscles or vice versa. However, in all such cases there is evidence (often in the form of some biological feature) that, in spite of symptom differences, the conditions are basically similar and also that they differ in a sys-tematic fashion from other diseases. Does this apply to MBD? Various attempts have been made to examine this possibility.

It has been claimed, for example, that specific hereditary influences produce different symptoms, and thus differentiate between syndromes. But do they? It is important to recognize that two questions are involved here: (a) Are there hereditary influences? and (b) If there are, are they of a kind that *differ* from those involved in other psychiatric syndromes (i.e., are different genes involved)? With respect to the first question, it has been shown that the rate of psychiatric illness (especially alcoholism, sociopathy, and hysteria) is increased in the *biological* relatives of hyper-kinetic children, but that it is not increased in the *adoptive* parents of such children (Cantwell, 1972, 1975; Morrison, 1973; Morrison & Stewart, 1971). The findings are interesting, although, of course, it is impossible to infer a genetic basis until there is also information on the biological relatives of adopted hyperkinetic and non-hyperkinetic children. This is because the difference could be simply a function of a generally lower rate of psychiatric disorder in adoptive parents as a result of selection policies on parents who are accepted as suitable for taking adoptive chil-dren. However, even if this were obtained, and even if it confirmed a hereditary influence, this would still *not* validate the syndrome as an entity. Before genetic findings could be used for this purpose, it would have to be demonstrated that the inheritance was *different* from that in other psychiatric disorders. Not only has this not been done, but also it is immediately apparent that the family history findings in the Morrison, the Morrison and Stewart, and the Cantwell studies were closely similar to those previously reported for aggressive antisocial children. We must conclude that so far genetic findings have not answered any questions of syndrome definition.

An alternative approach has been to invoke biochemical findings (Wender, 1971). There are some useful leads here from animal work (Shaywitz, Klupper, Yager, & Gordon, 1976; Grahame-Smith, 1978), and there is one report of low levels of dopaminergic activity in a very small sample of six children said to have MBD (Shaywitz, Cohen, & Bowers, 1977). However, it is far too early to draw firm conclusions. In the future, such research may come to provide a better guide to diagnosis and syndrome validation, but certainly we are not yet at that point.

Another approach involves good response to stimulant medication as the key feature defining MBD. If it were true that children with MBD responded differently to stimulants, this would indeed be a most useful validating feature. However, although claims of a specific drug response have been made (Wender, 1971; Wood, Reimherr, Wender, & Johnson, 1976), there is no good evidence that it exists. Numerous drug studies attest to the short-term benefits of stimulant medication in hyperkinetic children (Barkley, 1977), but that is not the point. The key issue from a nosological standpoint is whether the response is *different* from that in other psychiatric conditions. This has yet to be systematically studied, but, with the possible exception of anxiety states, most disorders seem to respond well to stimulants (Barkley, 1976; Sroufe, 1975). Indeed, at least over a few hours, even normal children seem to respond in much the same way to stimulants (Rapoport, Buchsbaum, Zahn, Weingartner, Ludlow, & Mikkelsen, 1977). Drug response, furthermore, does not appear to relate to differences in autonomic arousal, even though this is one mechanism hypothesized to underlie hyperactivity (Barkley & Jackson, 1977). Also, in spite of very different pharmacological actions, amitryptiline and methylphenidate were found in one study to have very comparable effects on hyperactivity (Yepes, Balka, Winsberg, & Bialer, 1977). The critical investigations have yet to be undertaken, but the evidence to date does *not* indicate that either the hyperkinetic syndrome or MBD is associated with a distinctive response to stimulants. Nevertheless, this is certainly a line of research worth pursuing.

The last strategy is to use prognosis as a guide to diagnosis. Unfortunately, this too is not of much help. Various follow-up studies indicated that hyperkinetic children often continue to show social problems in adolescence and adult life (Shaffer, 1978). However, this is also true of children with other forms of psychiatric disorder (Robins, 1979), and it remains uncertain whether the prognosis of children diagnosed as having MBD is any different from the prognosis of children having the hyperkinetic syndrome.

In conclusion, then, the hypothesis of MBD as a genetic or biochemical entity so far lacks empirical support.

References

Barkley, R. Predicting the response of hyperkinetic children to stimulant drop: A review. *Journal of Abnormal Child Psychology*, 1976, *4*, 327–348.

Barkley, R. A review of stimulant drug research with hyperkinetic children. *Journal of Child Psychology and Psychiatry*, 1977, *18*, 137–166.

Barkley, R. & Jackson, T. Hyperkinesis, autonomic nervous system activity and stimulant drug effect. *Journal of Child Psychology and Psychiatry*, 1977, *18*, 347–358.

Brown, G., Chadwick, O., Shaffer, D., Rutter, M., & Traub, M. A prospective study of children with head injuries. III. Psychiatric sequelae. *Psychological Medicine*, 1981, *11*, 63–78.

Cantwell, D. Psychiatric illness in the families of hyperactive children. *Archives of General Psychiatry*, 1972, *27*, 414–417.

Cantwell, D. Genetic studies of hyperactive children. In R. Fieve, D. Rosenthal, & H. Brill (Eds.), *Genetic research in psychiatry*. Baltimore: Johns Hopkins Press, 1975.

Chadwick, O., Brown, G., Rutter, M., Shaffer, D., & Traub, M. A prospective study of children with head injuries. II. Cognitive Sequelae. *Psychological Medicine*, 1981, *11*, 49–61.

Craft, A., Shaw, D., & Cartlidge, N. Head injuries in children. *British Medical Journal*, 1972, *3*, 200–203.

Dixon, P. (1981) Paper in preparation.

Grahame-Smith, D. Animal hyperactivity syndromes: Do they have any relevance to minimal brain dysfunction: In A. Kalveboer, H. van Praag, & J. Mentlewica (Eds.), *Minimal brain dysfunction: Fact or fiction: Advances in biological psychiatry* (Vol. I). Basel: Karger, 1978.

Meyer, E. & Byers, R. Measles encephalitis: A follow-up study of sixteen patients. *American Journal of Diseases in Childhood*, 1952, *84*, 543–579.

Morrison, J. The psychiatric status of the legal families of adopted hyperactive children. *Archives of General Psychiatry*, 1973, *28*, 888–891.

Morrison, J. & Stewart, M. A family study of the hyperactive child syndrome. *Biological Psychiatry*, 1971, *3*, 189–195.

Rapoport, J., Buchsbaum, M., Zahn, T., Weingartner, H., Ludlow, C., & Mikkelson, E. Dextroamphetamine: Cognitive and behavioral effects in normal prepubertal boys. *Science*, 1977, *199*, 560–563.

Robins, L. Longitudinal methods in the study of normal and psychological development. In K. Kisker, J. Meyer, C. Muller, & E. Stromgren (Eds.), *Psychiatrie der Gegenwart*, B and 1, "Grundlagen und Methoden der Psychiatrie" Heidelberg: Springer-Verlag, 1979.

Roff, M., Sells, S., & Golden, M. *Social adjustment and personality development in children*. Minneapolis, MN: University of Minnesota Press, 1972.

Rutter, M. Brain damage syndromes in childhood: Concepts and findings. *Journal of Child Psychology and Psychiatry*, 1977, *18*, 1–22.

Rutter, M. Diagnostic validity in child psychiatry. *Advances in Biological Psychiatry*, 1978, *12*, 2–22.

Rutter, M. Psychological sequelae of brain damage in children. *American Journal of Psychiatry*, 1981a, *138*, 1533–1544.

Rutter, M. Epidemiological/longitudinal strategies and causal research in child psychiatry. *Journal of the American Academy of Child Psychiatry*, 1981b, *20*, 513–544.

Rutter, M. Syndromes attributed to "minimal brain dysfunction" in children. *American Journal of Psychiatry*, 1982, *139*, 21–33.

Rutter, M. & Chadwick, O. Neurobehavioural associations and syndromes of "minimal brain dysfunction." In F. Rose (Ed.), *Clinical Neuro-Epidemiology*. London: Pitman, 1980.

Rutter, M., Chadwick, O., Shaffer, D., & Brown, G. A prospective study of children with head injuries. I. Description and Methods. *Psychological Medicine*, 1980, *10*, 633–645.

Rutter, M., Graham, P., & Yule, W. A neuropsychiatric study in childhood. *Clinics in Developmental Medicine No. 35/36*. London: Heinemann Medical School Press, 1970.

Rutter, M., Maughan, B., Mortimore, P., & Ouston, J. *Fifteen thousand hours: Secondary schools and their effects on children*. London: Open Books. Cambridge, MA: Harvard University Press, 1979.

Sandberg, S., Rutter, M., & Taylor, E. Hyperkinetic disorder in clinic attenders. *Developmental Medicine and Child Neurology*, 1978, *20*, 279–299.

Schachar, R., Rutter, M., & Smith, A. The characteristics of situationally and pervasively hyperactive children: Implications for syndrome definition. *Journal of Child Psychology and Psychiatry*, 1981, *22*, 375–392.

Seidel, U., Chadwick, O., & Rutter, M. Psychological disorders in crippled children: A comparative study of children with and without brain damage. *Developmental Medicine and Child Neurology*, 1975, *17*, 563–573.

Shaffer, D. Longitudinal research and the minimal brain damage syndrome. In A. Kalveboer, H. van Praag, & J. Mendlewicz (Eds.), Minimal brain dysfunction: Fact or Fiction? *Advances in Biological Psychiatry* (Vol. 1). Basel: Karger, 1978.

Shaffer, D., Chadwick, O., & Rutter, M. Psychiatric outcome of localized head injury in children. In R. Porter & D. Fitzsimmons (Eds.), *Outcome of Severe Damage to the Central Nervous System* (Ciba Foundation Symposium 34, New Series). Elsevier: Amsterdam-North-Holland, 1975.

Shaffer, D., McNamara, N., & Pincus, J. Controlled observations on patterns of activity, attention and impulsivity in brain damaged and psychiatrically disturbed boys. *Psychological Medicine*, 1974, *4*, 4–18.

Shaywitz, B., Cohen, D., & Bowers, D. CSF monoamine metabolites in children with minimal brain dysfunction—Evidence for alteration of brain dopamine. *Journal of Pediatrics*, 1977, *90*, 67–71.

Shaywitz, B., Klupper, J., Yager, R., & Gordon, J. Paradoxical response to amphetamine in developing rats treated with 6-hydroxy dopamine. *Nature*, 1976, *261*, 153–155.

Solomon, G., Holden, R., & Denhoff, E. The changing picture of cerebral dysfunction in early childhood. *Journal of Pediatrics*, 1963, *63*, 113–120.

Sroufe, L. Drug treatment of children with behavior problems. In F. Horowitz (Ed.), *Review of child development research* (Vol. 4). Chicago: University of Chicago Press, 1975.

Tizard, B. & Hodges, J. The effect of early institutional rearing on the development of eight-year-old children. *Journal of Child Psychology and Psychiatry*, 1978, *19*, 99–118.

Wender, P. *Minimal Brain Dysfunction in Children*. New York: Wiley, 1971.

Wood, D., Reimherr, F., Wender, P., & Johnson, G. Diagnosis and treatment of minimal brain dysfunction in adults. *Archives of General Psychiatry*, 1976, *33*, 1453–1460.

Yepes, L., Balka, E., Winsberg, B., & Bialer, I. Amitriptyline and methylphenidate treatment of behaviourally disordered children. *Journal of Child Psychology and Psychiatry*, 1977, *18*, 39–52.

5. Developmental disorders: Etiology and outcome

Ralph E. Tarter and Andrea M. Hegedus

The most recent definition of a developmental disability is contained in the Rehabilitation, Comprehensive Services and Developmental Disabilities Amendment to Public Law 95-602. Unlike its forerunner (PL 94-103), the new law emphasizes central nervous system (CNS) dysfunction underlying the disability. Signed into law in 1978 by President Carter, this new law defines a developmental disability according to the following criteria:

1. The deficit has a "mental" and/or physical basis
2. The impairment persists indefinitely
3. The onset is prior to 22 years of age
4. Limitations exist in at least three aspects of functioning in such areas as self-care, learning capacity, language ability, self-direction, mobility, and capacity to live independently
5. Individualized treatment services are needed that are of lifelong duration

Disturbances of CNS functioning can be divided into two types: those in which there are verified brain lesions and those in which there is no direct evidence of brain pathology. The former group includes a variety of neurological disorders such as strokes, tumors, degenerative processes, and congenital brain malformations. Neuroradiological and other laboratory procedures can readily confirm the presence of brain pathology. In the latter group of disorders, *inferences* are made about a neurogenic etiology. These inferences range from highly probable to speculative. In the case of idiopathic epilepsy, for example, the inference of disturbed CNS functioning is very strong. It is often less convincing in developmental disorders.

Some developmental conditions, like infantile autism, are characterized by such severe functional incapacity that a neurological etiology would seem obvious, but even here a theory of psychological causation has been advanced (Bettelheim, 1967). In other conditions, such as mental retardation, hyperactivity, and learning disability, no neurological signs or symptoms are observed in a significant proportion of cases (Benton, 1970; Rutter et al., Chapter 5; Satz & Morris, Chapter 6). Genetics, parental rearing style, and social deprivation are non-neurological factors that could cause a developmental disorder. Thus, it is highly unlikely that disturbed brain functioning is a universal etiological factor in the developmental disabilities.

This chapter will address the multiple causes and long-term outcome of several developmental disorders. For a discussion of short-term outcome and classification, see Chapters 1, 4, and 6. Certain disorders, such as autism and mental retardation will not be considered, since very little is known about the factors that affect their outcome in terms of either clinical or cognitive status. Thus, this chapter will be confined to a discussion of those conditions for which outcome in adulthood can be determined.

Hyperactivity and minimal brain dysfunction

Labels such as "hyperkinetic reaction of childhood," "hyperactive child syndrome," "minimal cerebral dysfunction," "minimal brain damage," and "minimal brain dysfunction" (MBD) are frequently used to describe children of adequate intelligence who do fulfill their potential in school, who exhibit interpersonal problems with peers, and who present management problems at home. Distractibility, impulsivity, excessive purposeless activity, restlessness, temper tantrums, lability, and unpredictability are commonly reported characteristics of these children.

Initially, an organic cause was hypothesized for the disturbed behavior, even though there was no clear evidence of brain damage in most cases. It was reasoned that since hyperactive children and children with known brain lesions behaved similarly, the same anatomical substrate must be disrupted. Hence, Strauss and Lehtinen (1947) advanced the notion of a "brain damage syndrome" to describe children who were undercontrolled, overly active, and unable to adjust adequately. Subsequently, Laufer, Denhoff, and Solomons (1957) described a similar behavior pattern, which they labeled "hyperkinetic impulse disorder." The salient features were hyperactivity, short attention span, poor concentration, irritability, impulsiveness, and poor quality schoolwork. Inspired by Bradley and Bowen's (1941) observation that amphetamines had a quieting effect in some hyperactive children, Laufer et al. (1957) postulated that the diencephalon was the locus of the brain dysfunction. They also suggested that emotional problems could cause hyperactivity in children, thereby raising the possibility of multiple etiologies for this disorder.

Once it was recognized that many hyperactive children could not be unequivocally diagnosed as brain damaged, emphasis shifted to "soft" neurological signs. These signs, usually behavioral in nature, are assumed to reflect subtle brain pathology. Greenberg and McMahon (1977), however, found that soft signs tend to diminish or disappear during maturation. Rutter, Graham, and Yule (1970) observed up to five soft signs in 16% of hyperactive children who had no known neurological disorder, thereby raising doubts about the pathognomic significance of these characteristics. Moreover, it has been reported that hyperactive children do not have more neurological soft signs than do other children (Werry & Aman, 1976). Despite evidence to the contrary, the notion of soft signs has remained quite popular, due, in large part, to the belief in a neurological causation for hyperactivity. As will be seen below, hyperactivity has numerous causes, one of which is a neurological disturbance.

ETIOLOGY

Numerous hypotheses have been advanced regarding the etiology of hyperactivity. Genetic, neurochemical, metabolic, traumatic, and toxic causes have been proposed. Space limitations prevent a detailed review of each hypothesis, but as will be seen below, a hyperactive behavior pattern can emerge via a number of different etiological pathways.

Genetic factors. The observation that hyperactivity runs in families even when the children are reared away from their biological parents has been interpreted as evidence for a genetic etiology (Cantwell, 1975; Stewart, 1970). Silver (1971) reported up to a 40% incidence of hyperactivity and learning disorders in children if a parent had these disorders. Safer (1973) observed a higher concordance for MBD in full sibs than in half sibs who were placed in foster homes. All the full sibs were hyperactive, whereas only two of the 14 half sibs were. A higher concordance for hyperactivity in monozygotic than in dizygotic twins has also been demonstrated (Willerman, 1973).

The evidence that activity level may be genetically mediated raises an interesting issue; namely, whether or not hyperactive children are categorically different from their peers or, instead, simply manifest quantitatively more extreme characteristics along the putative dimensions. As discussed by Rutter et al. (Chapter 4), support for a distinct clinical entity has not been forthcoming. Alternatively, it can be argued that hyperactivity characteristics (e.g., impulsivity, restlessness, distractibility) range along a continuum from age congruent normal to a more pronounced form that reflects a temperament style (Chess, Thomas, & Birch, 1968) to an extreme manifestation in which the behaviors are severely disruptive. Temperament is defined by the same characteristics (emotionality, impulsivity, activity level, and sociability) as hyperactivity (Buss & Plomin, 1975). Chess et al. (1968) described nine temperament traits: activity level, rhythmicity, adaptability, intensity, mood, threshold level, distractibility, attention-span persistence, and social approach-withdrawal. Thus, a child who exhibits high emotionality, impulsivity, and activity level may be diagnosed as suffering from a clinical hyperactivity disorder when, in fact, these characteristics constitute a temperament style.

There is no validated objective procedure to differentiate temperament style from a hyperactivity disorder. Both can be inherited and are defined by similar overt characteristics. Moreover, certain temperament characteristics and hyperactivity have been observed to be associated with an unfavorable outcome. The need to distinguish the clinically disturbed from those whose behaviors reflect an extreme temperament style poses an important treatment concern, inasmuch as drugs may be inappropriately utilized as an expedient means of controlling disruptive behavior.

Intrauterine and perinatal factors. Fetal stress and traumatic injury suffered during or soon after the birth process place the neonate at increased risk for a hyperactivity disorder. The use of drugs, alcohol, and tobacco by the mother during gestation, in addition to placental dysfunction and infection in the mother, also heighten the risk. Nichols (1976) reported that certain prenatal factors were associated with cognitive, motor, and perceptual impairments, as well as academic underachievement, hyperactivity, and neurological soft signs at a seven-year follow-up. Maternal proteinuria and the smoking of three packages of cigarettes per day during gestation were the most salient factors that augmented the child's risk for an unfavorable outcome. In a review of the teratogenic effects of alcohol, Streissguth, Landesman-Dwyer, Martin, and Smith (1980) concluded that children of alcohol-abusing mothers are at risk for hyperactivity and numerous neurological disturbances.

Asphyxia during delivery, infection, prematurity, and low birth weight, as well as cardiac and respiratory problems, have frequently been shown to increase the risk for neurological and behavioral disturbances. Recent research, however, has revealed that the effects of these factors may not be as great as they were once thought to be. Nichols (1976) reported that the risk for a negative outcome was increased by only 5% at a seven-year follow-up. In addition, Werner and Smith (1977) found that perinatal stress alone could not predict subsequent academic achievement. Sameroff and Chandler (1975) found that prenatal and perinatal risk variables were initially associated with problems during infancy, but by school age, the risk factors were predictive of only very severe conditions, such as mental retardation. Thus, although prenatal and perinatal factors are associated with an increased risk for subsequent neurological and behavioral disorders, it appears that this association is rather weak. Indeed, it has also been found by Werner, Bierman, and French (1977) that a stimulating home environment can compensate for the effects of perinatal stress, thereby lowering the risk for an unfavorable outcome.

Postnatal factors. Strauss and Lehtinen (1947) observed that damage to the brain, particularly the frontal lobes, resulted in hyperactivity. However, it is now commonly recognized that the vast majority of hyperactive children do not have verifiable brain damage. The extent to which a brain injury places the child at risk for a hyperactivity disorder is discussed in detail in Chapter 4 and thus will not be reviewed here. Suffice it to say that a rather severe injury is required before such a disorder emerges.

PSYCHIATRIC SEQUELAE

Numerous investigations have demonstrated that children who present the characteristics of hyperactivity are at risk for a psychiatric disturbance and poor social adjustment in adulthood. Detre, Kupfer, and Koral (1975) found that the most frequently reported childhood problems in an adult psychiatric clinic were those usually accepted to be associated with MBD.

Borland and Heckman (1976) studied 20 men who were hyperactive as children, and observed that compared to their nonhyperactive brothers, they had achieved a lower socioeconomic standing. In addition, almost one-half the men were psychiatrically disturbed. Schuckit, Petrich, and Chiles (1978) found that features typically considered characteristic of a hyperactivity disorder were evident in 20% of patients admitted for drug abuse rehabilitation or psychiatric treatment. The most common psychiatric diagnosis was "antisocial personality of late adolescence." Quitkin and Klein (1969) examined a group of 19 young adults who were impulsive, affectively labile, and manifested destructive and explosive outbursts; 12 individuals had a history of hyperactivity. Menkes, Rowe, and Menkes (1967) assessed a group of 14 adults who had been diagnosed hyperactive 25 years previously. Hyperactivity features were still present in three subjects. Delinquency, mental retardation, and psychosis were about equally distributed in their sample. Morris, Escoll, and Wexler (1972) studied the outcome of children who presented features of MBD. Only 20% were well adjusted 20 to 30 years later. Psychosis was found in 16.6% of the cases; other psychopathological disorders were observed in 63.4% of the sample. A study by Milman (1979) examined the outcome of 73 MBD children. A psychiatric disorder was observed in 93% of the adolescent subjects. Of this group, 80% exhibited a personality disorder, whereas 14% were diagnosed as borderline psychotic.

The above investigations suggest that childhood hyperactivity or MBD increases the risk for a psychiatric disturbance in adulthood, although this has not been confirmed by all investigators (Hechtman, Weiss, Perlman, Hopkins, & Wener, 1979). Although the subjects in this latter study viewed themselves as inferior, they did not present more psychopathology or sociopathy than controls on a self-rating psychiatric symptoms checklist. The results of this investigation notwithstanding, the weight of available evidence indicates that hyperactivity in childhood is a risk for future maladjustment. To clarify further the extent to which hyperactive children are at risk for a psychiatric disturbance, it is necessary to ascertain whether it antedates one particular disorder, or, if instead, it comprises a general vulnerability for a range of different conditions.

Antisocial and aggressive behavior. An association between hyperactivity and sociopathy has been frequently observed. Morrison and Minkoff (1975) reported three cases of explosive personality in which hyperactivity could be implicated as an etiological factor. Morrison (1979) reported that psychiatric patients with a history of hyperactivity were more likely to be sociopathic, have an alcohol problem, or exhibit a personality disorder than patients without a hyperactivity disorder. Menkes et al. (1967) found on follow-up that three out of fourteen hyperactive children had been arrested at least once for either delinquency or a criminal offense. Quitkin and Klein (1969) noted that the majority of their patients who exhibited lability, impulsiveness, and destructiveness had a history of hyperactivity. In a 10-year follow-up study conducted by Huessy, Metoyer, and Townsend (1974), there was a higher incidence of incarceration in hyperactive children than in controls. Mendelson, Johnson, and Stewart (1971) observed a high incidence of truancy, aggressiveness, and running away from home in a group of 83 children who had been diagnosed as hyperactive two to five years earlier.

The above studies demonstrate an association between childhood hyperactivity and subsequent antisocial or aggressive behavior. Although evidence exists for an association, a causal connection between these disorders cannot be advanced. Suffice it to say, most children with a conduct disorder are not diagnosed as hyperactive, and most hyperactive children do not become antisocial. Those who do become antisocial tend to come from families where there is parental psychopathology, punitive child-rearing practices, and poor parent-child relationships (Weiss, Minde, Werry, Douglas, & Nemeth, 1971).

Alcoholism. Schuckit et al. (1978) and Morrison (1979) observed a high incidence of hyperactivity characteristics in persons who abused drugs or alcohol. Blouin, Bornstein, and Trites (1978) compared hyperactive children to controls who had school adjustment problems. Upon five-year follow-up, it was found that the hyperactive children consumed alcohol more frequently than their learning-disabled peers. Wood, Reimherr, Wender, and Johnson (1976) also reported an association between alcohol and drug abuse in individuals who had been previously diagnosed as having MBD. Tarter, McBride, Buonpane, and Schneider (1977) conducted a retrospective survey of alcoholic and psychiatric patients. They identified two subgroups of drinkers who they labeled "primary alcoholics" and "secondary alcoholics." The primary alcoholics reported almost four times as many characteristics of childhood hyperactivity than the secondary alcoholics. The primary group also began their drinking career earlier than the secondary group, had a higher incidence of familial drinking problems, and manifested less psychopathology. The primary alcoholics scored lower on the psychopathic deviate scale of the MMPI, suggesting that their self-reported hyperactivity symptomatology did not simply reflect an antisocial personality disorder. They did, however, score higher on the mania scale, indicating a disposition toward higher energy or activity. One interesting finding was that the psychiatric patients also reported more hyperactivity symptoms than normal controls. Thus, on a checklist that describes hyperactivity or MBD features, it was found that primary alcoholics and psychiatric inpatients could be differentiated from secondary alcoholics and normal controls.

In a subsequent series of studies, Tarter (1981) replicated the dichotomy between primary and secondary alcoholism. Primary alcoholics reported significantly more hyperactivity characteristics in four out of five studies, and also presented themselves as more impulsive, psychosocially immature, and neurotic, with more serious drinking patterns than the secondary alcoholics. The primary alcoholics also admitted experiencing a greater craving for alcohol than the secondary alcoholics. Perceptual and cognitive tasks did not discriminate between the two groups. Although these findings indicate that hyperactivity may be associated with one type of alcoholism, its precise role as an etiological factor in alcohol abuse is unclear.

The results of family studies also support an association between hyperactivity and risk for alcoholism. The parents of hyperactive children tend to have been hyperactive themselves. Moreover, between 20 to 30% of the fathers of hyperactive children suffer from alcoholism (Cantwell, 1972; Morrison & Stewart, 1971). It has also been found that an association between alcoholism in the father and hyperactivity in male offspring exists only when the parents and children are biologically related, but not when they are adoptively related (Cantwell, 1975; Morrison & Stewart, 1973). Goodwin et al. (1975) also found evidence for childhood hyperactivity in alcoholics who were reared away from their alcoholic biological fathers.

There is no obvious reason why hyperactive children should be prone to drinking excess, even though there is some evidence that this is indeed the case (Mendelson et al., 1971). It would be very useful to know if hyperactive children metabolize alcohol differently than other children do, or if they experience a unique subjective effect. It is also possible that drinking excess in hyperactive adolescents is the culmination of a psychological disturbance stemming from longstanding frustration, school failure, peer rejection, and low self-esteem. The reasons for consuming drugs and alcohol are many and varied (Tarter, 1978). The specific etiological role, if any, that hyperactivity plays in the development of alcoholism still remains to be elucidated.

Affective disorders. Stewart and Morrison (1973) conducted a family study of affective illness and concluded that hyperactivity was not a childhood precursor to adult manic depression. Morrison (1979) studied 48 adult psychiatric patients who were hyperactive as children. Compared to patients without such a history, the hyperactive subjects were less likely to exhibit an affective disorder, but were more inclined to exhibit alcoholism, sociopathy, or a personality disorder. In contrast, Huessy (1979) found a 70% incidence of depressive symptoms in individuals who were previously diagnosed as having MBD. Anxiety symptoms were noted in 56% of the patients. Alcoholism and drug abuse were evident in 16 and 44% of the patients, respectively. Depression, however, was the most frequently reported condition and was accompanied by a relatively high incidence of suicide attempts (31%), mood swings (31%), and sleep problems (33%).

In another study, Cohen, Oliveau, and Huessy (1979) compared 12 adults who exhibited both depressive and aggressive symptoms with 12 subjects who exhibited only depression. In the former group, 11 subjects were described as hyperactive and distractible, in contrast to 5 patients in the depression only group. One-third of the depression-aggression group had a hyperactive relative, compared to none in the depression group. In addition, there was a higher incidence of impulsivity (12/12 vs. 0/12), alcohol abuse (10/12 vs. 4/12), insomnia (8/12 vs. 3/12), and antisocial behavior (7/12 vs. 1/12) in the depression-aggression group. Mann and Greenspan (1976) also reported anxiety and depressive symptoms in patients exhibiting "adult brain dysfunction."

Low self-esteem is a common characteristic of hyperactive children (Minde, Lewis, & Weiss, 1971). This is not very surprising considering the difficulties such children have in social, academic, and athletic situations in which attention, self-control, and perceptual-motor skills are essential for successful performance. A diminished sense of self-worth may, therefore, emerge upon repetitive failure and rejection, thus contributing to a depressive disturbance.

Psychosis. Rieder and Nichols (1979) assessed seven-year-old male offspring of schizophrenics. Hyperactivity was evident in eight of twenty-nine subjects. The most frequent neurological sign was mild incoordination, but symptoms of impulsivity, distractibility, and emotional lability were also noted. In contrast, 15 female offspring of schizophrenics did not exhibit a higher incidence of these characteristics than controls.

Several researchers have examined the association between a psychotic outcome and childhood MBD. Morris et al. (1972) found that 16.6% of psychotic adults had features of childhood MBD. Menkes et al. (1967) observed that about 25% of their adult subjects, who 24 years previously were diagnosed as suffering from MBD, presented a psychotic disorder. Milman (1979) traced 73 MBD children into adolescence and observed that 14% suffered from a borderline psychosis. Malmivara, Keinanen, and Saarlema (1978) found that psychotic and borderline children had more MBD signs than antisocial children.

Summary of outcome studies. Thus, in the few studies that have been conducted to date, it appears that a significant proportion of psychotics had the childhood characteristics typically associated with MBD and hyperactivity. Alcoholism, antisocial personality, and depression have also been found to be sequela of a hyperactivity disorder. From these studies, it can be concluded that a hyperactivity disorder increases the risk for a psychiatric disorder in adulthood, but is not predictive of a specific disorder.

These findings, however, should be considered tentative, inasmuch as the definition and description of hyperactivity and MBD are used inconsistently between investigators. Furthermore, the distinction between hyperactivity as a clinical entity and high activity level as a dimension of temperament remains to be clarified. This latter point is particularly important in light of Sameroff's (1978) finding that a poor attitude by the parents and anxiety over the pregnancy contributes to a difficult temperament in the child. Difficult children are more likely to be abused and assaulted by their parents (Klein & Stern, 1971). Thus, it is not surprising that such children are at higher risk for an unfavorable outcome. Whether outcome is related to the specific nature of a presumed genetic or constitutional disorder, or is mediated by the quality of interaction by parent and child, remains to be ascertained.

Learning disability

Learning disability is defined by a failure to perform academically at a level that is commensurate with age and intellectual capacity. Labels such as "specific reading disability" and "dyslexia" have been applied to children who, for reasons other than emotional maladjustment, are unable to acquire basic academic skills that meet community standards in reading, spelling, and arithmetic. Between 1 to 3% of school age children are estimated to have a learning disability (Lerner, 1976).

As Satz and Morris (Chapter 6) point out, learning disabled children comprise a heterogeneous population. Moreover, there are diverse etiologies for a learning disability. A genetic influence has been inferred from both family and twin studies. Hallgren (1950) surveyed 112 dyslexics and found that 90% had either a sibling or a parent with a similar problem, whereas only 10% of the controls had a relative with a learning problem. Frisk and his colleagues (Frisk, Wegelius, Tenbunen, Widholm, & Hortling, 1967) reported that 65% of dyslexics had either a parent or another relative with a learning disorder. Matheny, Dolan, and Wilson (1976) found a higher concordance for dyslexia in identical than in fraternal twins.

Intrauterine and perinatal stress have also been implicated as etiological factors in dyslexia. Kawi and Pasamanick (1958) noted an association between pregnancy complications and dyslexia. Steg and Rapoport (1975) found a higher incidence of minor physical anomalies (due to defects in embryogenesis) in learning disabled children than in controls. A breech presentation at birth has also been demonstrated to be related to learning problems (Matheny et al., 1976).

Studies of outcome, although not conclusive, indicate that children with learning difficulties are more vulnerable than their peers to emotional and behavioral disturbances. It is not known whether this reflects a neurological predisposition linked to the learning disability, or is rather a psychological reaction to low self-esteem, frustration, and chronic failure in the academic setting. Nevertheless, there is a body of evidence demonstrating higher rates of psychopathology, delinquency, and antisocial behavior in learning disabled adolescents (Robins, 1966; Yule & Rutter, 1968). The relationship appears to be reciprocal; that is, dyslexics are at risk for developing an antisocial disorder (Yule & Rutter, 1968), and antisocial children have a very high incidence, estimated by Robins (1966) to be 68%, of academic problems.

Several major differences between learning disabled children who were mainstreamed compared to those who were placed in special classes have been observed (Koppitz, 1971). At a five-year follow-up, the latter group exhibited more restlessness (96 vs. 88%), aggressiveness (30 vs. 23%), and attention seeking behavior (35 vs. 16%). A greater proportion of those who were placed in special classes also demonstrated low frustration tolerance (55 vs. 48%), withdrawal (52 vs. 32%), and rebelliousness (20 vs. 13%) compared to those who were mainstreamed. As can be seen from the percentages, the group differences are rather modest. Interestingly, however, it was observed that anxiety symptoms were *less* frequently reported for children in the special class than for those enrolled in regular classes. Delinquency, schizoid tendencies, and explosive outbursts did not discriminate the mainstreamed group from the group placed in special classes.

The specially placed and mainstreamed children had the same incidence of abnormal EEGs and verified brain injuries. The children in special classes, however, more frequently came from deprived circumstances (14 vs. 5%) or from an unstable home environment (32 vs. 25%). Surprisingly, early childhood neglect was more characteristic of the children enrolled in regular classes (25 vs. 14%) than of those in special classes. Children who were still in special classes five years after the diagnosis of a learning disability were distinguishable from learning disabled mainstreamed children on environmental factors and clinical features, but not on neurological disturbance. These group differences, however, are relatively small.

A subgroup of children with learning disabilities in the Koppitz (1971) investigation were subsequently placed in a residential setting. This group revealed a high incidence of delinquency (38%), explosive temper outbursts (73%), restlessness (95%), and anxiety (86%). Additional disturbances were found in language and perceptual and motor functions; illustrating that dyslexia is not necessarily, or even typically, a circumscribed syndrome in the majority of cases (Rutter, Tizard, & Whitmore, 1970).

In summary, the causes, characteristics, and outcome of a learning disability are variable. A large proportion of impaired children can be mainstreamed into regular classes, and after five years, are apparently able to make an adequate adjustment. A subgroup, however, exhibits persisting behavioral disturbances that necessitate placement in an institution.

Epilepsy

As in the other disorders, there are multiple etiologies for epilepsy. Trauma, malnutrition, allergies, drugs, endrocrinological disorders, encephalitis, and kidney disease, as well as an inherited predisposition, place individuals at risk for a seizure disorder (Broida, 1958; Conner, 1958; Lennox, 1954). Cognitive and intellectual disturbances in epileptic children are not uniform. A number of factors, such as age of onset, seizure frequency, seizure type, and presence or absence of verifiable brain damage, are associated with the pattern and severity of cognitive deficits (Tarter, 1972). Neither a specific personality type nor a particular trait characterize all epileptics (Tizard, 1962).

Epileptic children are at increased risk for a psychiatric disturbance. Graham and Rutter (1968) reported that 7.2 per 1,000 children in the general population suffer from seizures. Of these children, 29% (in contrast to 6.8% of normals) manifest a psychiatric disorder. A seizure disorder concomitant with confirmed brain damage results in a 58% rate of psychiatric disturbance. No specific psychiatric disorder is characteristic of epileptic children, although neurotic and antisocial features are the most frequently noted conditions.

Seizure type may be associated with certain clinical and personality characteristics. Graham and Rutter (1968) found that children with temporal lobe epilepsy were the most disturbed. Nuffield (1961) surveyed over 200 children and found that petit mal seizures were associated with neurotic symptoms, whereas a greater propensity for aggressive behavior was found in those suffering from temporal lobe seizures. Gibbs (1951), in a large scale study of adult epileptics, reported that a personality disorder was most likely if the focus was anterior temporal (32%) compared to the mid-temporal (13%) or frontal (5%) regions. Pond (1952) examined 150 referred cases and found that aggressive and explosive outbursts in children were associated with focal seizures. Temporal lobe epilepsy in both children and adults produced the most disturbance.

Factors other than clinical presentation and etiology also influence outcome. Pond (1952) reported that the home environment in petit mal cases was marked by anxiety, but the family was also gentle and accepting. In contrast, the brain-injured child more often came from a home marked by emotional disturbance and family instability. Taylor and Falconer (1968) observed that low socio-economic status, low intelligence, and poor academic adjustment negatively influenced prognosis. Community attitudes, prejudices, low self-concept of the affected person, and the stigma of being labeled epileptic also have been demonstrated to affect outcome (Grunberg & Pond, 1957). In addition, individuals with an early age onset have a poorer prognosis and are more frequently diagnosed as psychopathic (Lennox, 1954). There is also a fourfold increased incidence of epilepsy in their relatives. It still remains to be determined, however, whether or not there exists a subgroup of seizure disordered individuals who, because of disturbed inherited neurological organization, are predisposed to antisocial and aggressive behavior.

Cerebral palsy

Cerebral palsy comprises a group of heterogeneous neurological conditions of which the most salient manifestation is a disturbance of neuromotor capacity. Usually there are also disturbances of varying severity in language capacity, memory, attention, and visuospatial skill. Intelligence is often impaired and emotional adjustment is frequently poor.

A number of etiological factors that adversely affect the developing organism during the prenatal, perinatal, and postnatal periods have been identified. In the prenatal stage, congenital morphological malformations, asphyxia, and infection are risk factors. Maternal characteristics include adolescent pregnancy, low socioeconomic status, poor health, vaginal bleeding, and excessive vomiting. Heineman, Slone, and Shapiro (1977) reported that drugs, chronic hypertension, and a convulsive disorder during gestation, as well as hydramniosis (excessive amniotic fluid), were associated with an increased risk for cerebral palsy in the offspring. Niswander and Gordon (1972) identified several additional maternal risk factors that included chronic asthma, urinary tract infection, hypothyroidism, and heart disease. Thus, a variety of maternal characteristics and fetal insults can increase the risk for cerebral palsy.

Perinatal and postnatal risk factors have been identified as well. The incidence of cerebral palsy in premature births is three to four times greater than that in full term births. Events surrounding the birth process, such as prolonged labor, breech presentation, and trauma also increase the risk for neurological sequelae. During the early postnatal period, when the immune defense system is not fully functional, the neonate is particularly susceptible to such infections as meningitis and encephalitis. In addition, hypoxia and asphyxia may exacerbate neurological vulnerability in the newborn. During postnatal development, head trauma, child abuse, and infection can increase the risk for cerebral palsy, although in as many as 25% of affected cases no definite etiological factor can be implicated.

Only a few outcome studies have been conducted on cerebral palsied children. O'Reilly (1975) surveyed 336 adults and found that 26% of them were productively employed. The remainder either died, had to be institutionalized, or otherwise lead an unproductive existence. Only 28% were intellectually normal and self-sufficient. Spastic and paraplegic or hemiplegic individuals had a better outcome than those with athetoid symptoms or ataxia. Educational adjustment was also better for the spastic group. Of the spastic group, 35% graduated from regular schools and/or institutions of higher learning, whereas only 19% of athetoid and 17% of ataxic individuals achieved this level of success. And 80% of those who married were in the spastic group. Moreover, the mortality and institutionalization rates for the athetoid and ataxic patients were about twice as high as for those suffering from spastic disorders. The above findings strongly indicate that the specific neurological characteristics of cerebral palsy are associated with differential levels of social and educational adjustment.

Emotional adjustment is also generally poor in cerebral palsied individuals. Dunsdon (1952) observed that they are incapable of modulating their emotions to the particular situation. Cruickshank, Hallahan, and Bice (1976) reported that afflicted adolescents are often sad, angry, and resentful and suffer from a poor self-image. Considering the disease's incapacitating nature, combined with negative or indifferent public attitudes, these findings are not very surprising. Rutter, Graham, and Yule (1970) observed a psychiatric disturbance in 16 out of 36 cases, which is far in excess of the rate of psychiatric illness in the general population. Four of the subjects were neurotic, three exhibited antisocial tendencies, four manifested "mixed" patterns, three were hyperactive, one was psychotic, and one was classified as "other." The authors concluded that there are "many different psychiatric disorders resulting from interaction between neurological dysfunction, family disturbance and social circumstances."

In summary, it appears that cerebral palsy places the child at elevated risk for a cognitive and psychiatric disturbance. The severity of deficit is largely determined by the particular form of neurological disruption, although psychosocial factors also appear to be quite influential in affecting outcome.

References

Benton, A. Neuropsychological aspects of mental retardation. *Journal of Special Education,* 1970, *4,* 3–11.

Bettelheim, B. *The empty fortress: Infantile autism and the birth of the self.* New York: The Free Press, 1967.

Blouin, A., Bornstein, R., & Trites, R. Teenage alcohol use among hyperactive children: A five-year follow-up study. *Journal of Pediatric Psychology,* 1978, *3*, 188–194.

Borland, B. & Heckman, H. Hyperactive boys and their brothers: A 25-year follow-up study. *Archives of General Psychiatry,* 1976, *33*, 669–675.

Bradley, C. & Bowen, M. Amphetamine (Benzedrine) therapy of children's behavior disorders. *American Journal of Orthopsychiatry,* 1941, *11*, 92.

Broida, C. Psychosocial aspects of epilepsy in children and youth. In W. Cruickshank & G. Johnson (Eds.), *Psychology of exceptional children and youth.* Englewood Cliffs, N.J.: Prentice-Hall, 1958.

Buss, A. & Plomin, R. *A temperament theory of personality development.* New York: Wiley, 1975.

Cantwell, D. Psychiatric illness in the families of hyperactive children. *Archives of General Psychiatry,* 1972, *27*, 414–417.

Cantwell, D. Genetics of hyperactivity. *Journal of Child Psychology and Psychiatry and Allied Disciplines,* 1975, *16*, 261–264.

Chess, S., Thomas, A., & Birch, H. Behavior problems revisited: Findings of an antereospective study. In S. Chess & A. Thomas (Eds.), *Annual progress in child psychiatry and child development.* New York: Brunner/Mazel, 1968.

Cohen, S., Oliveau, D., & Huessy, H. Depression, hyperkinesis and violence: A new syndrome. Unpublished manuscript. University of Vermont, 1977. Cited by Huessy, H., Cohen, S., Blair, C., & Rood, P. Clinical explorations in adult minimal brain dysfunction. In L. Bellak (Ed.), *Psychiatric aspects of minimal brain dysfunction in adults.* New York: Grune & Stratton, 1979.

Connor, F. The education of children with chronic medical problems. In W. Cruickshank & G. Johnson (Eds.), *Education of exceptional children and youth.* Englewood, N.J.: Prentice-Hall, 1958.

Cruickshank, W., Hallahan, D., & Bice, H. Personality and behavioral characteristics. In W. Cruickshank (Ed.), *Cerebral palsy: A developmental disability.* Syracuse, N.Y.: Syracuse University Press, 1976.

Detre, T., Kupfer, D., & Koral, J. Relationship of certain childhood "traits" to adult psychiatric disorders. *American Journal of Orthopsychiatry,* 1975, *45*, 74–80.

Dunsdon, M. *The educability of cerebral palsied children.* London: National Foundation for Educational Research, 1952.

Frisk, M., Wegelius, B., Tenbunen, T., Widholm, O., & Hortling, H. The problem of dyslexia in teenagers. *Acta Paediatrica Scandinavica,* 1967, *56*, 333–343.

Gibbs, F. Ictal and non-ictal psychiatric disorders in temporal lobe epilepsy. *Journal of Nervous and Mental Disease,* 1951, *113*, 522–528.

Goodwin, D., Schulsinger, F., Hermansen, L., Guze, S., & Winokur, G. Alcoholism and the hyperactive child syndrome. *Journal of Nervous and Mental Disease,* 1975, *160*, 349–353.

Graham, P. & Rutter, M. Organic brain dysfunction and child psychiatric disorder. *British Medical Journal*, 1968, *3*, 695–700.

Greenberg, L. & McMahon, S. Serial Neurologic examination of hyperkinetic children. *Pediatrics*, 1977, *59*, 584–587.

Grundberg, F. & Pond, D. Conduct disorders in epileptic children. *Journal of Neurology, Neurosurgery and Psychiatry*, 1957, *20*, 65–68.

Hallgren, B. Specific dyslexia (congenital word blindness): A clinical and genetic study. *Acta Psychiatrica et Neurologica Scandinavica* (Suppl. 65), 1950.

Hechtman, L., Weiss, G., Perlman, T., Hopkins, J., & Wener, A. Hyperactive children in young adulthood: A controlled, prospective ten-year follow-up. *International Journal of Mental Health*, 1979, *8*, 52–66.

Heineman, O., Slone, D., & Shapiro, S. *Birth defects and drugs in pregnancy.* Acton, MA: Publishing Sciences Group, 1977.

Huessy, H. Clinical explorations in adult minimal brain dysfunction. In L. Bellak (Ed.), *Psychiatric aspects of minimal brain dysfunction in adults.* New York: Grune & Stratton, 1979.

Huessy, H. & Cohen, A. Vulnerability of hyperkinetic (MBD) children to subsequent serious psychopathology: A controlled 7-year follow-up. In E. J. Anthony, C. Koupernik, & C. Chiland (Eds.), *The child in his family* (Vol. 4). New York: Wiley, 1978.

Huessy, H., Metoyer, M., & Townsend, M. Eight to ten year follow-up of 84 children treated for behavioral disorder in rural Vermont. *Acta Paedopsychiatrica*, 1974, *40*, 230–235.

Kawi, A. & Pasamanick, B. Association of factor of pregnancy with reading disorders in children. *Journal of the American Medical Association*, 1958, *166*, 1420–1423.

Klein, M. & Stern, L. Low birth weight and the battered child syndome. *American Journal of Diseases of Children*, 1971, *122*, 15–18.

Koppitz, E. *Children with learning disabilities: A five-year follow-up study.* New York: Grune & Stratton, 1971.

Laufer, M., Denhoff, E., & Solomons, G. Hyperkinetic impulse disorder in children's behavior problems. *Psychosomatic Medicine*, 1957, *19*, 38–49.

Lennox, W. The epileptic child. In H. Miehal-Smith (Ed.), *Pediatric problems in clinical practice.* New York: Grune & Stratton, 1954.

Lerner, J. *Children with learning disabilities.* Boston, MA: Houghton Mifflin, 1976.

Malmivara, K., Keinanen, E., & Saarlema, M. Fate of child psychiatric risk groups: A 10- to 15-year follow-up. In E. J. Anthony, C. Koupernik, & C. Chiland (Eds.), *The child in his family* (Vol. 4). New York: Wiley, 1978.

Mann, H. & Greenspan, S. The identification and treatment of adult brain dysfunction. *American Journal of Psychiatry*, 1976, *133*, 1013–1017.

Matheny, A., Dolan, A., & Wilson, R. Twins with academic learning problems: Antecedent characteristics. *American Journal of Orthopsychiatry*, 1976, *46*, 464–469.

Mendelson, W., Johnson, N., & Stewart, M. Hyperactive children as teenagers: A follow-up study. *Journal of Nervous and Mental Disease*, 1971, *153*, 273–279.

Menkes, M., Rowe, J., & Menkes, J. A 25-year follow-up study on the hyperkinetic children with minimal brain dysfunction. *Pediatrics*, 1967, *39*, 393–399.

Milman, D. Minimal brain dysfunctions in childhood: Outcome in late adolescence and early adult years. *Journal of Clinical Psychiatry*, 1979, *40*, 371–380.

Minde, K., Lewis, D., & Weiss, G. Hyperactive child in elementary school: A five-year controlled follow-up. *Exceptional Child*, 1971, *38*, 215–221.

Morris, H., Escoll, P., & Wexler, R. Aggressive behavior disorders of childhood: A follow-up study. *American Journal of Psychiatry*, 1972, *112*, 55–72.

Morrison, J. Diagnosis of adult psychiatric patients with childhood hyperactivity. *American Journal of Psychiatry*, 1979, *138*, 955–958.

Morrison, J. & Minkoff, K. Explosive personality as a sequel to the hyperactive child syndrome. *Comprehensive Psychiatry*, 1975, *16*, 343–348.

Morrison, J. & Stewart, M. A family study of the hyperactive child syndrome. *Biological Psychiatry*, 1971, *3*, 182–195.

Morrison, J. & Stewart, M. The psychiatric status of the legal families of adopted hyperactive children. *Archives of General Psychiatry*, 1973, *130*, 791–792.

Nichols, P. *Minimal brain dysfunction: Association with perinatal complications.* Paper presented at the Society for Research in Child Development, New Orleans, LA: 1976.

Niswander, K. & Gordon, M. *The collaborative perinatal study of the National Institute of Neurological Diseases and Stroke: The women and their pregnancies.* Philadelphia: Saunders, 1972.

Nuffield, E. Neuro-physiology and behavior disorders in epileptic children. *Journal of Mental Science*, 1961, *107*, 438–458.

O'Reilly, D. Care of the cerebral palsied: Outcome of the past and need for the future. *Developmental Medicine and Child Neurology*, 1975, *17*, 141–149.

Pond, D. Psychiatric aspects of epilepsy in children. *Journal of Mental Science*, 1952, *98*, 404–410.

Quitkin, F. & Klein, D. Two behavioral syndromes in young adults related to possible minimal brain dysfunction. *Journal of Psychiatric Research*, 1969, *7*, 131–142.

Rieder, R. & Nichols, P. Offspring of schizophrenics III: Hyperactivity and neurological soft signs. *Archives of General Psychiatry*, 1979, *36*, 665–674.

Robins, L. *Deviant children grow up: A sociological and psychiatric study of sociopathic personality.* Baltimore, MD: William & Wilkins, 1966.

Rutter, M., Graham, P., & Yule, W. *A neuropsychiatric study in childhood.* London: William Heinemann, 1970.

Rutter, M., Tizard, J., & Whitmore, K. *Education, health and behavior.* London: Longman, 1970.

Safer, D. A familial factor in minimal brain dysfunction. *Behavior Genetics,* 1973, *3,* 175–186.

Sameroff, A. Infant risk factors in developmental deviancy. In E. J. Anthony, C. Koupernik, & C. Chiland (Eds.), *The child in his family* (Vol. 4). New York: Wiley, 1978.

Sameroff, A. & Chandler, M. Reproductive risk and the continuum of caretaking casualty. In F. Horowitz (Ed.), *Review of child development research* (Vol. 4). Chicago: University of Chicago Press, 1975.

Schuckit, M., Petrich, J., & Chiles, J. Hyperactivity: Diagnostic confusion. *Journal of Nervous and Mental Disease,* 1978, *166,* 79–87.

Silver, L. Familial patterns in children with neurologically based learning disabilities. *Journal of Learning Disabilities,* 1971, *4,* 349–358.

Steg, J. & Rapoport, J. Minor physical anomalies in normal, neurotic learning disabled, and severely disturbed children. *Journal of Autism and Childhood Schizophrenia,* 1975, *5,* 299–307.

Stewart, M. Hyperactive children. *Scientific American,* 1970, *222,* 94–99.

Stewart, M. & Morrison, J. Affective disorder among the relatives of hyperactive children. *Journal of Child Psychology and Psychiatry,* 1973, *14,* 209–212.

Strauss, A. & Lehtinen, L. *Psychopathology and education of the brain-injured child.* New York: Grune & Stratton, 1947.

Streissguth, A., Landesman-Dwyer, S., Martin, J., & Smith, D. Teratogenic effects of alcohol in humans and laboratory animals. *Science,* 1980, *209,* 353–361.

Tarter, R. Intellectual and adaptive functioning in epilepsy: A review of fifty years of research. *Diseases of the Nervous System,* 1972, *33,* 763–770.

Tarter, R. Etiology of alcoholism: Interdisciplinary integration. In P. Nathan, G. Marlatt, & T. Loberg (Eds.), *Alcoholism: New directions in behavioral research and treatment.* New York: Plenum Press, 1978.

Tarter, R. Minimal brain dysfunction as an etiological predisposition to alcoholism. In R. Meyer, B. Glucek, J. O'Brien, T. Babor, J. Jaffe, & J. Stabereau (Eds.), *Evaluation of the alcoholic: Implications for research theory and treatment.* Rockville, MD: U.S. Department of Health and Human Services, 1981.

Tarter, R., McBride, H., Buonpane, N., & Schneider, D. Differentiation of alcoholics according to childhood history of minimal brain dysfunction, family history and drinking pattern. *Archives of General Psychiatry,* 1977, *34,* 761–768.

Taylor, D. & Falconer, M. Clinical, socioeconomic, and psychological changes after temporal lobotomy for epilepsy. *British Journal of Psychiatry,* 1968, *114,* 1247–1261.

Tizard, B. The personality of epileptics: A discussion of the evidence. *Psychological Bulletin,* 1962, *59,* 196–210.

Weiss, G., Minde, K., Werry, J., Douglas, V., & Nemeth, E. Studies in the hyperactive child VIII: five-year follow-up. *Archives of General Psychiatry,* 1971, *24,* 409–414.

Werner, E. & Smith, R. *Kauai's children come of age.* Honolulu, HI: University of Hawaii Press, 1977.

Werner, E., Bierman, J., & French, F. *The children of Kauai: A longitudinal study from the prenatal period to age ten.* Honolulu, HI: University of Hawaii Press, 1971.

Werry, J. & Aman, M. The reliability and diagnostic validity of the physical and neurological examination for soft signs (PANESS). *Journal of Autism and Childhood Schizophrenia,* 1976, *6,* 253–263.

Willerman, L. Activity level and hyperactivity in twins. *Child Development,* 1973, *44,* 288–293.

Wood, D., Reimherr, F., Wender, P., & Johnson, G. Diagnosis and treatment of minimal brain dysfunction in adults. *Archives of General Psychiatry,* 1976, *33,* 1453–1460.

Yule, M. & Rutter, M. Educational aspects of childhood and maladjustment: Some epidemiological findings. *British Journal of Educational Psychology,* 1968, *38,* 7–9.

6. Classification of learning disabled children[1]

Paul Satz[2] and Robin Morris[2]

The classification of individuals into objective, homogeneous groups is a basic goal of the behavioral sciences. A homogeneous group is one in which all the subjects have the same attributes. Where such is not possible, a polythetic classification system is employed to classify individuals who share some, but not all, the attributes that define the group (Bailey, 1973). Psychiatric diagnosis, for example, is based on a polythetic classification system (APA, 1980).

In this chapter, we will discuss recent developments in the classification of childhood learning disabilities. This problem has only recently been addressed in a literature that has traditionally ignored the heterogeneity of learning disabled children (Appelbee, 1971; Benton, 1978; Rutter, 1978). Moreover, the fact that these disorders persist into adolescence, at which time more severe maladaptive behaviors may develop, provides further impetus for the need to identify homogeneous subtypes that have specific causes, courses, and outcomes (Spreen, 1976; Schonhaut & Satz, in press). Currently, however, there is a dearth of information on the na-

[1] This chapter was supported in part by funds from the National Institutes of Health (MH 19415-09).
[2] The authors gratefully acknowledge the constructive criticism of Albert J. Harris in early preparation of this work. The early foundation of this research was conducted by Roy O. Darby. Also a special acknowledgment to Roger K. Blashfield, who has been an important influence on many aspects of this research.

ture of learning disability subtypes, their diagnostic validity, and their prognostic utility.

Learning disability subtypes: A review

Reading or learning disability has traditionally been viewed as a homogeneous diagnostic entity. Not surprisingly, therefore, investigators have fostered rather simplistic explanatory models concerning the determinants (Benton, 1978; Rutter, 1978). These include the synaptic transmission theory of Smith and Carrigan (1958), Delacato's (1959) central neurological organization theory, Bender's (1958) maturational hypothesis, Cruickshank's (1972) perceptual deficit hypothesis, and Vellutino's (1978) verbal mediation hypothesis. Perhaps the most strident criticism of these unitary deficit hypotheses has been voiced by Appelbee (1971):

Research has been successful only in showing that these simplest models do not fit the problem with which we are dealing; and that if we hope in the future to add anything of significance to our understanding of the problem, we must concentrate on new models which correspond more closely to the heterogeneity of the disorder. Such a shift will require more sophisticated methods of analysis than have been employed in the past, and will probably bring with them a whole new set of problems of interpretation and design. Nevertheless, to continue any longer with models which have outlived their usefulness seems as foolish as to abandon any attempts at resolution of the problem whatsoever.

Appelbee's (1971) comments may have been prophetic in light of the subtype studies that followed. These studies, reviewed by Satz and Morris (1980), can be classified according to their underlying assumptions, as well as the techniques of analysis, and are frequently referred to as the clinical-inferential and the statistical approaches to classification.

Clinical classification

Studies subsumed under the clinical approach classify subjects into presumably homogeneous groups on the basis of *a priori* considerations and visual inspection of the data. In other words, the investigator, prior to grouping, has certain assumptions or decision rules for partitioning the data set. The data set is then partitioned on the basis of visual inspection. Traditionally, three different criteria have been utilized to classify subjects: (a) exclusionary selection criteria; (b) performance on neuropsychological tests; or (c) direct measures of reading and learning (achievement variables).

One of the more popular methods has been to classify subjects on the basis of exclusionary criteria in order to identify subgroups of disabled readers whose impairments are presumed to have a constitutional origin (Critchley, 1970; Waites, 1968). Other examples include the diagnosis of "minimal brain dysfunction" (MBD) advanced by the Easter Seal Research Foundation and the National Institute of Neurological Diseases and Blindness (Clements, 1966), "specific learning disability," proposed by the National Advisory Committee on Handicapped Children (USOE, 1968), and "primary reading retardation," suggested by Rabinovitch, Drew, DeJong, Ingram, and Withey (1954). These diagnoses are all based on exclusionary criteria and are used to identify a subset of the population of disabled readers or learners who are presumed to have a constitutional or neurological etiology. The logic behind diagnostic formulations that attempt to define the condition by what it is not is open to serious criticism (Ross, 1976). Rutter (1978) succinctly states: "if all the known causes of reading disability can be ruled out, the unknown (in the form of dyslexia) should be invoked. A counsel of despair indeed."

An additional problem with such studies is the presumption that subjects who meet these criteria differ from those individuals who do not meet them. This problem speaks to the issue of subtype validation, which has virtually remained untested in the clinical studies.

The validity of developmental dyslexia, an exclusionary diagnosis, was recently subjected to empirical examination using data from the Florida Longitudinal Project (Taylor, Satz, & Friel, 1979). A sample of severely disabled readers was divided into two subgroups, of which one subgroup met the World Federation of Neurology definition of developmental dyslexia (Waites, 1968). The two subgroups were then compared on a number of test variables that were external to the formation of the groups. The results indicated that the dyslexia subgroup could not be distinguished from the non-dyslexic poor readers along any of several dimensions that included the initial severity and progression of reading disturbance, frequency of reversal errors, familial reading and spelling competency, mathematical skill, neurobehavioral performance, and personality functioning. Since these dimensions have been traditionally viewed to be distinctive in dyslexia, the results raised serious doubts as to the clinical or research value of this exclusionary diagnosis.

Another classification has been to identify subtypes of reading or learning disabled children on the basis of neuropsychological test scores (Denckla, 1972, 1979; Kinsbourne & Warrington, 1966; Mattis, 1978; Mattis, French, & Rapin, 1975) or from direct measures of achievement (Boder, 1973). Even though most of these studies pre-selected their cohorts on the basis of exclusionary criteria, they have managed to reveal different subtypes of learning disabled children. The subtypes have usually been characterized by difficulties in language usage and/or visual perception.

Although the above-cited investigations have provided rich clinical insights into the nature of the disabilities, they are weakened by a number of methodological flaws, not the least of which concerns the manner of data partitioning. When complex multidimensional data sets are employed, it is virtually impossible to "eyeball" the true hidden structure of the data. If a priori decision rules are used in partitioning, then one must question the formation of subgroups that conform to the rules. This problem might account in part for the variability of subtypes reported in the literature. In some of the studies, monthetic groups are identified, in which all members of each group possess all the attributes necessary to define the group (Mattis et al., 1975). In other studies, a majority of subjects either reveal a mixed pattern of deficits (Boder, 1973) or do not fit into any distinctive subtype, suggesting poor coverage (Denckla, 1972). A final weakness in these studies concerns the failure to validate the subtypes, either through data manipulation techniques (reliability) or on variables external to the formation of the subtypes (descriptive and predictive validity).

Statistical classification

Studies subsumed under this classification approach use descriptive multivariate statistics in the search for learning disability subtypes. The statistical studies contrast with the previously described clinical studies in two ways. First, they do not make any a priori assumptions concerning either the nature or the number of subtypes. Second, classifications are generated from complex multidimensional data sets. These data sets are usually comprised of neuropsychological and/or achievement measures.

Five studies have been reported using this statistical approach to classification (for a review, see Satz & Morris, 1980). Two of these studies utilized cluster analytic techniques when they were at an early period in their development and consequently have numerous statistical and methodological flaws (Smith & Carrigan, 1958; Naidoo, 1972). However, they were timely and innovative forerunners of the studies that followed. The first major attempt to apply statistical techniques in the search for learning disability subtypes was reported by Doehring and Hoshko (1977). Classification was based on a child's performance on a battery of achievement tests. The authors used a Q-technique factor analysis (Nunnally, 1967) for partitioning the data. Three distinctive language subtypes were found: a linguistic deficit group, a phonological deficit group, and a naming deficit group. These subtypes, which were replicated in a later study (Doehring, Hoshko, & Bryans, 1979), were believed to be compatible with those observed in other studies, such as the language disorder subtype (Mattis et al., 1975; Mattis, 1978), the dysphonetic subtype (Boder, 1973), and the auditory dyslexic subtype (Myklebust, 1968). The absence of a non-language disorder subtype in the Doehring and Hoshko (1977) study may have been due to the nature of the achievement tests, which primarily assessed reading skills.

Petrauskas and Rourke (1979) conducted a Q-technique factor analysis on data derived from a large neuropsychological test battery. Subjects were preselected on the basis of exclusionary criteria in order to search for subtypes within the learning disabled population. In contrast to the Doehring and Hoshko (1977) study, a smaller group of average readers was also included for comparison purposes. Petrauskas and Rourke (1979) found five subtypes, of which three were observed to be reliable by a split-half method. The largest subtype was comprised of a group of children who had difficulties in concept formation, word blending, immediate memory, and verbal fluency. Subtype 2 showed linguistic, sequencing, and finger localization deficits. Subtype 3 showed severe impairment in concept formation (verbal coding). The other subtypes showed a mixed pattern of language and non-verbal spatial information processing deficits. Because of the large number of tests employed, it was difficult to interpret some of the subtypes. Also, the classification technique failed to identify a subtype of normal readers. Some of the children with average reading ability were misclassified into the learning disability types (false positives), whereas others remained unclassified. Coverage was generally low, as only 50% of the subjects could be classified into subtypes. Although these investigations represent significant methodological advances over the earlier clinical approaches, they can be faulted on at least the three following points.

STATISTICAL ANALYSIS

The first point concerns the choice of statistical procedures. The Q-technique of factor analysis (Nunnally, 1967) utilizes product-moment correlations between subjects. A matrix of these coefficients is then factored and sometimes rotated. If each subject has a high factor load on only one factor, then individuals with similar high factor loadings on the same factor can be classified in the same group. However, if a subject has a significant loading on more than one factor, then problems of classification occur. There are no objective rules for how such multiple loadings should be dealt with.

Fleiss and associates (Fleiss & Zubin, 1969; Fleiss, Lawlor, Platman, & Fieve, 1971) point out other problems with the Q-technique. They object to the use of correlations as the index of similarity between subjects, since correlations do not measure elevation, a factor that may be of critical importance in revealing subtypes in multidimensional data. In addition, the technique is of questionable validity when assumptions of linearity cannot be justified. Finally, the number of subtypes, given a set of variables can never be more than one less the number of variables $(p - 1)$. Thus, the data description is restricted by the Q-technique's limitations.

VALIDITY

The second point pertains to the issue of subtype validity. A limited number of external (or independent) criteria were used for validation in the statistical studies (e.g., teacher assessments and WISC verbal/performance discrepancy scores), and even those were for qualitative comparisons. No objective statistical tests comparing subtypes were employed.

The need for subtype validation cannot be stressed enough. Blashfield and Draguns (1976) point out that reliability and coverage are two conditions that must be met in any classification schema; the more reliable the measures, the more reliable the resulting classification schema (Conger & Lipshitz, 1973). The validity of a classification schema cannot be greater than its reliability, but a reliable classification schema is not necessarily valid. Coverage refers to the extent to which the classification schema incorporates those subjects it is intended to represent. If a significant proportion of the subjects resist incorporation into the schema, as in the Petrauskas and Rourke (1979) study, then one must question both the usefulness and representativeness of the subtypes.

Another issue in subtype validation is whether the classification schema can withstand the manipulation of subjects into equal split-half sub-groups and the addition of other groups or test variables. Virtually all subtype studies, with the possible exception of those conducted by Doehring et al. (1977, 1979) and Petrauskas et al. (1979), have ignored these validation procedures. The ultimate consideration, of course, con-cerns the test of the subtypes on criterion variables that are external (or independent) to forming the types (Skinner, 1981). As was pointed out, this crucial validation issue has remained untested in virtually all the subtype studies to date.

SELECTION CRITERIA

The third and final point concerns the prevailing tendency, in both the clinical and the statistical studies, to preselect the learning disability cohorts on the basis of arbitrary and/or exclusionary criteria prior to the derivation of subtypes. If the rationale behind the use of these statis-tical techniques is to identify the hidden structure of complex multi-dimensional data sets, then logic would dictate that these techniques be used both in the selection of the subjects and in the subdivision of the learning disability cohorts. This could be readily accomplished by using achievement data in the first phase of analysis, followed by neuro-psychological measures for subtype classification. This classification would then primarily be based on those subgroup(s) that clustered at the lower end of the achievement distribution.

In the following section, recent efforts to address the problems of subtype classification are reviewed. The Florida Longitudinal Project will be discussed insofar as it exemplifies both the difficulties and advantages of multivariate statistical approaches to classification.

Specific learning disability subtypes: Florida longitudinal project

Phase 1

A recent report on the search for learning disability subtypes using data from the Florida Longitudinal Project was presented by Satz and Morris (1980). This study followed Darby's (1978) earlier unpublished work in the field. A unique feature of the Florida Project was the use of cluster analysis to identify the learning disabled group initially. This was accom-plished by initially analyzing Wide Range Achievement Test (WRAT) scores on a large and generally unselected sample ($N = 236$) of Caucasian boys who resided in Alachua County at the end of Grade 5 (six years later). The sample (mean age = 11) included children at all levels of achievement. This approach represented the first attempt to use cluster analysis to define the target subgroup and comparison subgroups prior to the search for subtypes. It therefore had the advantage of avoiding the use of exclusionary criteria in the selection of learning disabled subjects while providing an objective and statistical classification of the cohorts.

The WRAT Reading, Spelling, and Arithmetic subtests were first converted into discrepancy scores by comparing a child's grade level with the grade equivalent score obtained on each subtest. These difference scores were then subjected to a cluster analysis in order to group the subjects according to similarity of their performance. The data were subjected to an average linkage hierarchical agglomerative clustering method utilizing a squared Euclidian distance similarity measure. This method of multivariate analysis was preferred because of high intertest correlations (Jastak & Jastak, 1976) and its sensitivity to elevation. Consequently, the above method was utilized so that the clusters that emerged were different according to achievement levels.

Nine subgroups, which were then subjected to a K-means iterative partitioning clustering method, emerged. This additional analysis was conducted because of the fact that an individual, once placed in a given cluster by a hierarchical agglomerative method, cannot be reassigned to a later forming cluster, even if its similarity is greater. In this method, within-cluster variance is reduced so as to increase homogeneity, while between cluster variance increases, resulting in less overlap between the groups.

The nine subgroups, which included 230 of the 236 subjects, reveal a number of interesting patterns of reading, spelling, and arithmetic skill. In Figure 6-1, the discrepancy scores on each WRAT subtest are presented on a normalized scale having a population mean of zero and a standard deviation of one. It can be seen that subgroups 1 and 2 obtained superior scores in reading, whereas subgroup 3 achieved high reading, spelling, and arithmetic scores. Subgroup 4 exhibited above average reading and spelling skills, but average performance in arithmetic. Subgroup 5 constituted a unique group by virtue of its average reading scores, slightly below average spelling performance, and severely

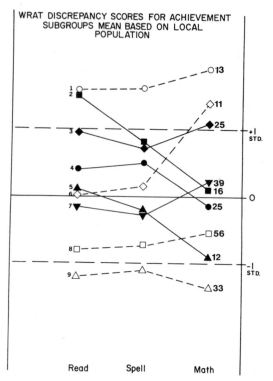

Fig. 6–1. Subgroups based on cluster analysis of Wide Range Achievement
Test at grade 5.

depressed arithmetic scores. Subgroup 6 demonstrated average reading
and spelling scores, but was superior in arithmetic skill. Subgroup 7 performed at about average levels across the three measures.

Subgroups 8 and 9 contained a large number of children who scored
at the lower end of the achievement spectrum. Achievement scores were
below average for both subgroups and were sufficiently depressed (two-
year deficit) to suggest that these children could be labeled learning
disabled.

The validity of these clusters was examined by determining if there
were group differences in Peabody Picture Vocabulary Test (PPVT)
IQ, neuropsychological test performance, neurological status, and socioeconomic level. Great differences between the groups were observed.
It was found that the verbal IQ scores differed between subgroups and
ranged from 90 (subgroup 9) to 116 (subgroup 1), with an overall sam-

ple mean of 103. Differences between the subgroups were also found on language and cognitive-perceptual capacity, with the lowest performance manifest by subgroups 8 and 9. The subgroups were also differentiated in terms of neurological and socioeconomic status. Subgroups 8 and 9 contained a much larger proportion of children with "soft" neurological signs and lower socioeconomic status.

CLASSIFICATION ON NEUROPSYCHOLOGICAL VARIABLES

Because differences were observed between the subgroups on the external criteria, it was decided to further subdivide subgroups 8 and 9 in order to detect subtypes of learning disabled children. As previously described, these two subgroups were severely impaired on all the WRAT subtests.

The neuropsychological scores obtained by the children in these two subgroups ($n = 89$) were then subjected to a cluster analysis. The particular tests selected were from a larger group of measures that had high loadings on a language factor (WISC Similarities, Verbal Fluency) and a perceptual factor (Beery Test of Visual-Motor Integration, Recognition Discrimination). A discussion of the tests and factor analyses can be found in Fletcher and Satz (1980). The rationale for this procedure of restricting the number of tests was to reduce test redundancy and random error variance, while increasing subtype interpretability. These variables also allowed employment of several different clustering procedures to ensure that the subtypes were replicable across different methods. Replication was felt to be mandatory in view of the controversy surrounding the potential uses and misuses of cluster analysis (Everitt, 1980).

Four different hierarchical agglomerative techniques were employed: complete linkage, average linkage, centroid method, and Ward's method. With each of these methods, squared Euclidian distance and error sum of squares similarity coefficients were used, yielding eight different methods. Following each cluster analysis, the individual solutions were subjected to a K-means iterative partitioning method.

Regardless of the method employed, five distinct clusters or subtypes emerged; these are graphically presented, jointly in Figure 6-2 and separately in Figures 6-3 through 6-7. The subtypes were derived from performance on the four neuropsychological tests. It can be seen that subtype 1 (Figure 6-3) was severely impaired on both of the language measures (Similarity and Verbal Fluency) and on PPVT IQ (used as a

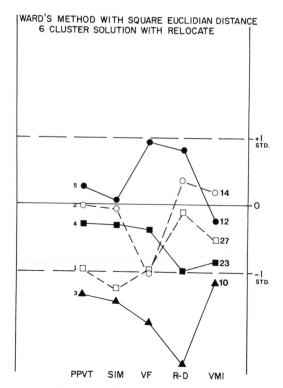

Fig. 6–2. Subtypes of the learning disabled children.

marker variable). In contrast, performance on the non-language perceptual tests was within normal limits. This subtype, which was defined as the *global language impairment type,* contained 27 children. Subtype 2 (Figure 6-4) was selectively impaired on only the verbal fluency test. Performance on the other neuropsychological and IQ tests was within normal limits. Fourteen children were classified in this group, which was defined as the *specific language-naming impaired subtype.*

Subtype 3 (Figure 6-5) was severely impaired on all the neuropsychological tests. Ten children were classified into this group, which was defined as the *global language and perceptually impaired subtype.* Subtype 4 (Figure 6-6) was selectively impaired on the nonlanguage perceptual tests. Their performance was normal on the language tests, including Peabody IQ. Twenty-three children were classified within this group, which was defined as the *visual-perceptual-motor impaired sub-*

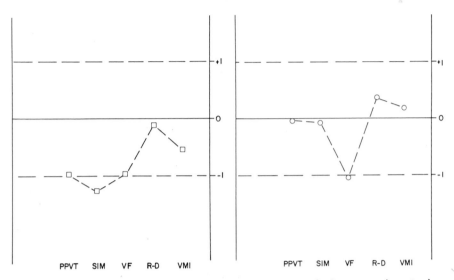

Fig. 6–3. Global language impaired subtype.

Fig. 6–4. Specific language (naming) impaired subtype.

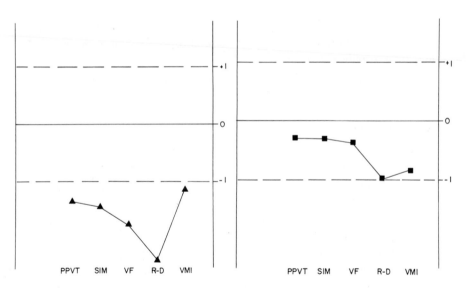

Fig. 6–5. Global language and perceptual impairment (mixed) subtype.

Fig. 6–6. Visual-perceptual-motor impaired subtype.

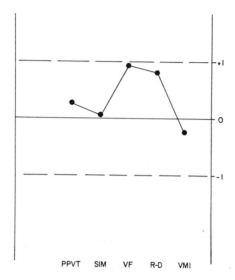

Fig. 6–7. Unexpected subtype.

type. Subtype 5 (Figure 6-7), in contrast to the preceding four subtypes, was not impaired on any of the neuropsychological measures. In
fact, their profile was characterized by average to superior performance
on all the cognitive tests. They were defined as the *unexpected learning
disabled subtype.* Twelve children were in this group.

VALIDATION OF SUBTYPES

Separate analyses were conducted on each subtype against various external criteria measures that included WRAT scores, SES level, neurological
status, and parental reading levels. A multivariate analysis of variance
was first computed on the WRAT scores to determine if the subtypes differed according to achievement level. The decision to conduct this analysis was prompted in large part by the high level of neuropsychological
performance in subtype 5 (unexpected). No significant main effect for
WRAT performance was found, thereby confirming the clustering solution for subgroups 8 and 9, which identified the learning disabled cohorts.
Significant differences between subtypes were observed, however, on neurological status and parental reading levels.

A higher proportion of positive findings (soft neurological signs) was
observed in subtypes 1 (global language), 3 (global language and perceptual), and 4 (visual-perceptual-motor) than in the other subtypes.

Moreover, a higher proportion of low SES children tended to be derived from subtypes 1 and 3. In contrast, subtypes 2 (specific language-naming) and 5 (unexpected) had a lower proportion of children with positive neurological findings. They also tended to come from higher socioeconomic backgrounds.

It was also observed that the biological parents of subtypes 2 and 5 achieved higher reading scores than those of the other three subtypes. In fact, their WRAT scores, when adjusted for education and SES level, were higher than the mean for total sample. This finding underscores the importance of subdividing learning disabled children into homogeneous subtypes when searching for familial-genetic determinants (Owen, 1978; Taylor et al., 1979).

Interpretation of the derived subtypes must be exercised with caution. The subtypes reported herein (especially subtypes 1 through 4) are concordant with findings from other studies (clinical and statistical), which typically report a language, a perceptual, and/or a mixed subgroup of learning disabled children, of which the language disordered subtype is the most frequently observed (Mattis et al., 1975; Mattis, 1978; Boder, 1973; Doehring & Hoshko, 1977; Petrauskas & Rourke, 1979). At least 60% of the children in the present study evidenced some type of language difficulty on the neuropsychological tests (subtypes 1 to 3). The clustering methods, however, classified the children into specific subtypes of language disorders. Also, the various profiles revealed in the present study are not uncommon to professionals working with learning disabled children; this adds a dimension of credibility to clinical impressions. Moreover, it is worth noting that the word production difficulties found in subtype 2, and the global language difficulties in subtype 1, have features that are commonly found in adult aphasics. Comparisons, however, between the present findings and adult aphasia must be considered speculative at this time.

The derivation of subtypes 4 (visual-perceptual-motor) and 5 (unexpected) should caution those who postulate a unitary language deficit model for learning disability (Vellutino, 1978). At least 40% of the sample of disabled readers did not show an impairment in language skills—at least as assessed by the present measures. Subtype 4 exhibited a selective impairment in non-language cognitive skills (visual perception), whereas subtype 5 demonstrated average to superior performance on all the neuropsychological measures.

The derivation of subtype 4 also conflicts with the theory advanced by

Satz and Sparrow (1970). They postulated that there are two general subtypes of learning disability, a predominantly language disorder type found in children between 11 and 12 years of age and a predominantly spatial-perceptual disorder type characteristic of younger children between 5 and 7 years of age. The presence of subtype 4 (visual-perceptual-motor), which was derived on children who were, on average, 11 years of age, lends little support for this hypothesis. In fact, this subtype, in contrast to previous studies (Boder, 1973; Mattis et al., 1975), contained the second largest number of children.

The identification of subgroup 5 was totally unexpected—hence its name. The significance of this subtype, however, should not be dismissed. Virtually no attention has been given to the subtype of learning disabled children who are seemingly free of neuropsychological deficits. In fact, they would be completely overlooked if the methods employed did not subdivide the children according to performance on achievement tests.

One could argue that this subtype was an artifact of either the clustering method or the variables that were used for the clustering. The former explanation, however, is unlikely in view of the fact that this subtype emerged regardless of the particular clustering method that was used. A more reasonable explanation is that this group of children had motivational or emotional problems or both. To examine for this possibility, a separate analysis was conducted using scores from the Children's Personality Questionnaire (CPQ) (Porter & Cattell, 1972). The CPQ assessed 14 independent factors or traits that are presumed to underlie the normal personality. The finding that this questionnaire did not differentiate between the subtypes is interpreted to indicate that specific personality characteristics were not associated with any of the learning disability subtypes, at least as measured by the CPQ. Hence, the unexpected subtype of learning disability was unrelated to either neurological capacity or personality characteristics. Nor did subtype 5 reveal a familial pattern of reading failure. In fact, the biological parents of these children obtained higher WRAT reading and spelling scores than the other parents.

The inability to explain the origins of this unexpected subtype should not be viewed as a limitation. The purpose of this study was to identify stable and homogeneous subtypes in a relatively unselected sample of children. In this respect, the objectives were primarily descriptive. By establishing the validity of these descriptive subtypes, there is now a firm basis for research to focus on the underlying causes.

Despite the promise that this study holds, particularly for establishing an empirically derived classification schema, the results should be considered tentative. None of the studies reviewed in this chapter are exempt from criticism, and the present study is no exception. One should note the following concerns.

First, one must question the use of achievement tests that sample a restricted range of reading skills. The WRAT is notoriously limited in this respect. In fact, it does not measure comprehension, a component of reading that could have improved the search for subgroups and subtypes. Second, one could fault the study for its use of a small number of neuropsychological tests. Despite the logic argued in defense of this approach, one still wonders whether the same subtype clusters would have emerged if a larger number of neuropsychological variables had been measured. Third, one should note that the subtype analyses were conducted on only subgroups 8 and 9, both of which showed a marked impairment on each of the WRAT subtests. Fourth, the subtypes were derived on a homogeneous group of children. This factor limits extrapolation of the results to disabled learners in the general population. Inasmuch as developmental factors are hypothesized to underlie different stages in the reading process (Fletcher & Satz, 1980; Rourke, 1978; Satz & Fletcher, 1979), it is necessary to apply the classified subtypes to other age groups.

Strengthening the validity of the subtypes by the use of additional criterion measures is a fifth consideration. For example, the relationships between subtypes and teacher observations, remedial programs, developmental histories, and other measures of personality functioning might have provided additional information that would have proved helpful, especially in understanding the unexpected subtype. A sixth concern pertains to the use of the PPVT as the measure of intellectual level. This test assesses comprehensional vocabulary and would appear to have been more appropriately utilized as a clustering variable in the subtype analysis. Finally, cluster analysis has certain limitations. There are numerous methods of cluster analysis, of which many have never been critically examined or even clearly defined. In general, they have not been built upon a firm statistical foundation and should be viewed as basically heuristic. In addition, there are also many different algorithms and computer software packages that may yield different results from the same procedures. Moreover, only limited attempts have been made to validate clustering methods.

Phase 2

As was pointed out earlier in this chapter, a useful classification schema must demonstrate adequate reliability, coverage, and validity. Despite efforts to address these issues, problems still remain. For example, although the clustering techniques classified 96% of the subjects, the question can be raised as to whether the various subtypes are statistical artifacts from homogeneous data or do not reflect the true hidden structure of the data. The validity of the clusters must be carefully considered, inasmuch as it has been observed that clusters emerge even with random data.

With this concern in mind, it was decided to submit the data to a series of statistical analyses to answer the following questions:

1. Would the same subtypes emerge using a split-half method of data partioning? This question addresses subtype reliability.
2. Would the same subtypes emerge in a random data set (Monte Carlo method) that mimics the neuropsychological data in terms of means, standard deviations, and inter-variable correlations? This question tests the null hypothesis that no subtypes exist.
3. Would the subtypes be influenced by the insertion of additional neuropsychological variables, especially those that load on similar factors? This question pertains to the reliability of the classification.
4. Would the subtypes be altered by the insertion of additional *subgroups*, such as an average reading subgroup (subgroup 6) or a specific mathematics disability subgroup (subgroup 5)? This question addresses the construct validity of the subtypes.

SPLIT-HALF

A split-half design was employed in which the 89 children were randomly assigned into two subsamples. It was expected that if the methods and subtypes were reliable, the subsamples would each yield similar results. This, in fact, was found to be the case. Both subsamples yielded the same basic results and replicated the original subtypes. Figure 6-8a illustrates the pattern of results from one of these subsamples. Less than 15% of the subjects changed from their original subtype clusters to another cluster in the split-samples.

MONTE CARLO

Clustering methods can find subtypes in random data. Thus, the null hypothesis can be tested by generating a random data set that mimics the known parameters of the original data. Data sets were generated with the same number of subjects, variables, means, and standard deviations, as well as the same correlation matrix between variables observed in the original data.

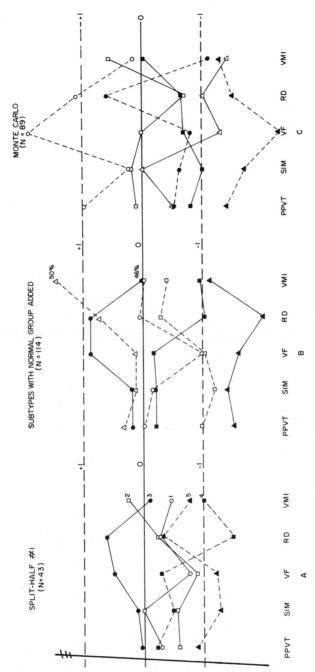

Fig. 6–8. Example results from reliability and validation studies.

The data were then clustered using the previously described methods and compared to the original subtypes. It can be seen in Figure 6-8c that the Monte Carlo technique yielded a somewhat different pattern of subtypes, thereby suggesting the rejection of the null hypothesis.

ADDITIONAL CLUSTERING VARIABLES

It was next asked what would happen if additional variables were included in clustering the subjects. The Peabody Picture Vocabulary Test (PPVT) and the Embedded Figures Test (EFT) were added to the original four clustering variables. It was found that less than 12% of the subjects changed subtype clusters. Nor did the cluster means change to any appreciable extent.

ADDITIONAL SUBGROUPS

In the first addition, the children in subgroup 5 (arithmetic disability) were added to the original 89 children. The sample was then subjected to the clustering procedure. All five of the original clusters maintained their original profiles. Moreover, only 4% of the subjects changed subtype clusters. Of the twelve children who were added, four (33%) clustered into subtype 5 (unexpected subtype), and six (50%) clustered into subtype 4 (visual-perceptual-motor subtype). This finding supported the stability of the original cluster solution, and provides new leads into the possible processes involved in mathematics disabilities.

In the second addition, the 25 children from subgroup 3 (above average achievement) were added to the original 89 children. It was hypothesized that these children would form a new cluster. The results of this analysis are illustrated in Figure 6-8b. It can be seen that this subgroup did not, in fact, fall into any deficit subtype, but instead formed a new cluster of average and above average abilities. Only nine subjects (10%) from the original sample changed clusters.

Thus, the above data manipulations provided additional support for the reliability and validity of the subtypes revealed in the Florida Longitudinal Project. To further the validation process, subsequent research should focus on collecting more information about the different subtypes, as well as replicating the findings with other samples and by other investigators.

In summary, our understanding of learning disabilities has been hampered by the absence of a classification system. Consequently, the relationship between learning disability subtypes and other childhood and adult disorders has yet to be clearly delineated. The development of a reliable and valid classification system is an essential first step toward these objectives. Without empirically established and validated classification systems, research on the etiology, prevention, and treatment of childhood disorders will invariably be unrewarding.

References

American Psychiatric Association. *Diagnostic and statistical manual of mental disorders.* DSM III. Washington, D.C.: Author, 1980.

Appelbee, A. Research in reading retardation: Two critical problems. *Journal of Child Psychology and Psychiatry and Allied Disciplines,* 1971, *12,* 91–113.

Bailey, K. Monothetic and polythetic typologies and their relation to conceptualization, measurement and scaling. *American Sociological Review,* 1973, *38,* 18–33.

Bender, L. Problems in conceptualization and communication in children with developmental alexia. In P. Hoch and J. Zubin (Eds.), *Psychopathology of communication.* New York: Grune & Stratton, 1958.

Benton, A. Some conclusions about dyslexia. In A. Benton & D. Pearl (Eds.), *Dyslexia: An appraisal of current knowledge.* New York: Oxford University Press, 1978.

Blashfield, R. & Draguns, J. Evaluative criteria for psychiatric classification. *Journal of Abnormal Psychology,* 1976, *85,* 140–150.

Boder, E. Developmental dyslexia: A diagnostic approach based on three atypical reading-spelling patterns. *Developmental Medicine and Child Neurology,* 1973, *15,* 663–687.

Clements, S. *Minimal brain dysfunction in children.* NINDB Monograph No. 3, Washington, D.C.: U.S. Department of Health, Education and Welfare, 1966.

Conger, A. & Lipschitz, R. Measures of reliability for profiles and test batteries. *Psychometrika,* 1973, *38,* 411–427.

Critchley, M. *The dyslexic child.* Springfield, IL: C. Thomas, 1970.

Cruickshank, W. Some issues facing the field of learning disabilities. *Journal of Learning Disabilities,* 1972, *10,* 57–64.

Darby, R. Learning disabilities: A multivariate search for subtypes. Unpublished doctoral dissertation, University of Florida, 1978.

Delacato, C. *The treatment and prevention of reading problems.* Springfield, IL: C. Thomas, 1959.

Denckla, M. Clinical syndromes in learning disabilities: The case for "splitting" vs. "lumping." *Journal of Learning Disabilities,* 1972, *5,* 401–406.

Denckla, M. Childhood learning disabilities. In K. Heilman & E. Valenstein (Eds.), *Clinical neuropsychology,* New York: Oxford University Press, 1979.

Doehring, D. & Hoshko, I. Classification of reading problems by the Q-technique of factor analysis. *Cortex,* 1977, *13,* 281–294.

Doehring, D., Hoshko, I., & Bryans, R. Statistical classification of children with reading problems. *Journal of Clinical Neuropsychology*, 1979, *1*, 5–16.

Everitt, B. *Cluster analysis* (2nd Ed.). London: Heineman Education Books, 1980.

Fleiss, J. & Zubin, J. On the methods and theory of clustering. *Multivariate Behavior Research*, 1969, *4*, 235–250.

Fleiss, J., Lawlor, W., Platman, S., & Fieve, R. On the use of inverted factor analysis for generating typologies. *Journal of Abnormal Psychology*, 1971, *77*, 127–132.

Fletcher, J. & Satz, P. Developmental changes in the neuropsychological correlates of reading achievement: A six year longitudinal follow-up. *Journal of Clinical Neuropsychology*, 1980, *2*, 23–37.

Jastak, J. & Jastak, S. *The Wide Range Achievement Test manual of instruction* (Rev. Ed.). Wilmington, Delaware: Guidance Associates of Delaware, Inc., 1976.

Kinsbourne, M. & Warrington, E. Developmental factors in reading and writing backwardness. In J. Money (Ed.), *The disabled reader: Education of the dyslexic child*. Baltimore: Johns Hopkins Press, 1966.

Mattis, S. Dyslexia syndromes: A working hypothesis that works. In A. Benton & D. Pearl (Eds.), *Dyslexia: An appraisal of current knowledge*. New York: Oxford University Press, 1978.

Mattis, S., French, J., & Rapin, T. Dyslexia in children and adults: Three independent neuropsychological syndromes. *Developmental Medicine and Child Neurology*, 1975, *17*, 150–163.

Myklebust, H. (Ed.), *Progress in learning disabilities* (Vol. 1). New York: Grune & Stratton, 1968.

Naidoo, S. *Specific dyslexia*. New York: Pitman Publishing, 1972.

Nunnally, J. *Psychometric theory*. New York: McGraw-Hill, 1967.

Owen, F. Dyslexia-genetic aspects. In A. Benton & D. Pearl (Eds.), *Dyslexia: An appraisal of current knowledge*. New York: Oxford University Press, 1978.

Petrauskas, R. & Rourke, B. Identification of subgroups of retarded readers: A neuropsychological multivariate approach. *Journal of Clinical Neuropsychology*, 1979, *1*, 17–37.

Porter, R. & Cattell, R. *Handbook for the children's personality questionnaire (The CPQ)*. Champaign, IL: Institute for Personality and Ability Testing, 1972.

Rabinovitch, R., Drew, A., DeJong, R., Ingram, W., & Withey, L. A research approach to reading retardation. *Association for Research in Nervous and Mental Disease*, 1954, *34*, 363–396.

Ross, A. *Psychological aspects of learning disabilities and reading disorders*. New York: McGraw-Hill, 1976.

Rourke, B. Reading, spelling, arithmetic disabilities: A neuropsychological perspective. In H. Myklebust (Ed.), *Progress in learning disabilities* (Vol. 4). New York: Grune & Stratton, 1978.

Rutter, M. Prevalence and types of dyslexia. In A. Benton & D. Pearl (Eds.),

Dyslexia: An appraisal of current knowledge. New York: Oxford University Press, 1978.

Satz, P. & Fletcher, J. Early screening tests: Some uses and abuses. *Journal of Learning Disabilities,* 1979, *12,* 65–69.

Satz, P. & Morris, R. Learning disability subtypes: A review. In F. Pirozzolo & M. Wittrock (Eds.), *Neuropsychological and cognitive process in reading.* New York: Academic Press, 1980.

Satz, P. & Sparrow, S. Specific developmental dyslexia: A theoretical formulation. In D. Bakker & P. Satz (Eds.), *Specific reading disability,* Rotterdam University Press, 1970.

Schonhaut, S. & Satz, P. Prognosis of the learning disabled child: A review of the follow-up studies. In M. Rutter (Ed.), *Behavioral syndromes of brain dysfunction in children.* New York: Guilford Press, in press.

Skinner, H. Toward the integration of classification theory and methods. *Journal of Abnormal Psychology,* 1981, *90,* 68–87.

Smith, D. & Carrigan, P. *The nature of reading disability.* New York: Harcourt, Brace & Co., 1958.

Spreen, O. Neuropsychology of learning disorders: Post conference review. In R. Knights & D. Bakker (Eds.), *The neuropsychology of learning disorders: Theoretical approaches.* Baltimore: University Park Press, 1976.

Taylor, H., Satz, P., & Friel, J. Developmental dyslexia in relation to other childhood reading disorders: Significance and utility. *Reading Research Quarterly,* 1979, *15,* 84–101.

USOE, *First Annual Report of the National Advisory Committee on Handicapped Children.* Washington, D.C.: U.S. Department of Health, Education and Welfare, 1968.

Vellutino, F. Toward an understanding of dyslexia: Psychological factors in specific reading disability. In A. Benton & D. Pearl (Eds.), *Dyslexia: An appraisal of current knowledge.* New York: Oxford University Press, 1978.

Waites, L. Report of the research group on development dyslexia and world illiteracy. *Proceedings of the World Federation of Neurology,* 1968.

7. Schizophrenia

Robert A. Asarnow

It is generally accepted that the diagnostic category of schizophrenia represents a heterogeneous group of individuals (Strauss, Carpenter, & Bartko, 1974). It is not known, however, if the interindividual variability in clinical presentation reflects several etiological pathways or if there is an underlying core disturbance common to all affected individuals. The research strategy that can best resolve this issue is to elucidate the developmental characteristics of children who are at heightened risk and follow them into adulthood. As Moffitt, Mednick, and Cudek (Chapter 3) point out, the high risk paradigm affords the opportunity to detect the characteristics of the disorder that are not confounded by pharmacotherapy, institutionalization, or other consequences of the illness.

Neuropsychological techniques, by virtue of their ability to describe behavior in relation to the underlying neuroanatomical substrate, have been responsible for many advances in understanding the functional organization of the brain (Geschwind, 1965; Gazzaniga & Sperry, 1967). Moreover, the clinical application of these procedures has proven to be very useful in identifying the anatomical locus underlying behavioral disturbances (Luria, 1966; Teuber, 1962). With respect to investigations of children at high risk for schizophrenia, certain prodromal features that implicate central nervous system dysfunction have also been revealed.

In this chapter, I will review the neuropsychological and neurological studies of children at risk for schizophrenia. It will be seen that an impressively consistent set of findings can be accommodated by a comprehensive model of neuropsychological development.

The McMaster/Waterloo study of schizophrenia

The McMaster/Waterloo study compared offspring of schizophrenic mothers living with foster parents with control subjects living in foster homes and in the community with their biological parents. The Psychiatric Status Schedule (PSS) and the MMPI were used to evaluate clinical status. The subjects were given eight tasks to assess their capacity (Zubin, 1975). These tasks were selected on the basis that they met the following criteria: (a) previous cross-sectional research with adult schizophrenic subjects had demonstrated their discriminating sensitivity; (b) they were applicable to adolescents; and (c) they had good psychometric properties and could be administered in a standardized fashion.

The central issue addressed in this project concerned whether or not children deemed to be at risk for schizophrenia could be differentiated from other children on information processing and attention tests. To answer this question, a group of foster children whose biological mothers were schizophrenic (the high risk group) were compared to a group of foster children without a family history of psychopathology (the foster control group) and to a group of children living with non-psychiatrically ill biological parents (the community control group). The high risk group of foster children provided the opportunity to identify deficits that were not confounded by destabilizing influences of severe psychopathology in their homes. This is not inconsequential, since Rodnick and Goldstein (1974) have found that it takes an appreciable period of time before a schizophrenic mother (particularly poor premorbids) can assume competent parenting functions after an acute episode. Thus, by studying foster children, any possible disruptive effect that could be the product of a psychiatric disorder in a parent, or the aftermath of an acute disorder, was avoided. Although the children had lived for a considerable period of time with their biological parents, they had spent, on average, the last eight years in foster homes. The community control group was included in order to assess the effects of foster placement, as well as to provide normative developmental data.

Sample description and recruitment

Foster child placement agencies in southern Ontario were contacted and a list compiled of children between the ages of 12 and 18 that also identified the biological mothers of the children. The list of biological mothers

was cross-checked with a central psychiatric registry. A history of psychiatric hospitalization was found in 161 of the mothers. Next, the case history files of psychiatric hospitals were checked in order to detect the
women who had a discharge diagnosis of schizophrenia. The case histories
of these mothers were then independently reviewed by two psychiatrists
in order to confirm the validity of the diagnosis. Cases were accepted for
inclusion in the study only if the two raters reached agreement independently. The foster parents of children whose biological mothers were diagnosed schizophrenic were then contacted and their cooperation sought
so that the child could be tested. This process yielded a total of nine subjects. A foster control group was subsequently constituted by selecting a
set of potential subjects from the same foster agency files from which the
high risk children were drawn. The foster controls were closely matched
to the index subject on the variables of sex, age, race, religion, and age at
the time of placement. The names of the biological parents of the foster
control cases were submitted to the central psychiatric registry, where a
search of the records of all Ontario hospitals was made. A report of hospitalization for either biological parent led to rejection of the control
case. One foster contact case was selected as a yoked control for each
index case.

The second group of controls, the community group, was consituted in
an effort to control for the effects of foster home placement. School au-
thorities compiled a list of students between the ages of 12 and 16 who
were performing at average levels and who were regarded by their teachers as well adjusted. From this list, a group was developed to match the
high risk and foster control groups according to age, sex, and grade level.
Children were excluded if there was a history of perinatal difficulties or
central nervous system disorder.

Test instruments and procedures

The test battery, which is described in more detail in Asarnow, Steffy,
MacCrimmon, and Cleghorn (1977, 1978), consisted of the following
tasks: a competing-voices task (Rappaport, 1968); a concept-formation
task (Walker & Bourne, 1961); a continuous performance test (Kornet-
sky, 1972); the Digit Symbol Substitution subtest from the Wechsler
Adult Intelligence Scale; a simple reaction time procedure (Bellissimo &
Steffy, 1972); a span-of-apprehension task (Neale, McIntyre, Fox, &
Cromwell, 1969); the Spokes test from the Halstead-Reitan Neuropsycho-

logical Battery (Reitan, 1957); and the Stroop color-word test (Wapner & Krus, 1960).

Clinical interview data was obtained using the Psychiatric Status Schedule (PSS). It is comprised of an interview schedule and an inventory of 321 true-false items. When completed and scored, the PSS yields 17 symptom and 6 role scales. The Minnesota Multiphasic Personality Inventory (MMPI) was also administered to each subject.

Results

HIGH RISK VS. CONTROL GROUPS

The performance of the three groups of children on the eight attention-demanding tasks was compared by a simple analysis of variance. It was found that the high risk group generally performed less adequately than the foster control group, who, in turn, performed less competently than the community control group. Several of the measures significantly differentiated the high risk group from the two control groups. On the span-of-apprehension task, group differences were found on the complex stimulus array component. The high risk group made significantly fewer detections than the foster and community control groups. On the concept-formation task, the high risk group also made significantly more errors than the foster and community control groups on the second most simple condition. In addition, they performed more poorly than the community control group when three dimensions comprised the task. Similarly, on the Spokes test, the high risk group took significantly longer, on the complex version, to complete the maze than the foster and community control groups. The differences were only marginally significant on the simple version of the Spokes test.

In view of the number of statistical tests conducted, a question arose as to whether the observed differences were fortuitous. If such were the case, then one would *not* expect to find that a subgroup of high risk subjects was responsible for the differences across tasks. The next analysis was computed to determine if the tasks that differentiated the high risk group from the control groups were representative of all the high risk children or reflected a subgroup with extreme scores. This analysis assumed special importance in light of the fact that with a risk marker of maternal history of schizophrenia one would expect only about 8 to 12% of the children in the present study to become schizophrenic as adults (Rosenthal, 1970). For this reason, it would not be surprising to find that a small subset of children shifts the group means in the direction that magnified the differences between the high risk and the control groups.

VARIATION WITHIN THE HIGH RISK GROUP SCORES

The next analysis was conducted, therefore, to determine if a subset of children within the high risk group was impaired on the various tasks. By examining the intercorrelations between the measures, it could be determined if the subjects were consistent in their performance across tasks. Indeed, a high correlation was observed between the Spokes B test and the most complex condition of the span-of-apprehension task ($r = -.61$). In contrast, the correlations between the most discriminating condition of the concept-formation task and the Spokes B test ($r = .27$), as well as the correlation between the most discriminating condition of the concept-formation task and the most complex condition of the span-of-apprehension task ($r = -.14$), were substantially lower. From this analysis, it appeared that the subjects' scores were relatively comparable for the complex versions of the span-of-apprehension task and the Spokes test, but that a somewhat different subset of subjects was contributing to impaired performance on the concept-attainment task.

Another way to evaluate the origin of the differences is to identify the subjects who scored in the bottom one-third on the three most discriminating tasks. On the complex versions of the span-of-apprehension task and the Spokes Test, seven high risk children had scores in the bottom one-third (ten worst scores) on both tasks. Five of these seven high risk children scored in the bottom one-third on the concept-formation task. Thus, there appeared to be a subset of children in the high risk group whose performance was deviant across the tasks, which, in turn, resulted in this latter group performing more poorly than the foster and community control groups. To corroborate the above impressions, a cluster analysis was used to detect whether there were subsets of children within the high risk group who were identifiable on the basis of performance patterns on the test battery. To perform the cluster analysis, the ratio of variables to subjects had to be reduced. This was accomplished by submitting the 25 scores from the battery to a factor analysis followed by a varimax rotation of the axes. It was observed from this analysis that five factors could account for 79% of the variance within the matrix.

The five factor scores were then computed for each subject and submitted to a hierarchical cluster analysis (Howard & Harris, 1966). Cluster analysis is a multivariate procedure that classifies subjects on the basis of

Table 7-1. Distribution of four attentional clusters across the high risk and foster and community control groups.

| | Cluster | | | |
	I	II	III	IV
High risk	1	3	1	**4**
Foster control	4	5	0	1
Community control	9	1	0	0

commonalities along specific dimensions. Groups of subjects generated by the Howard-Harris program at each level of clustering showed minimal within-cluster variance and maximal between-cluster variance. The subject clusters so generated were, in effect, empirically derived typologies of the subjects classified on the basis of commonalities in attentional functioning. Hierarchical cluster analysis, as opposed to other forms of cluster analysis, classifies all subjects at each level of resolution. Table 7-1 presents the distribution of the subjects classified in a four-cluster resolution on the basis of commonalities in their attentional performance. It can be seen that the patterns of performance represented by clusters 3 and 4 occurred predominantly in the high risk group and accounted for five of the nine high risk children.

Table 7-2 presents the means, standard deviations, and F values for the four clusters. Because cluster 3 consisted of only one child, analyses of variance were conducted between clusters 1, 2, and 4. It was found that subjects in cluster 1 performed in a superior fashion across all tasks that differentiated clusters 1, 2, and 4; whereas cluster 3, consisting of the one high risk child, exhibited impaired performance across all tasks.

The most interesting subgroup was cluster 4, comprising four high risk children and one foster control child. This cluster differed significantly from clusters 1 and 2 on the two most complex levels of the span-of-apprehension task and on the complex version of the Spokes test. In addition, the children in cluster 4 were significantly impaired, relative to those in cluster 1, on the condition in the competing-voices task in which seven voices were presented. Across a number of tasks, the subjects in cluster 4 tended to demonstrate a differential impairment as a function of an increase in the amount of information that had to be processed, a characteristic we have interpreted as reflecting an "overload" on performance capacity. Also, cluster 4 subjects exhibited greater decrements than the other subjects on the span-of-apprehension and competing-voices tasks in

Table 7-2. Attentional performance of four attentional clusters.

Task	Score	Variable		I Mean	I S.D.	II Mean	II S.D.	III Mean	III S.D.	IV Mean	IV S.D.	F-Values
Competing Voices	Number of errors	Number of voices	−1	0.07	0.21	0.19	0.50	2.00	—	1.10	2.19	2.31
			−3	3.03	1.94	4.50	2.02	29.50	—	7.70	11.12	1.75
			−7	6.32	1.76	9.22	2.37	29.00	—	12.30	9.97	3.69
			−13	4.64	2.79	7.55	3.49	27.50	—	7.30	3.21	3.15
Concept Attainment	Errors to criterion	Number of stimulus dimensions	−3	2.14	1.23	2.67	1.12	5.00	—	2.60	1.82	0.51
			−4	2.14	0.95	2.55	1.13	3.00	—	2.40	1.14	0.45
			−5	4.28	1.98	5.44	2.19	10.00	—	6.60	3.65	1.90
			−6	6.78	2.52	8.00	3.08	12.00	—	9.80	3.27	2.15
Continuous Performance Test	Number of errors of commission and omission	Errors of commission		2.35	4.29	0.80	0.83	11.00	—	0.00	0.0	1.32
		Errors of omission		1.07	1.14	2.49	1.51	11.00	—	0.00	0.0	7.45
Digit Symbol Substitution Test	Number completed	DSST		57.30	10.48	45.60	6.84	30.00	—	47.80	5.12	5.58
Simple Reaction Time	Latency difference (msec) between irregular and regular trials at preparatory interval of 1, 4, and 7 sec (−1000 added to difference)	Preparatory interval	−1	961.70	29.46	919.60	35.76	1015.40	—	937.90	53.59	0.90
			−4	985.30	32.82	988.20	41.92	850.70	—	1014.40	14.17	1.39
			−7	991.70	40.44	1011.30	37.27	1093.60	—	1000.40	32.86	2.71

Test	Measure		285.50	37.88	307.10	108.41	459.00	—	261.80	20.50	2.75
Span of Apprehension	Latency (msec)	Series of 15 irregular trials	285.50	37.88	307.10	108.41	459.00	—	261.80	20.50	2.75
	Number of correct detections	Number of elements in array									
		−1	39.90	0.27	39.70	0.44	34.00	—	39.40	0.89	2.25
		−3	39.20	1.05	39.20	0.83	37.00	—	38.80	1.10	0.35
		−5	37.80	2.08	37.40	1.67	32.00	—	34.20	2.49	5.99
		−7	34.50	2.53	32.80	3.49	26.00	—	28.20	1.92	9.30
Spokes Test	Total time (sec)	Spokes A	30.40	8.09	37.80	9.11	59.90	—	36.60	12.02	2.05
		Spokes B	49.80	9.97	62.90	20.92	145.10	—	99.20	24.02	15.80
Stroop Test	Total time (sec)	Read color words	5.75	0.94	8.54	2.05	7.50	—	6.14	0.57	11.28
		Name colors	7.32	1.02	9.91	1.24	12.00	—	8.06	1.06	13.81
		Read color words (interference condition)	7.12	1.59	9.26	1.44	8.40	—	6.80	0.91	6.73
		Name colors (interference conditions —4 trials)	55.82	8.17	71.14	12.55	84.80	—	67.68	4.64	7.56

accuracy of detection of target stimuli as the noise-to-signal ratio increased. In addition, this "overload" pattern was seen on the Spokes test in which differentially greater impairment occurred as the complexity of the task increased. The subjects in this group also revealed impaired performance on the Digit Symbol Substitution Test in comparison to cluster 1, but did not differ from the subjects in cluster 2. In contrast to their performance on the other measures, the subjects in cluster 4 were not differentially affected by an increase in complexity on the Stroop and concept-attainment tasks. The subjects in cluster 2, with one exception (the Stroop test), were intermediate in performance between the subjects in clusters 1 and 4.

The five high risk children in clusters 3 and 4 were the same subset of subjects who were previously found to perform in the bottom one-third of all subjects across the span-of-apprehension tasks, the Spokes test, and the concept-attainment task. Thus, using three different methods of analysis, five high risk subjects were identified who performed in a deficient manner across a number of tasks. One of these children manifested an impairment across all tasks. The other four high risk children, along with one foster control child in cluster 4, exhibited a deficit on primarily perceptual-motor tasks when the task was complex.

RELATIONSHIP BETWEEN ATTENTION/INFORMATION PROCESSING
AND CLINICAL ASSESSMENTS

In an effort to validate the differences between subtypes and to replicate the clinical/behavioral characteristics reported in other studies of children at risk for schizophrenia, the MMPI and Psychiatric Status Schedule were administered (Asarnow, Steffy, Cleghorn, & MacCrimmon, 1979; MacCrimmon, Cleghorn, Asarnow, & Steffy, 1980). This was done to determine if the attentionally impaired subjects exhibited some of the prodromal behavioral and clinical characteristics of schizophrenia and to provide preliminary evidence for information processing deficits as markers of schizophrenia. Moreover, these analyses also provided a basis for determining whether the attentional and behavioral/clinical features were markers for different developmental pathways to schizophrenia.

The subjects who exhibited attentional impairments also obtained higher PSS and MMPI scores than the subjects in the other clusters. Thus, on the MMPI, the cluster 4 subjects scored higher on the schizophrenia and psychopathic deviate scales than the subjects in the other two clusters. An item analysis of the schizophrenia scale indicated that a number of the subjects in cluster 4 reported some "micropsychotic experiences." On the PSS, they also reported more problems with social isolation and greater difficulty in meeting the student role than other children. Although the attentionally impaired subjects in the high risk group were more symptomatic overall, it should be noted that symptoms were not concentrated in any one of the clinical scales and that none of the high risk subjects exhibited psychotic symptoms. Table 7-3 presents some of the clinical and behavioral characteristics of the attentionally impaired subjects. It can be seen that two children demonstrated attentional impairments and also obtained elevated scores on the PSS and MMPI. The picture that emerged of these two children was such that, on a number of attentional tasks, they demonstrated an "overload" pattern of performance; that is, a differential decrement in the accuracy of their detection of target stimuli as the amount of information they were required to process was increased. These two children reported scholastic difficulty, problems concentrating in school, few friendships, social isolation, and "micropsychotic" experiences. During the interview, they reported instances in which they engaged in aggressive and antisocial behavior. They were also described as belligerent by the psychiatrist who conducted the interview.

The characteristics of these two children are consistent with those observed by Offord and Cross (1969) and are typical of schizophrenics who have a history of childhood difficulties prior to the onset of overt schizophrenic illness. Roff, Knight, and Wertheim (1976) similarly found that a poor outcome in adult schizophrenics was associated with low school performance, poor peer relations, and unsocialized aggression. Roff et al. concluded that this pattern of behavior (particularly in boys) represented one of a number of different developmental pathways to adult schizophrenia—the process schizophrenic pathway. The two children in the McMaster/Waterloo study who showed both attentional and clinical impairment appeared to fit this description. Moreover, on some of the attention/information processing tasks, these children exhibited levels of performance that were similar to overtly schizophrenic adults, and, on the span-of-apprehension test, they functioned at a level that was *identical* to that of acute and remitted adult schizophrenics. In conclusion, it would appear that this subgroup of children are at a heightened risk, relative to other children, for developing schizophrenia. Whether or not these two multiply handicapped high risk children actually succumb to schizophrenia can, of course, only be determined through follow-up investigation.

Table 7-3. PSS scores and MMPI T-scores over 70 for attentionally impaired subjects.

Attentional cluster	Group	PSS*				MMPI													
		DA	SI	SR	TO	L	F	K	Hs	D	Hy	Pd	Mf	Pa	Pt	Sc	Ma	SI
III	HR	3	5	0	13		87									74		
	HR	10	4	9	28		83			75	71	83		87		91		75
	HR	10	6	11	40		76			77	71	71			81	80		
IV	HR	0	0	1	2			79										
	HR	0	0	0	0		78					71				75		
	FC	0	0	0	0												96	

* PSS scales: DA = depression anxiety, SI = social isolation, SR = student role, TO = total score.

The Minnesota studies

The Minnesota studies (Neuchterlein, 1982a, b, in press; Neuchterlein, Phipps-Yonas, Driscoll, & Garmezy, in press) also investigated problems of attention in groups of children at risk for schizophrenia. This research program consists of a series of doctoral dissertations conducted by Keith Neuchterlein, Susan Phipps-Yonas, and Regina Driscoll in the Department of Psychology at the University of Minnesota, under the Supervision of Norman Garmezy. The research was initiated, in part, to test a model proposed by Zubin (1975) who theorized that attention could be differentiated into three basic components: sustained, shift, and selective. Sustained, or maintenance of attention was defined as the extension of a focus over time after the selection of focus has been completed. Shift of attention was defined as a switching mechanism that moves the attentional focus between temporally successive stimuli. Selective attention was defined as the separation of relevant from irrelevant simultaneous stimuli. The Minnesota studies are, thus, similar to the McMaster/Waterloo project in broadly surveying various aspects of attention.

Multiple measures of each of these components of attention were administered to several rigorously defined contrast groups of children who were between nine and sixteen years of age. One group consisted of children born to mothers who had nonschizophrenic forms of psychiatric disturbance. This group permitted the determination of whether maternal psychiatric distress was associated with attention deficits in their children. Thus, only children whose mothers' psychiatric diagnosis fell outside the schizophrenic spectrum (Rosenthal, 1970) were included. The diagnoses of the mothers were predominantly depressive neurosis, adjustment reactions, and personality disorders. A second group consisted of hyperactive children. Since these children suffer from attentional problems, their inclusion afforded the opportunity to determine the specificity of attentional deficits that are exhibited by children who are at risk for schizophrenia. The high risk group consisted of offspring of schizophrenic mothers.

Each of the children in these three groups was matched with a normal comparison child drawn from the same classroom. Because the investigators were concerned with the possibility of the groups being systematically unmatched on factors other than the matching variables, a larger comparison group was selected by stratified sampling based on sociometric status.

Measures of attention

As indicated above, the Minnesota project used multiple measures of various components of attention. Neuchterlein et al. (in press, b) examined sustained attention using adapted versions of the continuous performance test (Rosvold, Mirsky, Sarason, Bransome, & Beck, 1956). This test requires the subject to monitor a series of briefly presented visual stimuli, usually numbers or letters, and to press a button each time a predesignated target stimulus appears. Phipps-Yonas (Neuchterlein et al., in press) studied shift of attention using a cross-modal reaction time paradigm (Sutton, Hakarem, Zubin, & Portnoy, 1961; Sutton & Zubin, 1965). In this task, two blocks of trials are first presented in which reaction time to a light stimulus and to a tone stimulus are recorded. Next, the subjects are presented with a condition in which lights and tones are randomly ordered across trials. The longer reaction time latencies on the cross-modal sequences, compared to the ipsimodal sequences, are attributed to the time required to shift attention from one modality to the other.

Driscoll (Neuchterlein et al., in press) employed two discrimination learning tasks to study selective attention. The tasks varied the extent to which incidental, but simultaneous stimuli would be scanned as an intrinsic part of the basic learning task. The central task entailed learning a series of pictures of objects, each of which was presented with pictures of two other irrelevant objects. On other trials, irrelevant names of objects were auditorily presented. The amount of intentional focused learning was measured by recall and recognition of the relevant pictures. Incidental learning was indexed by parallel measures for the irrelevant pictures and the auditorily presented object names.

Results

To reduce the number of variables and to stabilize the scale of measurement, each of the three components of attention were factor analyzed, and factor scores were computed for each subject. The factor scores were then analyzed for group differences. These analyses determined whether an unusual number of children from any group obtained extreme scores. To accomplish this objective, the number of children in each group who scored on the most extreme ten percentile of each tail of the theoretical factor score distribution were counted. This analysis revealed that there were more children of schizophrenic mothers than normal children, who obtained scores in the extreme low CPT-d' group. Relatively few children born to non-psychotic, psychiatrically disturbed mothers or hyperactive children fell into the low CPT-d' factor score group. On the other hand, the CPT beta factor, reaction time, intentional learning, and incidental learning factors did not isolate a disproportionately large group of extreme scoring offspring of schizophrenic mothers.

The comparison between the children of schizophrenic mothers and hyperactive children revealed some interesting qualitative differences in attentional functioning. Relative to the children in the stratified normal group, the hyperactive children obtained significantly lower mean CPT beta factor scores and also contributed a disproportionate number of cases to the group with low CPT beta factor scores. Unlike the children of schizophrenic mothers, they did not demonstrate a significant deviation on the CPT-d' factor. This latter finding suggests that the children of schizophrenic mothers can be differentiated from other children who are defined, in part, by their attentional problems. The children of schizophrenics were characterized by impaired sequential discrimination of relevant and irrelevant stimuli in a task demanding sustained attention. The hyperactive children, in contrast, tended to respond to stimuli as relevant, even when there was meager sensory evidence for their relevance.

ANALYSIS OF SUBGROUPS

A cluster analysis was used to examine the possibility that a subgroup of offspring of schizophrenic mothers could be identified by performance scores across attentional tasks. Factor scores for all subjects on the CPT-d', reaction time, and intentional learning were entered into a cluster analysis. Five clusters were isolated. One cluster consisted of 14 cases whose average scores on the CPT-d', reaction time, and intentional learning factors were in the bottom ten percentile for the entire sample. This cluster included a disproportionate number of children born to schizophrenic mothers. A second cluster consisted of one case, a child of a schizophrenic mother, who scored poorly on the CPT-d', but not on the other two performance factors. Thus, two of the five clusters contained disproportionate numbers of children of schizophrenic mothers.

Additional analyses revealed a small subset of children who scored very poorly on the three central factors, which were derived from the three sets of information processing tasks. There was also a tendency for the children of schizophrenic mothers to be overly represented in the clusters of children who manifested impairments across a number of different information processing tasks. Interestingly, the best discrimination between groups was achieved by the CPT-d' task, which measures the capacity of the subject to sustain attention while sequentially discriminating relevant from irrelevant stimuli.

Two children in the stratified normal control group showed a pattern of deviant attentional performance that closely approximated that of the children of schizophrenic mothers. They also scored quite low on a measure of sociometric status. It is noteworthy that low peer appraisal ratings are predictive of psychopathological problems and psychiatric contact in adulthood (Cowen, Pederson, Babigian, Izzo, & Trost, 1973; Roff, 1961, 1963).

The New York High Risk Project

In the New York High Risk Project (Cornblatt & Erlenmeyer-Kimling, in press; Erlenmeyer-Kimling, Marcuse, Cornblatt, Friedman, Ranier, & Rutschman, in press), multiple measures of attention were administered to children of schizophrenic parents. One of the unique features of this research program was that it was concerned with prospectively studying children who varied in their genetic loading for schizophrenia. This was accomplished by examining children who had either one or two schizophrenic parents and comparing them to contrast groups of children who had a parent with a psychiatric disorder other than schizophrenia and to children of parents without a history of psychiatric disorder.

Three rounds of assessment have been conducted to date. Two attentional measures were used in the first round of testing, at which time the children were between 7 and 12 years old. A version of the continuous performance test was employed; it required the subject to respond to either a target stimulus whenever it appeared or when it was immediately preceded by another specified stimulus. On one-half the blocks of trials, a distractor, consisting of a tape recording of a woman's voice reciting digits at rates of presentation varying from fast to slow, was also presented. The other one-half of the trial blocks did not contain distracting stimuli. Signal detection analyses were then conducted to obtain estimates of d' and $beta$.

The second measure was an auditory attention-span task. In this task, sequences of either three or five letters were recited by a female voice at either a fast or a slow rate of presentation. The subject was required to recall each sequence immediately following its presentation. On one-half of the trials, a distractor consisting of a male voice reciting letters in the interval between the target letters was presented. During this part of the task, the subjects were instructed to ignore the male voice.

When children with one schizophrenic parent were compared to normal control children, the high risk subjects made more errors of omission on target trials on the CPT under both the distractor and non-distractor conditions (Erlenmeyer-Kimling & Cornblatt, 1978). The high risk group also made significantly more errors of commission than the control group. There were, however, no differences between the groups in reaction time, nor was there a differential effect of the distractor condition. On the attention-span task, there was no difference between the groups on the three-letter sequence or slow rate of presentation under either the distraction or the non-distraction condition. On the five-letter sequence and fast rate of presentation procedure, the high risk group performed significantly more poorly than the control group, but only under the non-distraction condition. Under the distraction condition, there was a large decrement in performance for both groups and, thus, no differential effect in the children of schizophrenic mothers was revealed.

Comparisons between the groups were complemented by an analysis of eight performance indices in which standardized scores were obtained. Subjects who fell into the extreme 5% of the distribution that was derived from the normal subjects were tallied. It was found that 29% of the control subjects and 60% of the high risk subjects were in the bottom 5% of the distribution for at least one performance index. None of the control subjects obtained extreme scores for more than four performance indices, in contrast to 6.9% of the high risk subjects.

A third round of testing[1] (Cornblatt & Erlenmeyer-Kimling, in press) on these subjects included a revised computerized version of the CPT, an information overload task (IOT), and the Wisconsin Card Sorting Task. In the revised version of the CPT, double digit numbers were flashed on a visual monitor. Two CPT tasks were administered. The first required subjects to respond whenever the digits "08" were presented; the second, when any two identical stimuli appeared in a row. The IOT required subjects to point to one of four pictures that matched a target word that was recited during different auditory background distractors. Under one condition, the pointing task was presented in the absence of background noise to establish base-line response levels. Under the second condition, the dis-

---

[1] The second round of testing is not discussed here because different versions of the CPT were administered to each one-half of the sample.

tracting stimuli presented to the subjects consisted of sounds in a busy school cafeteria, whereas the third condition consisted of a tape-recorded voice telling a simple story. Subjects were required to process, and not simply screen out, the distracting stimuli. This was achieved by informing them that they would be questioned about the stories when the pointing task was terminated. It was found that the high risk subjects performed the pointing task significantly more poorly than the normal control subjects under both distraction conditions. They also answered significantly fewer questions about the background story under the third condition. The Wisconsin Card Sorting Task and the CPT did not reveal differences between groups, in part because of ceiling effects.

A new sample of children between the ages of seven and twelve was tested in order to replicate the findings of the first study. The revised CPT was administered to this sample, but it did not discriminate between the groups. However, on the more complex conditions, the high risk subjects made significantly fewer correct responses and also obtained significantly lower d' scores than the control group, findings that were consistent with the results obtained during the first round of testing.

A visual-aural digit span task (Koppitz, 1973) was also administered. Digit strings of increasing length in both the visual and aural modalities were presented. It was observed that the high risk subjects recalled significantly fewer digits than the normal control subjects under all the conditions except when the stimuli were orally presented and recalled. This is not surprising, since it was the easiest condition.

The data from the third round of testing of the original sample were further examined by tallying of the number of response indices in which each subject performed deviantly relative to the normal control group. Of the high risk subjects, 30% versus 3% of the normal control group performed deviantly on four or more of the indices.

The increased prevalence of deviant performance in the high risk group was corroborated by an interesting longitudinal analysis. A deviance score, consisting of 13 indices generated by the CPT and IOT measures, was computed. The deviance scores, spanning seven years between round one and round three, were found to be significantly correlated in the high risk subjects, but not in the normal controls. Cornblatt and Erlenmeyer-Kimling (in press) interpreted these results to indicate that performance in the control group, when deviant, was due to random fluctuations, whereas in the high risk subjects, their performance pattern suggested a stable characteristic.

The New York High Risk Project also provided important preliminary data concerning the relationship between early attentional dysfunction and subsequent behavior problems. The high risk subgroup, characterized on initial assessment by attentional dysfunction, was the most likely to show behavioral problems in adolescence. Indeed, these subjects tended to manifest increasingly deviant behavior as they grew older. Cornblatt and Erlenmeyer-Kimling (in press) suggest that this finding is consistent with the hypothesis that an attentional dysfunction is an early predictor of later psychopathology.

The Boston studies

A number of investigators from settings in the Boston area have collaborated in the study of young children of psychotic mothers (Grunebaum, Weiss, Gallant, & Cohler, 1974). The mothers were schizophrenic, schizoaffective, depressed, manic-depressed, or borderline schizophrenic. As part of the original assessment, children who were three, five, and six years old were tested with age-appropriate versions of the children's embedded figures test (CEFT) (Kagan, 1971). A version of the continuous performance test (CPT) was also used, wherein children were required to press a key when they detected a pre-designated stimulus (the letter X for six-year-olds and the color red for five-year-olds).

It was observed that among the five-year-olds, the children of schizophrenic mothers made more errors of omission than the children of schizoaffective, psychotic, non-schizophrenic mothers and children of mothers with no history of a psychiatric disorder. The five-year-old children of both schizophrenic and schizoaffective mothers made significantly more errors of commission than control children. No differences were found among the six-year-old children in either errors of omission or errors of commission. On the CEFT, the five-year-old children of schizophrenic and schizoaffective mothers did not differ from each other. However, these two groups failed more stimuli than did the children of non-psychiatric controls. Again, there were no differences among the six-year-old children.

In another investigation, Gamer, Gallant, Grunebaum, and Cohler (1977) compared three-year-old children whose mothers were psychotic (62% of the mothers were diagnosed as schizophrenic or schizoaffective psychosis, 29% as depressed or manic depressive psychosis) to a group of low risk children on the CEFT. The high risk subjects performed less competently than the low risk group, particularly on the more difficult stimuli, despite the fact that the groups did not differ from each other on the Peabody Picture Vocabulary Test. No significant differences were noted between children whose mothers were diagnosed as suffering from schizophrenia, schizoaffective, or depressive psychosis on the CEFT or the Peabody. The lack of differentiation between the groups was interpreted as indicating that CEFT performance might be a marker of impairment in children that arises from the stress of living with a psychotic mother.

Herman, Mirsky, Ricks, and Gallant (1977) retested six children of schizophrenic mothers who were in the original cohort investigated by Grunebaum et al. (1974). In addition to the attention test, EEG tracings and visual-evoked potentials were recorded. The electrophysiobiological data were gathered while the children were performing the attentional task so as to provide a clearer account of the nature of the attentional impairment during a visual information processing task.

The investigation (Herman et al., 1977) failed to detect a difference between the high risk children and controls on the CPT. Moreover, the high risk group demonstrated a significant improvement over their previous performance, whereas no such change was observed in the control subjects.

The Stony Brook High Risk Project

The Stony Brook High Risk Project (Weintraub & Neale, in press; Neale, in press) assessed the specificity of information processing impairments exhibited by children at risk for schizophrenia. Children of depressed and schizophrenic parents were compared. The children ranged in age from 6 to 15 years and were divided into two subgroups of 6 to 10 and 11 to 15 years of age. Although the Stony Brook Project used an extensive set of measures that tapped academic, social, clinical, and familial variables, the present discussion will be limited to a review of the information processing tasks and findings. Two tests were utilized that measured the ability of the child to ignore irrelevant input and to sustain attention. A visual search task that required the subject to scan a list of 30 strings of four letters was used. Two variables were manipulated to assess the influence of task difficulty on score time: the physical similarity between the target and noise letters and the location of the target letters. A digit-span task developed by Oltmans and Neale (1975) was used as a measure of distractability. In this task, numbers were presented on a tape recording at the rate of one digit every two seconds. The child was instructed to report as many digits as possible after listening to the series. In the distractor condition, the interval between each relevant digit was filled by an opposite-sex voice reciting an irrelevant digit.

Weintraub and Neale (in press) found that on the visual search task the children of both schizophrenic and depressed parents were slower than the offspring of controls, but the former two groups did not differ significantly from each other. An analysis of deviant responders corroborated the above findings; 17% of the offspring of schizophrenics, 21% of the offspring of depressives, and only 7% of the offspring of controls scored more than one standard deviation above the mean in search time.

On the digit-span task, there were no significant differences between the three groups under the non-distractor condition. Under the distractor condition, the offspring of schizophrenic and depressed mothers scored significantly lower than the children of normal parents. The former two groups, however, did not differ from each other. A deviant responder analysis yielded a somewhat sharper discrimination between the groups than was revealed by an analysis of group means. A tendency was observed for the offspring of schizophrenic parents to score more than one standard deviation from the mean than the offspring of either the depressed or the normal parents.

Comment

The studies reviewed above indicate that children of schizophrenic mothers exhibit impaired performance on measures of information processing. The consistency of this finding across studies is impressive considering the differences in the tasks employed and the characteristics of the samples. Moreover, the results obtained by Cornblatt and Erlenmeyer-Kimling (in press) illustrated that high risk children who demonstrate early attentional difficulties are also the most likely to exhibit social maladjustment during adolescence. MacCrimmon et al. (1980) similarly found that attentionally impaired high risk subjects show some of the prodromal behavioral and clinical characteristics of individuals who subsequently develop schizophrenia. These findings suggest that measures of information processing may have some predictive validity.

Nonetheless, a number of important issues on the specificity of the impaired attention/information performance, and discrepancies between studies, remain to be clarified. Particularly relevant are the findings obtained by Weintraub and Neale (in press), in which no differences between children of depressed and schizophrenic mothers were found. Similarly, Grunebaum et al. (1974) failed to obtain significant differences, although the children of schizophrenic mothers tended to be the most impaired, followed by the children of schizoaffective and depressed mothers. Perhaps discriminable differences could not be found because the nature of the information processing deficit is quite specific in schizophrenia, and not all measures will reveal group differences. It will be recalled that in the Minnesota project, the offspring of schizophrenic mothers were more likely than other children to score low on a d' factor when tested on a continuous performance test. This finding is particularly impressive considered in light of the fact that one of the comparison groups was comprised of children with an attention deficit disorder. Thus, the inability of the same studies to differentiate children at high risk for schizophrenia from other children may be due in part to the fact that the instruments did not specifically tap the vulnerability for schizophrenia.

Other factors also need to be considered. The removal of the parent from the home or the return of the parent from the hospital are events that likely have a very substantial impact on the family (Rodnick & Goldstein, 1974). In the Stony Brook Project, children were tested relatively close to the time of the parent's hospitalization. It is possible, therefore, that the parent's removal or return to the family, being contiguous to the time of testing, induced a state of generalized psychological distress in the children. Asarnow and MacCrimmon (1981) have recently suggested that generalized states of distress can obscure the specific, but subtle manifestations of psychopathology. The fact that the children in the McMaster/Waterloo project were living with foster parents, and the offspring in the Minnesota and New York projects were tested an appreciable time after the mother's hospitalization, may thus partially account for the discrepancies found in the Stony Brook study.

Another potential factor contributing to the discrepancies may stem from the fact that the Stony Brook Project selected a somewhat unusual sample of high risk children. This project, by virtue of its broad interest in the assessment of social, familial, and environmental factors, was primarily concerned with studying children in intact families. One could theorize that their parents were better compensated schizophrenic individuals, with probably a later onset of the disorder. In contrast, the mothers in the McMaster/Waterloo study were so impaired that their psychiatric status was an important factor in removing the child from their care.

It is, therefore, reasonable to hypothesize that the children in the Stony Brook Project, having better adjusted and less impaired parents than the children in the other projects, had a lower genetic loading for schizophrenia. There is some evidence to support this notion as indicated by the observation that the degree of genetic loading, as indexed by the presence of a family history for the disorder, *within* samples of schizophrenics, is correlated with the severity of an information processing impairment (Asarnow, Cromwell, & Rennick, 1978).

Another factor that may contribute to the differences between investigations relates to the task requirements. It is noteworthy that the visual search task in the Stony Brook Project did not feature the use of a brief stimulus presentation time. It may be that one task parameter required for the elicitation of an impairment is a very brief exposure time that involves rapid processing of information.

Clearly, the above explanations for the discrepant findings between investigations are speculative and *ex post facto* in nature. Indeed, any generalization about the meaning of information processing impairments detected in high risk children must be considered speculative until it can be determined if these deficits are predictive of schizophrenia. This ultimate criterion variable, the occurrence of clinical schizophrenia, may, however, take as long as 40 years to be determined. Obviously, this is too great a period of time to elapse between the generation and testing of a hypothesis. One approach in dealing with this problem is to examine intermediate outcome variables that occur at some point in the pathogenesis of schizophrenia and that are related to the subsequent development of the disorder. An alternative strategy is to determine if the impairments exist in other groups of individuals who are vulnerable to schizophrenia, but who are not actively disturbed at the time of testing (Asarnow & MacCrimmon, 1981).

The convergence paradigm

The convergence strategy consists of *cross sectionally* studying the prodromal, active, and post-psychotic stages of schizophrenia. It provides an opportunity to determine if a particular measure taps the core aspects of schizophrenia when administered to individuals who are vulnerable to the disorder, but who are not necessarily symptomatic at the time of testing. Adult schizophrenics in remission, who are vulnerable but not symptomatic, are one such group.

A number of studies will be reviewed to illustrate the application of

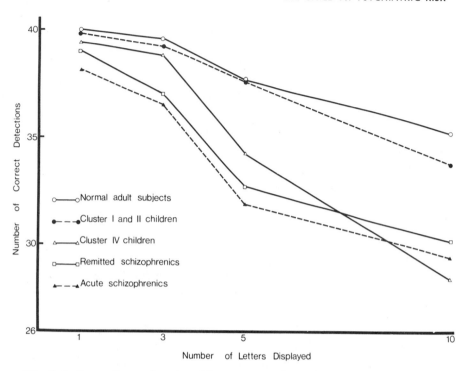

Fig. 7–1. Span-of-apprehension. The mean number of correct detections as a function of the number of letters displayed.

the convergence strategy. Asarnow and MacCrimmon (1981) administered the span-of-apprehension test that was used in the McMaster/ Waterloo project with groups of acute and remitted schizophrenics, as well as normal control subjects. As the number of non-relevant elements was increased, both acute and remitted schizophrenics showed a progressively greater decrement than normal controls in the accuracy of detection of the target stimuli. In Figure 7-1, it can be seen that the schizophrenics' pattern of performance was similar to that of a subset of the foster children at risk for schizophrenia. This finding suggests that performance on this task may be tapping core schizophrenic processes that are relatively independent of clinical status.

Figure 7-2 presents the span-of-apprehension data from another recently completed study (Asarnow & MacCrimmon, 1981) in which a subgroup of schizophrenics were differentiated from a group of partially recovered manic-depressive patients. Figure 7-3 graphically illustrates that performance on this test could correctly classify 100% of the normal

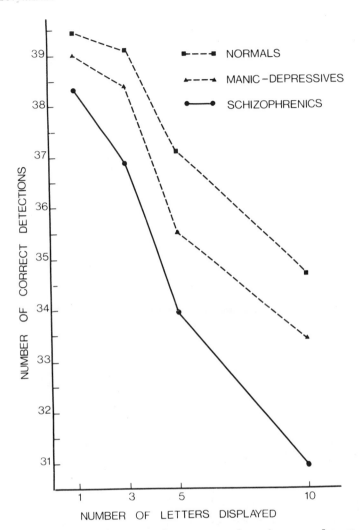

Fig. 7–2. Span-of-apprehension. The mean number of correct detections as a function of the number of letters displayed.

controls, 85% of the manic-depressives, and a subgroup comprising 40% of remitted schizophrenic patients. Interestingly, the subgroup of schizophrenics identified by test performance did not differ from the remainder of the schizophrenic group in specific symptoms, overall clinical status, or general performance efficiency. Taken collectively, these findings suggest that performance on the span-of-apprehension test may be a marker of vulnerability in one subset of the schizophrenias.

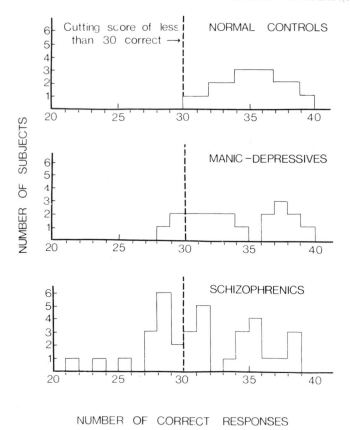

Fig. 7–3 Span-of-apprehension. The frequency distributions of the number of correct detection on the 10-letter array.

Asarnow and MacCrimmon (1978) also tested patients on a version of the continuous performance test, in which subjects were instructed to press a button when a predesignated digit appeared. It was found that the acute and remitted schizophrenics made significantly more errors of commission and omission than the normal controls. The two groups of schizophrenics did not differ from each other, although there was a tendency for the remitted schizophrenics to be more impaired when tested under the distractor condition. These results replicated Wohlberg and Kornetsky's (1973) finding that remitted schizophrenics were deficient on the CPT, particularly when distracting stimuli were present. The above findings, considered in conjunction with the results obtained by Grunebaum et al. (1974) and Cornblatt and Erlenmeyer-Kimling (in press), in which children at risk for schizophrenia were more impaired on the CPT than normals (particularly under the distractor condition), indicate that this task may measure certain core disturbances associated with schizophrenia.

Genetic studies

Investigations of attention/information processing capacity in first-degree relatives of schizophrenic probands have revealed that (a) non-symptomatic first-degree relatives of process schizophrenics are impaired on reaction time tasks (DeAmicis & Cromwell, 1979); (b) siblings of schizophrenics are deficient on an auditory vigilance task and choice reaction time (Wood & Cook, 1979); and (c) there is a positive correlation between CPT omission errors between schizophrenic mothers and their sons (Grunebaum et al., 1974). These findings, considered collectively, suggest the possibility of a genetic basis for the impairments observed in individuals at risk for schizophrenia.

The above observations also suggest a strategy that could clarify some of the ambiguities concerning the transmission of schizophrenia. Little doubt exists that there is a significant genetic contribution to the transmission of schizophrenia (Gottesman, 1978). For example, unlike the biological relatives, members and relatives of the family into which a schizophrenic is adopted do not have elevated rates of schizophrenia. In addition, the concordance rates for schizophrenia in identical twins are about three times higher than in fraternal twins, and at least 30 times higher than in the general population. On the other hand, more than one-half of monozygotic twins are discordant for schizophrenia, despite their identical genetic makeup. These findings have been interpreted (Gottesman, 1978; Kidd, 1978) as indicating that environmental and genetic factors interact to cause schizophrenia and that the importance of these major factors may vary from case to case. Cromwell (1978) has extended these points to argue that since schizophrenia may represent the final common behavioral pathway for a number of different disorders, studies of symptoms are limited by their incapacity to elucidate the nature of the genotypes specific to subgroups of schizophrenics. He also argues that further progress in understanding the inheritance of schizophrenia must be based on studies of the inheritance of factors more closely related to the manifestation of the genotype than simply their symptoms. The suggested alternative to the study of symptoms is the study of impairments in information processing as the possible core aspects of schizophrenia.

Neurophysiological studies of high risk children

Itil, Hsu, Saletu, and Mednick (1974) found that a group of high risk children were significantly different from a matched control group in their EEG and auditory-evoked potentials. The children who were at risk had EEG tracings characterized by high frequency beta activity, fewer fast alpha waves, and slower low voltage delta activity than their controls. The latencies of their auditory-evoked potentials were also shorter than those of the control group. Itil et al. (1974) noted similarities of the electrophysiological patterns in their subjects to those seen in psychotic children and in adult chronic schizophrenics, leading them to hypothesize that these neuropsychological patterns may predispose to schizophrenic illness.

Herman et al. (1977) obtained EEG recordings while children were performing the CPT, as well as under a resting condition when there was no stimulation and under a resting condition when they received visual stimulation consisting of flashes from a photic stimulator. In contrast to the findings of Itil et al. (1974), they did not find differences between high risk and control children in the spectral analyses of base-line EEG data. Although no gross deficits were observed in the high risk group on the CPT test, this group did, however, differ from the controls in evoked responses to the CPT stimuli. This took the form of larger amplitudes mostly in response to positive stimuli. The high risk group also had longer response latencies, a finding that was particularly evident with respect to negative stimuli. In addition, greater response amplitudes were observed in the high risk group in the early component of the evoked response across all stimulus intensities generated by a photic stimulator.

An explanation involving a maturational lag was advanced to account for the above findings. The investigators noted that the evoked potentials in the high risk children were similar to those seen in younger normal children. A less mature nervous system was thus hypothesized to underlie a "slower development of visual stimulus processing mechanisms in children at risk for schizophrenia" (Herman et al., 1977).

Friedman, Vaughan, and Erlenmeyer-Kimling (1979) also studied the evoked potentials to CPT stimuli in high risk and control children. Under the first experimental condition, the subjects were instructed to respond to the number 08; under the second condition, they were told to respond upon the repetition of the immediately preceding number. A principal components factor analysis was conducted, and scores were computed for each individual. It was observed that the high risk group tended to have a greater amplitude on a factor that tapped the P_{240} component of the evoked response. This group also returned to base line faster than the control group. An analysis of the outliers revealed that ten high risk and two normal subjects were represented in four or more of the factors. Within this subgroup, four of the subjects, all of whom were high risk, revealed a consistent pattern of factor scores marked by large amplitude frontal P_{450} to signal stimuli, large amplitude P_{240} to both stimuli and tasks, little initial negativity, the absence of late positive activity, and faster returns to base line. Friedman et al. (1979) also noted that the morphology of the outlier's wave forms was quite similar to that found in adult schizophrenics.

In another study, Friedman, Erlenmeyer-Kimling, and Vaughan (in press) obtained evoked responses to relevant, irrelevant, and background auditory events. A principal components analysis was used in order to identify the components of the waveform. This was followed by a comparison of the mean factor scores between the high risk and control groups. The most striking finding was the low factor score, indicating late positivity in the waveform for both the missing stimulus and frequent stimulus conditions in the high risk subjects.

A reduced amplitude of late ERP components when the eliciting event is relevant was replicated in another subsample from the New York High Risk Project. Given the consistency of this finding, and also its presence in adult schizophrenics, the author concluded that "it may be one of the premorbid indicators for schizophrenia" (Friedman et al., 1979).

The studies described above suggest that there may be characteristic neurophysiological patterns that are associated with an increased risk for schizophrenia. These patterns are thought to tap mechanisms of selective attention (Friedman et al., 1979). In the studies cited above, deficits are most likely to be observed on tasks that require selective attention, while the subject makes rapid discriminations. These neurophysiological findings offer an intriguing confirmation and extension of the psychological studies of information processing, suggesting that when high risk children are engaged in specific information processing tasks, characteristic neurophysiological anomalies are observed.

Neurological and neuropsychological dysfunction

Interest in neurobiological factors has in large measure been stimulated by Fish's seminal investigations of 24 infant offspring of schizophrenic mothers (Fish, 1957, 1963, 1975, 1977). Infant development was monitored by standard tests that were repeated ten times during the first decade of life. Physical growth curves were plotted (Wetzel, 1946) to detect changes in pattern or rate of development. Developmental quotients were computed for postural-motor, visual-motor, and language development, using the Gesell examination (1947). Independent psychological and psychiatric assessments were also conducted when the children reached 10 and 18 years of age. On these occasions, the children were diagnosed psychiatrically and rated for global impairment. The psychological examination included the Wechsler Intelligence Scale for children or adults, the Rorschach, the Thematic Apperception test, the Bender-Gestalt, and a perceptual-motor battery.

Two of the 24 children developed childhood schizophrenia. According to Fish (1977), they exhibited "a major disorganization of neurological maturation that involved postural-motor, visual-motor and physical development as early as the first month of life." The neurological defect appeared to be related to the timing and integration of neurological maturation, which resulted in unusual fluctuations in the rate of development. By 10 years of age, the high risk children tended to exhibit a number of perceptual disturbances. Impaired performance was observed on the block design subtest of the WISC, the Bender-Gestalt (Koppitz, 1964), fine motor coordination tests, and a finger schema test. Fish and Hagin (1973) suggest that the antecedents of the perceptual impairments noted at ages seven and ten could be detected when the child reached two years of age by, for example, impaired performance on the formboard.

To describe this pervasive, but fluctuating disability, Fish introduced the term "pan-developmental retardation." None of the children exhibiting this disorder had complications during either pregnancy or birth. They characteristically demonstrated periods of marked developmental acceleration that alternated with periods of retardation. Their disabilities, as noted above, were both far ranging in nature and detectable early in life.

Fish's neurointegrative deficit hypothesis was examined in a series of studies conducted by Marcus and his co-workers in Israel. In the Jerusalem Infant Development Study (Marcus, Auerbach, Wilkinson, &

Burack, 1981), the infant offspring of schizophrenic, affectively disturbed and personality-disordered mothers were compared to a normal control group. The children, at three and fourteen days of age, were tested with the Neonatal Behavioral Assessment Scale (NBAS) and rated on such functions and capacities as motor reactivity, habituation to stimulation during sleep, and auditory and visual orientation to stimuli, as well as ability to cope with other kinds of stimulation. At four, eight, and twelve months of age the children were evaluated on the Bayley Scales of Infant Development (Bayley, 1969), to chart mental, motor, and behavior development.

No differences at three and fourteen days of age were noted between the two groups on the NBAS. However, at four and eight months of age, the children of schizophrenics obtained lower scores on the Bayley Scale than controls on the mental development index and the psycho-motor development index. Similar trends persisted to the 12-month assessment, but the group differences at that time were only marginally significant.

To evaluate individual differences, Marcus et al. (1981) then selected items from the Neonatal and Bayley Scales to comprise a scale of motor and sensorimotor functioning. It was found that 13 infants in the schizophrenic group consistently performed poorly on the motor and sensorimotor measures during the first year of life. The capacity of the remaining seven infants who were born to schizophrenics, as well as most of the controls, was not impaired. An examination of the birth records of these subjects revealed that poor motor and sensorimotor performance during the first year of life tended to be associated with a low birth weight and mild to moderate prenatal problems.

A subgroup of children was identified who, at 14 days of age, demonstrated a number of disturbances that were characterized by weakness in upper body muscle control, poor, free-flowing limb movements, and a tendency toward elevated muscle tone. At four months of age, almost none of the infants in this subgroup showed visually guided reaching or age-level hand coordination. Most of them could not raise themselves to a sitting position, pull themselves to a standing position, or stand up by furniture at eight months of age. In addition, the majority of children did not acquire the motor skills necessary for picking up small objects, nor did they develop mid-line coordination. By the age of 12 months, most of them exhibited gross motor difficulties. They could not stand alone or from a supine position. Many could not walk without help. Most exhibited signs of object permanence; that is, they searched for disappearing objects. Their retrieval of objects was also impaired when complex motor behavior and memory abilities were required for successful performance.

The possible sequelae of these anomalies were examined in a different study of seven- to fourteen-year-old children (Marcus, 1974). Children of schizophrenic mothers were compared to matched controls. One-half of the children in each group lived on a kibbutz; the remainder were reared by their nuclear families. In addition to a variety of tests that were administered to the children, extensive information was obtained from interviews with parents and teachers. A neurological examination was conducted in order to assess for gross damage, as well as developmental deficiencies and "soft" neurological signs.

It was found that among the younger children, almost one-half of the offspring of schizophrenic parents clustered together and obtained scores indicative of a poor level of functioning. However, the difference between groups was not statistically significant, primarily because the distribution of scores in the high risk children was skewed. Further analyses revealed that the high risk subjects had delayed motor development that appeared to be accompanied by asymmetry and unilateral weakness of the musculature. Other deficit capacities were noted in right-left orientation, audio-visual integration, and perception.

Hanson, Gottesman, and Heston (1976) studied 116 children who were part of a larger prospective investigation of child development sponsored by the Perinatal Branch of the National Institute of Neurological Disease and Stroke. From this pool of subjects, there were 33 children who had at least one schizophrenic parent and 36 children who had a parent who was hospitalized, but for a non-schizophrenic psychiatric disorder. These children were compared to a group with no family history of psychiatric disorders.

The data, primarily comprising measures of motor performance from the year four assessment, were then analyzed. It was found that the children of schizophrenic parents more often performed poorly on tests of gross and fine motor control (e.g., pegboard, bead stringing), than children in the other groups. Neurological abnormalities, however, were not consistently present. Rather, the high risk children presented variable types and severity of neurological abnormality.

An analysis of variation within the high risk group was conducted in which three *a priori* indicators of schizophrenia were evaluated. The indicators selected were poor motor skills, large intraindividual variation on psychological tests, and schizoid behavior at ages four and seven.

Hanson et al. (1976) were then able to detect a subgroup of five children of schizophrenic parents who exhibited similar profiles on the three indicators. It was observed that all five subjects demonstrated persisting maladjustment throughout early childhood. The investigators pointed out that the probability of any one child manifesting all three indicators by chance is quite low and suggested that it is children with the above features who might be vulnerable to a future schizophrenia-like disability.

Some corroboration of the findings of Hanson et al (1976) was provided by Rieder and Nichols (1979), who examined a sample of children who were also drawn from the National Institute of Neurological and Communicative Diseases and Stroke Collaborative Perinatal Project. These researchers factor analyzed the scores from psychological and physical-neurological examinations that were conducted on 29 seven-year-old male offspring of schizophrenics. The psychological examination consisted of the WISC, Bender-Gestalt test, Auditory-Vocal Association Test from the Illinois Test of Psycholinguistic Abilities, Draw a Person, and Wide Range Achievement Test. The neurological examination involved scoring the child on a standardized 110-item protocol that focused on physical and neurological impairments. All the examination variables were factor analyzed to yield four factors with loadings of .20 or more. The factors identified were hyperactivity; immaturity (clinging to mother, fearfulness, shyness, or dependence on examiner); neurological signs (poor coordination; abnormal gait, movement, or reflexes; and mirror movements); and low school achievement. The 92nd percentile was used as the threshold for abnormal values for three of the factors; the 97th percentile was used as the threshold point for the factor describing neurological signs.

An examination of the children who scored beyond the threshold values revealed that the male offspring of schizophrenics were more frequently in the abnormal ranges than the matched control group on the hyperactivity and immaturity factors. The differences between the groups on the neurological factor were only marginally significant. An items analysis of this factor indicated that the difference was due primarily to one item, coordination of hand and arm movements.

Erlenmeyer-Kimling et al. (in press) have similarly detected impaired motor functioning measured by a modification of the Lincoln-Oseretsky Test of Motor Proficiency. This battery of tests discriminated between the high risk and normal subjects in two independent samples. In the initial sample, only a trend toward greater neurological impairment was noted in the high risk males under 11 years of age. A version of the neurological examination, administered to the second sample, revealed significant differences on items that tested right-left orientation, gait and position, and eye movement and on scales that measured fine motor coordination. In general, it was observed that inferior neurological functioning was characteristic of the high risk subjects, particularly in the younger boys, in whom the most salient impairment was fine motor coordination. It was also observed that low scores on the neurological summary scale were related to overall difficulties in adjustment. Moreover, the high risk subjects who had adjustment problems during adolescence, also had relatively poor neurological summary scores (Erlenmeyer-Kimling, Kestenbaum, Bird, & Hilldoff, in press).

Orvaschel, Mednick, Schulsinger, and Rock (1979) obtained results that were quite consistent with those obtained by Erlenmeyer-Kimling and her colleagues. The offspring of schizophrenic parents were compared to a group of children who had a non-schizophrenic, but psychiatrically disturbed parent and to children whose parents had no history of psychiatric disorder. The children were given a number of information processing tests that included a dichotic listening task and a signal detection task. Each child received a neurological examination and was given a revision of the Lincoln-Oseretsky battery of motor tests. It was found that children with a schizophrenic mother and children with a non-schizophrenic, psychiatrically disturbed mother had heightened tactile sensitivity and were motorically more clumsy and awkward than children of normal mothers. The specific items that comprised these disturbances were graphesthesia, two-point discrimination deficit, figure agnosia, impairments in the Kinsborne simultaneous touching test, disturbed side touching sense, and steriagnosis. The offspring of schizophrenic parents also tended to show evidence of neurological dysfunction in the areas of motor impersistence, associated movements, and posture and gait. It should be emphasized, however, that these disturbances were not specific to children at risk for schizophrenia.

Comment

The investigations conducted to date illustrate that children of schizophrenic parents are more likely than normal children to exhibit neurological impairments, particularly on tasks that measure neuromotor functioning. These impairments are more frequent in males than in females. Moreover, these neurological disturbances have been found to be associated with adjustment problems and/or major psychiatric symptoms.

The developmental persistence of these anomalies has been partially confirmed by Quitkin, Rifkin, and Klein (1976), who observed that adult schizophrenics with premorbid histories of asociality evidenced more neurological soft signs than schizophrenics without a premorbid history of asociality. The features that were more frequently found in adult schizophrenics with a premorbid history of asociality included dysdyadochokinesia (awkwardness on rapidly alternating pronation-supination); difficulty in identifying the area of the face upon being touched; left- and right-sided agraphesthesia (difficulty in detecting letters traced on the hand); mirror movements (movement of the contralateral limb that occurs when a patient has been instructed to move only the opposite limb); and awkwardness of fine motor movement.

It is quite striking to note that in the investigations conducted so far, there are by and large no impairments of vegetative or passive neurological functions. With the exception of disturbances in tactile hypersensitivity (Orvaschel et al., 1979), and agraphesthesia (Quitkin et al., 1976), most of the neurological deficits observed have involved tasks in which the child had to initiate motor output, either in response to sensory stimulation or verbal commands. Impaired visual motor coordination and fine motor control appear to be the most frequent neurological characteristics of children at risk for schizophrenia.

Psychobiological substrate

A rather striking convergence of findings emerges from the studies of children who are at risk for schizophrenia. A number of psychobiological disturbances have been noted across studies despite differences in the defining and selecting of subjects, as well as method of measurement. Though the long-term predictive significance of these impairments is unknown, the results obtained so far are encouraging. The finding that impaired information processing performance during early childhood predicts a poor level of adjustment during early adolescence suggests that the deficits manifested during childhood do have later consequences. The fact that a subset of high risk children with impaired performance across a number of attention/information processing tasks also exhibited some of the prodromal behavioral characteristics of children who subsequently became schizophrenic adults supports the clinical relevance of the findings (Asarnow et al., 1979). Neurological anomalies in infants at risk for schizophrenia (Fish, 1977) have also, in a number of cases, been found to antedate the development of childhood schizophrenia. Finally, many of the disturbances observed in children at risk for schizophrenia have also been found in actively schizophrenic, as well as in partially recovered schizophrenic adults. Taken collectively, these findings suggest that the impairments manifested by children at risk tap core aspects of the disorder, which may represent developmental precursors of a florid schizophrenic syndrome.

Despite these findings there is some doubt concerning the specific diagnostic sensitivity of these impairments. For example, it has been found that children of schizophrenic parents did not differ from children of depressed parents on a visual search task or a measure of distractability (Neale, in press). Nor have children of schizophrenics been found to differ on the CEFT from children of parents with schizoaffective and major affective disorders (Gamer et al., 1977). In another study (Orvaschel et al., 1979), children of schizophrenic mothers did not significantly differ neurologically from children of mothers suffering from other psychiatric disturbances; and, in a study by Rieder and Nichols (1979), the differences between high risk and control children were only marginally significant. Clearly, further research is required to delineate the specific diagnostic sensitivity of these impairments and to elucidate both the sample and task characteristics that might account for some of the inconsistent findings.

Since only 10% of schizophrenic adults have a schizophrenic parent, there are practical limitations concerning the extent to which impairments can be detected in the offspring of schizophrenics. It may well be that the most important contribution from the type of studies discussed in this chapter will be the isolation of high risk individuals who share a common psychobiological substrate.

What might the general outlines of this psychobiological substrate look like? It is important to note at the outset that the impaired functions described in this chapter cannot readily be seen as classical neurological signs with relatively narrow localizing significance. Indeed, the diversity of the impaired functions with regard to their presence *across* sensory and motor systems argues against a relatively narrow focal lesion. The converging findings reviewed above, which are a start in specifying the nature of the behavioral dysfunction found in some schizophrenias, provide the first step in a neurobehavioral analysis of these disorders.

We have noted the interesting finding of intact processing of tactile and proprioceptive/kinesthetic stimuli as well as intact sensory processes and simple motor functioning in schizophrenia (Buss & Lang, 1965; Lang & Buss, 1965). But under conditions when some of the individuals at risk for schizophrenia have to make a rapid series of discriminations, which require the integration of a number of constituent cognitive processes, and/or when such an individual is required to rapidly and efficiently integrate sensory input with a motor response, an impairment is observed. Neurophysiological studies also suggest that when an impairment is observed, it is under these particular task demands.

This matrix of specific information processing dysfunctions, which may perhaps elicit relatively predictable, though episodic changes in brain state must be accounted for in any neuropsychological model of schizophrenia. The term "neurointegrative deficit" (Meehl, 1962) aptly describes these impairments.[2]

Luria (1966) has argued that the tertiary association areas of the cortex are major neural substrates underlying sequential cognitive operations. These cortical areas, which include much of the temporal, parietal-occipital, the inferoparietal, and frontal regions, continue to develop well into early childhood. Development, according to Luria (1966), involves a hierarchical structuring of behavior, with the later developing control areas assuming an increasingly important role in behavioral integration, organization, and regulation. The tertiary association cortex, particularly the frontal lobes, are the substrate for the increasingly important role that language and speech play in organizing and integrating activity. Luria ascribes the following functions to the frontal lobes:

primary integration of all stimuli reaching the organism and the attachment of informative or regulatory significance to some of this information of the "provisional basis of action" and the creation of complex programs of behavior; the constant monitoring of the performance of these programs and the checking of behavior with comparison of actions performed and the original plan; the provisions of the systems of feedback on the basis of which complex forms of behavior are regulated—all these phenomena in man take place with the intimate participation of the frontal lobes, and they account for the exceptionally important place of the frontal lobes in the general organization of behavior.

The impairments observed in organizing constituent acts into complex responses, as the integration of sensory input and motor response, may reflect a disruption in the frontal region. On the other hand, the neurologi-

2 These findings differ from earlier neuropsychological models that emphasized subcortical, and specifically limbic system involvement.

cal impairments found in children at risk for schizophrenia involving tactile, kinesthetic, and proprioceptive sensation could possibly stem from a disruption of the tertiary association cortex in the parietal lobes. Many of the tasks involving visual-motor integrating, in which children at risk for schizophrenia show deficits, make multiple demands on the tertiary association cortex. These tasks require the processing of proprioceptive stimuli to provide the feedback to modify ongoing motoric acts, and they also necessitate adequate spatial orientation to direct those acts.

The tertiary association cortex not only serves as a substrate for some of the instrumental functions impaired in schizophrenia, but is also interconnected with structures that mediate affect. Both the frontal and parietal tertiary cortex have many connections with limbic structures, which are known to underlie affective behavior. For example, the parietal cortex is intimately connected via the nucleus accumbens septi to the hippocampus and amygdala (Mesulam & Geschwind, 1978). In support of the above hypothesis implicating frontal and parietal disturbance, it is of interest to note that Farkas (1980), using positron emission tomography, observed less metabolic activity in these brain areas in most of a sample of chronic schizophrenic patients in contrast to normal subjects. In addition, Asarnow et al. (1977) found that children at risk for schizophrenia showed impairment on the Spokes Test, a test that taps frontal lobe functions.

One intriguing characteristic of the tertiary association cortex is that it is a late developing part of the brain and therefore it is modifiable by environmental influences. This is not surprising, since even the primary visual and somatosensory cortex require environmental stimulation for normal anatomical development (Hubel & Wiesel, 1970; Hirsch & Spinelli, 1970). It is, therefore, possible that some of the wide variation in the clinical manifestations of schizophrenia may be the result of a developmental arrest of this system. Since the functional characteristics of brain damage in animals have been shown to be related to the status of the developing brain at the time of damage (Rodier, 1980), it is possible that some of the variations in manifestations of schizophrenia reflect the point in development at which brain dysfunction first occurs. The tertiary association cortex, because of its rather late development and, therefore, greater amenability to external influences, would appear likely to be implicated as an area influenced by the environment in the genesis of schizophrenia.

It is interesting to note that families of schizophrenic patients, and children at risk for schizophrenia, often exhibit communication deviances (Singer, Wynne, & Tooley, 1978; Goldstein, Rodnick, Jones, McPherson, & West, 1978). The deviances take the form of a difficulty in maintaining a shared focus of attention and meaning during a conversation, thereby making it difficult for listeners to attend in a regular and predictable manner to what is being communicated (Singer, 1978). Such a difficulty during the course of development might perhaps affect the amount of systematically patterned social stimulation an individual receives, particularly when it involves the juxtaposition of cognitive and affective stimuli. It is tempting to speculate that these deviant environmental transactions, especially when experienced by individuals with subtle dysfunctions in the neural structures that are the substrate for integrative and goal directed activity, contribute to inadequate development of these cortical systems. In this way, a subtle psychobiological dysfunction could be augmented by environmental factors so that development is increasingly abnormal.

The model briefly sketched out above needs to be fleshed out by new data in order to provide the epigenetic model that is required to account for both the ontogenetic development of schizophrenia, as well as its transgenerational transmission. If the high risk and other complementary investigative strategies could isolate the psychobiological substrate of schizophrenia, an enormous step forward in our understanding of this disorder would result. The development of rationally derived treatment procedures, and perhaps even more importantly, preventive intervention programs (Asarnow & Asarnow, in press) await this development.

Implications for preventive intervention

The model of schizophrenia described herein has implications for developing preventive intervention strategies. Two hypotheses could be postulated to explain the pattern of information processing dysfunction: (a) specific stages or components of information processing are impaired; and (b) the impaired performance of schizophrenia-prone individuals arises because of deficits in the central executive control functions that regulate the temporal and hierarchical processing of information. The first hypothesis would suggest that the manifest dysfunctions would be amenable to treatment that compensates for limitations in specific information processing capacities, such as number of slots or durability of short-term memory. The second hypothesis would be consistent with treatment aimed at engendering more efficient utilization of capacity by increasing the efficiency of executive control functions.

The research literature indicates that behavioral interventions are not very effective in altering structural features of the information processing system (Campione & Brown, 1978). Executive control processes, however, appear to be responsive to behavioral interventions, suggesting that executive functions may serve as a useful focus for preventive intervention. Key components of the executive system that have been emphasized are control processes and metacognition (i.e., a person's knowledge of his cognitive machinery and the way it operates). Optimal functioning is assumed to occur when metacognitive knowledge is integrated with control processes such that the most effective match of strategy to task is achieved.

Although behavioral intervention is not likely to be successful in directly remediating structural defects, there is ample precedent from work with brain-damaged (Luria & Tizard, 1961), and developmentally disabled individuals (Belmont & Butterfield, 1977) that behavioral intervention techniques would be useful in *compensating* for deficits by permitting schizophrenics to use their limited capacity more efficiently. Luria and Tizard (1961), for example, have stated that speech (overt self-instructions), can substantially improve the processes of sensory analysis and motor regulation to compensate for lesions in the sensory projection areas of the cortex. If, on the other hand, the dysfunction is consistent with the second hypothesis, in that some schizophrenics are deficient in temporally and hierarchically organizing the flow of information processing, then cognitive interventions focusing on executive functions would appear to be indicated.

Procedures utilizing cognitive behavior modification (Asarnow & Meichenbaum, 1979; Mahoney, 1974) and cognitive training techniques used with developmentally and learning disabled children (Belmont & Butterfield, 1977; Borkowski, in press) provide other strategies for enhancing behavior by increasing cognitive and/or verbal control of executive functions. For example, one might teach schizophrenics with an information processing impairment to recognize situations that are likely to involve an impairment and to activate "a plan to form a plan" when impairment is experienced. Self-regulatory procedures could then be taught for coping with the impairment. For example, on tasks such as the span-of-apprehension, a person could be taught how to consecutively scan letters to enable correct detection and identification.

It is important to note that the role of executive control functions in schizophrenics information processing dysfunction can be rigorously examined through (a) studies of strategies based on direct observation of behavior while the subject is performing a task and (b) evaluations of the effects of strategies that are elicited by manipulating the format of presentation of material (e.g., making task demands more salient). Thus, properly conceived and designed intervention programs can play a critical role in evaluating these two hypotheses; they also provide a first step toward the development of interventions aimed at enhancing the information processing abilities of some schizophrenic individuals.

References

Asarnow, J. The Waterloo studies of interpersonal competence. Paper presented at the Risk Research Consortium Plenary Conference, San Juan, Puerto Rico, March, 1980.

Asarnow, J. & Meichenbaum, D. Verbal rehearsal and serial recall: The meditational training of kindergarten children. *Child Development*, 1979, *50*, 1173–1177.

Asarnow, R. & Asarnow, J. Attention-information processing dynsfunction and vulnerability to schizophrenia: Implications for preventive intervention. In M. Goldstein (Ed.), *Preventive intervention in schizophrenia: Are we ready?* Washington, D.C., U.S. Department of Health and Human Services, Public Health Service, Alcohol, Drug Abuse and Mental Health Administration, in press.

Asarnow, R., Cromwell, R., & Rennick, P. Cognitive and evoked response measures of information processing in schizophrenics with and without a family history of schizophrenia. *Journal of Nervous and Mental Diseases*, 1978, *166*, 719–730.

Asarnow, R. & MacCrimmon, D. Span of apprehension deficits during the postpsychotic stages of schizophrenia: A replication and extension. *Archives of General Psychiatry*, 1981, *38*, 1006–1011.

Asarnow, R., Steffy, R., Cleghorn, J., & MacCrimmon, D. The McMaster Waterloo studies of children at risk for severe psychopathology. In J. Shamsie (Ed.), *New directions in children's mental health.* New York: Spectrum, 1979.

Asarnow, R., Steffy, R., MacCrimmon, D., & Cleghorn, J. An attentional assessment of foster children at risk for schizophrenia. *Journal of Abnormal Psychology*, 1977, *86*, 267–275.

Asarnow, R., Steffy, R., MacCrimmon, D., & Cleghorn, J. The McMaster Waterloo project: An attentional and clinical assessment of foster children at risk for schizophrenia. In L. Wynne, R. Cromwell, & S. Matthysse (Eds.), *The nature of schizophrenia: New approaches to research and treatment.* New York: Wiley, 1978.

Bayley, W. *Bayley scales of infant development.* New York: Psychological Corporation, 1969.

Bellissimo, A. & Steffy, R. Redundancy-associated deficit in schizophrenia reaction time performance. *Journal of Abnormal Psychology*, 1972, *80*, 229–307.

Belmont, J. & Butterfield, E. The instructional approach to developmental cognitive research. In R. Kail & J. Hagen (Eds.), *Perspectives on the development of memory and cognition*. Hillsdale, NJ: Lawrence Erlbaum Associates, 1977.

Borkowski, J. Signs of intelligence: Strategy generalization and metacognition. In S. Yussen (Ed.), *The development of reflection*. New York: Academic Press, in press.

Buss, A. & Lang, P. Psychological deficit in schizophrenia: Affect, reinforcement, and concept attainment. *Journal of Abnormal Psychology*, 1965, *70*, 2–24.

Campione, J. & Brown, A. Toward a theory of intelligence: Contributions from research with retarded children. *Intelligence*, 1978, *2*, 279–304.

Cornblatt, B. & Erlenmeyer-Kimling, L. Early attentional predictors of adolescent behavioral disturbances in children at risk for schizophrenia. In J. Anthony, L. Wynne, & N. Watt (Eds.), *Children at risk for schizophrenia*. New York: Cambridge University Press, in press.

Cowen, E., Pederson, A., Babigian, H., Izzo, L., & Trost, M. Long-term follow-up of early detected vulnerable children. *Journal of Consulting and Clinical Psychology*, 1973, *41*, 438–446.

Cromwell, R. Genetic transmission—concluding comments. In L. Wynne, R. Cromwell, & S. Matthysse (Eds.), *The nature of schizophrenia: New Approaches to research and treatment*. New York: Wiley, 1978.

DeAmicis, L. & Cromwell, R. Reaction time crossover in process schizophrenia patients, their relatives, and control subjects. *Journal of Nervous and Mental Disease*, 1979, *167*, 593–600.

Erlenmeyer-Kimling, L. & Cornblatt, B. Attentional measures in a study of children at high-risk for schizophrenia. In L. Wynne, R. Cromwell, & S. Matthysse (Eds.), *The nature of schizophrenia: New approaches to research and treatment*. New York: Wiley, 1978.

Erlenmeyer-Kimling, L., Kestenbaum, C., Bird, H., & Hilldoff, V. Assessment of the New York high-risk project studies in a sample who are now clinically deviant. In J. Anthony, L. Wynne, & N. Watt (Eds.), *Children at risk for schizophrenia*. New York: Cambridge University Press, in press.

Erlenmeyer-Kimling, L., Marcuse, Y., Cornblatt, B., Friedman, D., Ranier, J., & Rutschman, J. The New York high-risk project. In J. Anthony, L. Wynne, & N. Watt (Eds.), *Children at risk for schizophrenia*. New York: Cambridge University Press, in press.

Farkas, I. *Positron emission tomography in nuclear schizophrenics*. Paper presented at the Department of Psychiatry, U.C.L.A. School of Medicine, November, 1980.

Fish, B. The detection of schizophrenia in infancy. *Journal of Nervous and Mental Disease*, 1957, *125*, 1–24.

Fish, B. The maturation of arousal and attention in the first months of life: A study of variations in ego development. *Journal of the American Academy of Child Psychiatry*, 1963, *2*, 253–270.

Fish, B. Biologic antecedents of psychosis in children. In D. Freeman (Ed.), *The biology of the major psychoses: A comparative analysis.* New York: Raven Press, 1975.

Fish, B. Neurobiological antecedents of schizophrenia in children: Evidence for an inherited congenital neurointegrative defect. *Archives of General Psychiatry,* 1977, *34,* 1297–1313.

Fish, B. & Hagin, R. Visual-motor disorder in infants at risk for schizophrenia. *Archives of General Psychiatry,* 1973, *28,* 900–904.

Friedman, D., Vaughan, H., & Erlenmeyer-Kimling, L. Event-related potential investigations in children at high-risk for schizophrenia. In D. Lehman & E. Calloway (Eds.), *Human evoked potentials: Applications and problems.* New York: Plenum, 1979.

Friedman, D., Erlenmeyer-Kimling, L., & Vaughan, H. Event-related potential (ERP) methodology in high-risk research. In J. Anthony, L. Wynne, & N. Watt (Eds.), *Children at risk for schizophrenia.* New York: Cambridge University Press, in press.

Gamer, E., Gallant, D., Grunebaum, H., & Cohler, B. Children of psychotic mothers: Performance of 3-year-old children and tests of attention. *Archives of General Psychiatry,* 1977, *34,* 592–597.

Gazzaniga, M. & Sperry, R. Language after section of the cerebral commissures. *Brain,* 1967, *90,* 131–148.

Geschwind, N. Disconnection syndromes in animals and man. I and II. *Brain,* 1965, *88,* 237–294, 585–644.

Gesell, A. *Developmental diagnosis* (Vol. 2). New York: Paul B. Hoeber, 1947.

Goldstein, M., Rodnick, E., Jones, J., McPherson, S., & West, K. Familial precursors of schizophrenia spectrum disorder. In L. Wynne, R. Cromwell, & S. Matthysse (Eds.), *The nature of schizophrenia: New approaches to research and treatment.* New York: Wiley, 1978.

Gottesman, I. Schizophrenia and genetics: Where are we? Are you sure? In L. Wynne, R. Cromwell & S. Matthysse (Eds.), *The nature of schizophrenia: New approaches to research and treatment.* New York: Wiley, 1978.

Grunebaum, H., Weiss, J., Gallant, D., & Cohler, B. Attention in young children of psychotic mothers. *American Journal of Psychiatry,* 1974, *131,* 887–891.

Hanson, D., Gottesman, I., & Heston, L. Some possible childhood indicators of adult schizophrenia inferred from children of schizophrenics. *British Journal of Psychiatry,* 1976, *129,* 142–154.

Herman, J., Mirsky, A., Ricks, N., & Gallant, D. Behavioral and electrographic measures of attention in children at risk for schizophrenia. *Journal of Abnormal Psychiatry,* 1977, *86,* 27–33.

Hirsch, H. & Spinelli, D. Visual experience modifies distribution of horizontally and vertically oriented receptive fields in cats. *Science,* 1970, *168,* 869–871.

Howard, H. & Harris, B. A hierarchical grouping routine (IBM 360/65 Fortran program). University of Pennsylvania Computer Center, 1966.

Hubel, D. & Wiesel, T. The period of susceptibility to the physiological effects of unilateral eye closure in kittens. *Journal of Physiology,* 1970, *206,* 419–436.

Itil, T., Hsu, W., Saletu, B., & Mednick, S. Computer EEG and auditory evoked potential investigations in children at risk for schizophrenia. *American Journal of Psychiatry,* 1974, *131,* 892–900.

Kagan, J. *Change and continuity in infancy.* New York: Wiley, 1971.

Kidd, K. A genetic perspective on schizophrenia. In L. Wynne, R. Cromwell, & S. Matthysse (Eds.), *The nature of schizophrenia: New approaches to research and treatment.* New York: Wiley, 1978.

Koppitz, E. *The Bender Gestalt test for young children.* New York: Grune & Stratton, 1964.

Koppitz, E. Visual and digit span performance of boys with emotional and learning problems. *Journal of Clinical Psychology,* 1973, *29,* 463–466.

Kornetsky, C. The use of a simple test of attention as a measure of drug effects in schizophrenic patients. *Psychoparmacologia,* 1972, *24,* 99–106.

Lang, P. & Buss, A. Psychological deficit in schizophrenia: Interference and activation. *Journal of Abnormal Psychology,* 1965, *70,* 77–106.

Luria, A. *Higher cortical functions in man.* Basic Books, 1966.

Luria, A. & Tizard, J. (Eds.). *The role of speech in the regulation of normal and abnormal behavior.* New York: Liveright, 1961.

MacCrimmon, D., Cleghorn, J., Asarnow, R., & Steffy, R. Children at risk for schizophrenia: Clinical and attentional characteristics. *Archives of General Psychiatry,* 1980, *37,* 671–674.

Mahoney, M. *Cognition and behavior modification.* Cambridge: Ballinger, 1974.

Marcus, J. Cerebral functioning in offspring of schizophrenics: A possible genetic factor. *International Journal of Mental Health,* 1974, *3,* 57–73.

Marcus, J., Auerbach, J., Wilkinson, L., & Burack, C. Infants at risk for schizophrenia: The Jerusalem infant development study. *Archives of General Psychiatry,* 1981, *38,* 703–713.

Meehl, P. Schizotaxia, schizotypy, schizophrenia. *American Psychologist,* 1962, *17,* 827–838.

Mesulam, M. & Geschwind, N. On the possible role of neocortex and its limbic connections in attention and schizophrenia. In L. Wynne, R. Cromwell, & S. Matthysse (Eds.), *The nature of schizophrenia: New approaches to research and treatment.* New York: Wiley, 1978.

Neale, J. Information processing and vulnerability: High-risk research. In M. Goldstein (Ed.), *Preventive intervention in schizophrenia: Are we ready?* Washington, D.C., U.S. Department of Health and Human Services, Public Health Service, Alcohol, Drug Abuse and Mental Health Administration, in press.

Neale, J., McIntyre, C., Fox, R., & Cromwell, R. Span of apprehension in acute schizophrenics. *Journal of Abnormal Psychology,* 1969, *74,* 593–596.

Neuchterlein, K. Sustained attention among children vulnerable to adult schizophrenia and among hyperactive children. In J. Anthony, L. Wynne, &

N. Watt (Eds.), *Children at risk for schizophrenia*. New York: Cambridge University Press, in press.

Neuchterlein, K. Perspectives on future studies of attentional functioning in children at risk for schizophrenia. In J. Anthony, L. Wynne, & N. Watt (Eds.), *Children at risk for schizophrenia*. New York: Cambridge University Press, in press.

Neuchterlein, K., Phipps-Yonas, S., Driscoll, R., & Garmezy, N. The role of different components of attention in children vulnerable to schizophrenia. In M. Goldstein (Ed.), *Preventive intervention in schizophrenia: Are we ready?* Washington, D.C., U.S. Department of Health and Human Services, Public Health Service, Alcohol, Drug Abuse, and Mental Health Administration, in press.

Offord, D. & Cross, L. Behavioral antecedents of schizophrenia: A review. *Archives of General Psychiatry*, 1969, *21*, 167–283.

Oltmans, R. & Neale, J. Schizophrenic performance when distractors are present: Attentional deficit or differential task difficulty? *Journal of Abnormal Psychology*, 1975, *84*, 205–209.

Orvaschel, H., Mednick, S., Schulsinger, F., & Rock, D. The children of psychiatrically disturbed parents: Differences as a function of the sex of the sick parent. *Archives of General Psychiatry*, 1979, *36*, 691–695.

Quitkin, F., Rifkin, A., & Klein, D. Neurologic soft signs in schizophrenic and character disorders: Organicity in schizophrenia with premorbid asociality and emotionality unstable character disorder. *Archives of General Psychiatry*, 1976, *33*, 845–853.

Rappaport, M. Attention to competing voice messages by nonacute schizophrenic patients: Effects of message load, drugs, dosage levels and patient background. *Journal of Nervous and Mental Disease*, 1968, *146*, 404–411.

Reitan, R. The comparative effects of placebo, ultran, and meprobromate on psychological test performance. *Antibiotic Medicine and Clinical Therapy*, 1957, *4*, 158–163.

Rieder, R. & Nichols, P. Offspring of schizophrenics III: Hyperactivity and neurological soft signs. *Archives of General Psychiatry*, 1979, *36*, 665–675.

Rodier, P. Chronology of neuron development: Animal studies and their clinical implications. *Developmental Medical Child Neurology*, 1980, *22*, 525–545.

Rodnick, E. & Goldstein, M. Premorbid adjustment and the recovery of mothering function in acute schizophrenic women. *Journal of Abnormal Psychology*, 1974, *83*, 623–628.

Roff, M. Childhood social interactions and young adult bad conduct. *Journal of Abnormal Psychology*, 1961, *63*, 333–337.

Roff, M. Childhood social interactions and young adult psychosis. *Journal of Abnormal Psychology*, 1963, *19*, 152–158.

Roff, J., Knight, R., & Wertheim, E. Disturbed preschizophrenics: Childhood symptoms in relation to adult outcome. *The Journal of Nervous and Mental Disease*, 1976, *162*, 274–281.

Rosenthal, D. *Genetic theory and abnormal behavior.* New York: McGraw-Hill, 1970.

Rosvold, H., Mirsky, A., Sarason, I., Bransome, E., & Beck, L. A continuous performance test of brain damage. *Journal of Consulting Psychology,* 1956, *20,* 343–351.

Singer, M. Attentional processes in verbal behavior. In L. Wynne, R. Cromwell, & S. Matthysse (Eds.), *The nature of schizophrenia: New approaches to research and treatment.* New York: Wiley, 1978.

Singer, M., Wynne, L., & Tooley, M. Communication disorders and the families of schizophrenics. In L. Wynne, R. Cromwell, & S. Matthysse (Eds.), *The nature of schizophrenia: New approaches to research and treatment.* New York: Wiley, 1978.

Steffy, R., Asarnow, R., Asarnow, J., MacCrimmon, D., & Cleghorn, J. The McMaster Waterloo high risk project: Multifaceted strategy for high risk research. In J. Anthony, L. Wynne, & N. Watt (Eds.), *Children at risk for schizophrenia.* New York: Cambridge University Press, in press.

Strauss, J., Carpenter, W., & Bartko, J. An approach to the diagnosis and understanding of schizophrenia. *Schizophrenia Bulletin,* 1974, *11,* 35–79.

Sutton, S., Hakarem, G., Zubin, J., & Portnoy, M. The effect of shift of sensory modality on serial reaction time: A comparison of schizophrenics and normals. *American Journal of Psychiatry,* 1961, *74,* 224–232.

Sutton, S. & Zubin, J. Effect of sequence on reaction time in schizophrenia. In A. Welford & J. Birren (Eds.), *Behavior, aging and the nervous system.* Springfield, Ill.: C. C. Thomas, 1965.

Teuber, H. Efforts of brain wounds implicating right or left hemisphere in man: Hemispheric differences and hemispheric interaction in vision, audition, and somathesis. In V. Mouncastle (Ed.), *Interhemispheric relations and cerebral dominance.* Baltimore: Johns Hopkins Press, 1962.

Walker, G. & Bourne, I. The identification of concepts as a function of amounts of relevant and irrevelant information. *American Journal of Psychology,* 1961, *74,* 410–417.

Wapner, S. & Krus, D. Effects of lysergic acid diethylamide and differences between normals and schizophrenics on the Stroop color-word test. *Journal of Neuropsychiatry,* 1960, *2,* 76–81.

Weintraub, S. & Neale, J. The Stony Brook high-risk project. In J. Anthony, L. Wynne, & N. Watt (Eds.), *Children at risk for schizophrenia.* New York: Cambridge University Press, in press.

Wetzel, N. The baby grid. *Journal of Pediatrics,* 1946, *29,* 439–454.

Wohlberg, G. & Kornetsky, C. Sustained attention in remitted schizophrenics. *Archives of General Psychiatry,* 1973, *28,* 533–537.

Wood, R. & Cook, M. Attentional deficit in the siblings of schizophrenics. *Psychological Medicine,* 1979, *9,* 465–467.

Zubin, J. Problem of attention in schizophrenia. In M. Kietzman, S. Sutton, & J. Zubin, *Experimental approaches to psychopathology.* New York: Academic Press, 1975.

8. Alcoholism

Donald W. Goodwin

Introduction

The fact that alcoholism runs in families has been known for centuries. Aristotle, Plutarch, the writers of the Old Testament, and many others have commented on the familial patterns of alcoholism.

Until this century the explanation was simple and universal: alcoholism was inherited. Moreover, it was inherited in a certain way, that is, by the transmission of acquired traits. If the mother took piano lessons, then the children would be musical. If the mother or father drank too much, then the children would be alcoholic. Few questioned this interpretation.

Several events in the early twentieth century changed all of this. First, it was noted that many things that ran in families probably do not involve heredity. Speaking French or voting Republican are two examples. A second factor was the rediscovery of Mendel's work. This, in effect, sounded the knell for the Lamarkian doctrine of the transmission of acquired traits. The random shuffling and reshuffling of genes became the cornerstone of scientific genetics (leaving aside possible mutational or teratogenic effects of alcohol affecting the germ plasm or fetus directly). Whatever the reason was for alcoholism running in families, it clearly could not be ascribed to the fact that mother or father drank too much.

A third factor also contributed to the historical swing away from heredity as an explanation for almost everything. Psychoanalysis and social work came into their own in the second and third decades of the twentieth century, and both these movements focused strongly on upbringing and environmental factors in the production of alcoholism and other behavioral disorders. Although it was still recognized that alcoholism ran in families, the explanation generally was that poor parenting, role modeling, bad neighborhoods, and other psychosocial factors were responsible.

In the past decade, there has been renewed interest in hereditary factors as a possible influence in alcoholism. Scientists interested in this were faced with a dilemma. Ordinarily, the people who provide the child's genes also have powerful influences on the child's growth and development. Some said that no amount of effort could separate "nature" from "nurture," since they were intertwined. However, since the familialness of alcoholism was almost the only thing that students of alcoholism could agree about, attempts to separate nature from nurture were made.

Nature–nurture research in humans follows three lines. The oldest approach is to compare the prevalence of illness within identical and fraternal twins. A second approach involves studying individuals who are separated in infancy from their biological parents, in which the illness occurred, and are subsequently raised by adoptive parents who do not have the illness. A third approach is to determine whether known inherited traits, such as blood group type and color blindness, are associated with alcoholism.

This chapter will review these three approaches and then discuss the research approaches that seem most promising. Most of the information is nontechnical. However, the author feels that genetic counselors as well as concerned families should base their advice on the best scientific evidence available; presented, one hopes, without bias toward either genetic or psychosocial factors.

Twin studies

This method, originally proposed by Galton, compares identical twins with fraternal twins in which at least one member of each pair has the illness. The assumption is that the monozygotic (MZ) and dizygotic (DZ) twins differ only with respect to genetic makeup, and that the environment is the same for both types of twins. Given these assumptions, the prediction is that genetic disorders will be concordant more often among MZ twins than among DZ twins.

In Sweden, Kaij (1960) interviewed 90% of 174 male twin pairs, located through temperance boards, and established zygosity by anthropometric measurements and blood types. The concordance rate for alcohol abuse was 58% for the MZ group and 28% for the DZ group, a statistically significant difference. When alcohol abusers were compared according to severity of symptoms, the largest differences occurred between individuals who showed the most extensive use of alcohol. However, this investigator also found that social and intellectual "deterioration" was more correlated with zygosity than with extent of drinking. Kaij's interpretation of this was that "alcoholic deterioration" occurred more or less independently of alcohol consumption, and that it may be a genetically determined contributor to the disease, rather than a consequence.

Jonsson and Nilsson (1968) reported upon questionnaire data obtained from 7,500 Swedish twins, of which zygosity diagnoses were known for about 1,500 pairs. These authors found that MZ twins were significantly more concordant in regard to quantity of alcohol consumed. Socioenvironmental factors, however, seemed to explain much of the variation in consequences from drinking; a result corresponding closely to findings reported in a Finnish study by Partanen, Brunn, and Markkanen (1966), in which more equivocal evidence was found for a genetic predisposition toward alcoholism. These investigators studied 902 MZ and DZ male twins, 28 to 37 years of age. The zygosity diagnoses were based upon anthropometric measurements and serological analysis. The sample constituted a substantial proportion of all twins born in Finland during the years 1920–29. A sample of brothers the same age as the twins was also studied. In contrast to Kaij (1960), Partanen et al. (1966) found no differences between MZ and DZ twins with regard to addictive symptoms, drunkenness arrests, or other social consequences of drinking. Also, within-pair variations for DZ twins and for non-twin brothers were not significantly different. The frequency and amounts of drinking, as well as abstinence, however, were significantly more concordant among MZ than among DZ twins.

In another Finnish study, Forsander and Eriksson (1974) compared six MZ and eight DZ male twin pairs and found the ethanol elimination rate to be 80% inheritable, with acetaldehyde in venous blood 60 to 80% inheritable. These data support the finding of Vesell, Page, and Passananti (1971), who studied elimination rates of alcohol in 14 pairs of twins. The subjects were given 1 ml/kg of 95% ethanol solution orally and were tested for ethanol elimination rates by sampling the blood over a 4-hour period. The ethanol elimination rate was found to be 98% inheritable, that is, almost totally controlled by genetic factors. On the basis of these two studies, it would appear that alcohol elimination rates are under a high degree of genetic control, although further studies of larger samples are needed for confirmation.

In the United States, Loehlin (1972) studied 850 pairs of like-sex twins chosen from a group of some 600,000 high school juniors taking the National Merit Scholarship Questionnaire Test. Although conceding the "fragility" of his data, Loehlin found that putative MZ twins were more concordant for "heavy drinking" than were putative DZ twins, and also that zygosity did not appear to influence drinking customs and attitudes.

Like all approaches to the environment versus heredity problem, twin studies have weaknesses: twins represent a genetically select population, with higher infant mortality, lower birth weight, slightly lower intelligence, and older mothers. Also, the assumption that MZ and DZ twins have similar environments is open to question. In the Partanen et al. (1966) study, MZ twins differed from DZ twins in that they lived together longer, were more concordant in marital status, and were more equal in "social, intellectual and physical dominance relationship." In this and other ways, the interaction between physical characteristics and the environment may tend to reduce intrapair differences in MZ twins and increase differences in DZ twins.

Adoption studies

Another approach to separating environmental from hereditary factors is to study individuals who were separated from their biological relatives soon after birth and raised by nonrelative foster parents. In 1970, the author and his colleagues began a series of adoption studies in Denmark to investigate further the possibility that alcoholism has genetic roots (Goodwin, Schulsinger, Hermansen, Guze, & Winokur, 1973; Goodwin, Schulsinger, Knop, Mednick, & Guze, 1977; Goodwin, Schulsinger, Moller, Hermansen, Winokur, & Guze, 1974).

Phase one

In the first phase, a sample of 55 Danish males adopted in the first few weeks of life by nonrelatives was studied. Their biological parents, however, had been alcoholic. They were matched by age with a control group of 78 male adoptees whose biological parents, as far as was known, were not alcoholic. A psychiatrist conducted a "blind" interview of the total sample. The findings from phase one are as follows.

ALCOHOLISM

Of the 55 sons of alcoholics, ten were alcoholic, as determined both by specific clinical criteria and a history of treatment for alcoholism. Of the 78 controls, four met the criteria for alcoholism, but had never received treatment. The differences between the two groups were statistically significant.

HEAVY DRINKING

Sons of alcoholics were no more likely to be heavy drinkers than were controls. About 40% of each group were heavy drinkers, taking six drinks or more daily at least several times a month.

MENTAL DISTURBANCES

The sons of alcoholics were no more likely to receive a diagnosis of depression, sociopathy, drug abuse, or other diagnosable psychiatric conditions than were the controls. A number of individuals in both groups were diagnosed by a psychiatrist as having personality problems.

From these data, it was concluded that sons of alcoholics were about four times more likely to be alcoholic than were sons of nonalcoholics, although there was no exposure to the alcoholic biological parent after the first few weeks of life. Moreover, they were likely to become alcoholic at a relatively early age (in their 20's) and to have a form of alcoholism serious enough to warrant treatment. Having a biological parent who was alcoholic apparently did not increase their risk of developing psychiatric disorders, other than alcoholism, and did not predispose to heavy drinking in the absence of alcoholism. The familial predisposition to alcoholism in this group was specific for alcoholism and *not on a continuum* with heavy drinking.

Phase two

In the second phase of the study, the effects of rearing by the biological parents were studied. One member of one set of parents was alcoholic (primarily the father) and both members of one set were not alcoholic, as far as could be determined. Sons of alcoholics (the brothers of which had been studied in phase one) raised by the alcoholic parent were compared with matched controls raised by nonalcoholic parents. Sons of alcoholics raised by the biological parent had a high rate of alcoholism, when compared to controls, but no greater than the rate for the brothers raised by nonalcoholic foster parents, found in phase one. The rate of alcoholism was about 18% for both groups.

The conclusions drawn from the first two phases of the study were (a) alcoholism was transmitted in families and (b) increased susceptibility to alcoholism in men occurred about equally in the sons of alcoholics raised by alcoholic biological parents and in those raised by nonalcoholic foster parents. In other words, if indeed there was a genetic predisposition to alcoholism, *exposure to the alcoholic parent did not appear to augment this increased susceptibility.*

Phase three

Daughters of alcoholics were investigated in the third phase of the adoption study. The study sample consisted of 49 daughters of alcoholics, raised by adoptive parents, and, as controls, 48 daughters of presumed nonalcoholics also raised by adoptive parents. Subjects and controls both had a mean age of 35 years. As was the case in former studies, interviews were conducted blindly to eliminate interviewer bias. The major findings from this phase were as follows.

ALCOHOLISM

Of both the sample and the control group, 4% was either alcoholic or had a serious drinking problem. The sample was too small to draw definite conclusions, but as the estimated prevalence of alcoholism among Danish women is about 0.1 to 1.0%, the data suggest there may be an increased prevalence of alcoholism in the two groups. Nothing was known about the controls other than that none had a biological parent with a hospital diagnosis of alcoholism. Explanation of the appearance of alcoholism among controls was not readily apparent; however, it was interesting that both groups of women had adoptive parents described as alcoholic, suggesting that environmental exposure to alcoholism may contribute to alcoholism in women (although it did not appear to in men, as demonstrated by data from phase two of this study). It should be noted, also, that although controls were presumed to have nonalcoholic biological parents, this does not preclude their having parents with drinking problems, because the only index for the controls was the lack of a "hospital diagnosis" of alcoholism in their parents.

HEAVY DRINKING

More than 90% of the women in both groups were abstainers or very light drinkers. This contrasted with the case of the Danish male adoptees of whom about 40% were heavy drinkers.

MENTAL DISTURBANCES

Family history studies have suggested that alcoholics often have male relatives who are alcoholic or sociopathic and female relatives who are depressed (Winokur, Reich, Rimmer, & Pitts, 1970). In this study, however, there was a low rate of depression in both groups, with no more depression in the daughters of the alcoholics than in the control women. However, in a comparison between daughters of alcoholics raised by their biological parents and controls, there was a significant increase in depression in the former group. There was also evidence of increased susceptibility to other psychiatric disorders in the daughters of alcoholics.

From this study, it appears that alcoholism in women may have a partial genetic basis, but the sample size precluded any definitive conclusion. Since the great majority of the women drank very little, it is possible, also, that social factors discouraging heavy drinking may suppress a genetic tendency, if indeed one exists. There was no evidence of a genetic predisposition to depression in the daughters of alcoholics. If such a predisposition exists, environmental factors apparently are required to make the depression clinically manifest. Regarding daughters raised by alcoholic parents, it is not possible to determine whether their increased rate of depression was due to environmental factors and a genetic predisposition or due entirely to environmental factors. It should be noted that some evidence indicates that women develop alcoholism at a later age than do men and possibly some of these 35-year-old women had not yet entered the age group of risk.

Other adoption studies in this and other countries have, in general, supported the author's evidence that, at the least, alcoholism runs in families. Schuckit, Goodwin, and Winokur (1972) studied a group of individuals, reared apart from their biological parents, in whom either a biological parent or a "surrogate" parent had a drinking problem. The subjects were significantly more likely to have a drinking problem if their biological parent was considered alcoholic than if their surrogate parent was. In a study of 32 alcoholics and 132 nonalcoholics, most of whom came from broken homes, it was found that 62% of the alcoholics had an alcoholic biological parent compared to 20% of the nonalcoholics. This association occurred irrespective of personal contact with the alcoholic biological parent. Simply living with an alcoholic parent did not appear to be related to the development of alcoholism. Bohman (1978) studied 2,000 adoptees born between 1930 and 1949 by inspecting official registers in Sweden for notations about alcohol abuse and criminal offenses in adoptees and in biological and adoptive parents. There was a significant correlation between registrations for abuse of alcohol in biological parents and in their adopted-out sons. The greater the number of registrations for alcoholism in biological parents, the greater the incidence of registration for alcohol abuse in adopted-out children. These results closely parallel those found in the Goodwin (Goodwin, Schulsinger, Moller, Hermansen, Winokur, & Guze, 1974) study. Cadoret and Gath (1978) studied 84 adult adoptees, 18 years or older, who were separated at birth from their parents and had no further contact with their biological relatives. Alcoholism occurred more frequently in adoptees whose biological background included an individual with alcoholism. But alcoholism did not correlate with any other biological parental diagnosis.

Only one adoption study is discordant with this growing bank of data. Roe (1944) studied 49 foster children in the 20- to 40-year-old age group. Comparisons were made between 22 subjects who had "normal" parents with 27 subjects who had a biological "heavy drinking" parent. The conclusion reached was that the differences between the groups were not significant, and neither group had adult drinking problems. However, the data can be questioned on grounds that the sample was small and that the biological parents of the group of 27 did not receive a hospital diagnosis of alcoholism as did the subjects in the Danish study.

The preceding adoption studies suggest that genetic factors may play a role in alcoholism, but provide no clues of the genetics of transmission. Studies bearing upon possible modes of transmission are presented in the following paragraphs.

Kaij and Dock (1975) tested the hypothesis of a sex-linked factor influencing the occurrence of alcoholism by comparing alcohol abuse rates in 136 sons of the sons versus 134 sons of the daughters of 75 alcoholics. No substantial difference between the groups of grandsons was found in frequency of alcoholism, suggesting that a sex-linked factor was not involved. The total sample was also used to calculate both the risk and actual rate of registration for alcohol abuse among grandsons. The rate of registration by the grandsons' fifth decade of life was found to be 43%, approximately three times that of the general male population. This result is incompatible with an assumption of a recessive gene being involved in the occurrence of alcoholism, although, it is compatible with the assumption of a dominant gene.

Investigating the possibility that children of alcoholics metabolize alcohol differently than do children of nonalcoholics, Utne, Hansen, Winkler, and Schulsinger (unpublished) compared the disappearance rate of blood alcohol in two groups of adoptees: 10 adoptees had a biological parent who was alcoholic and 10 adoptees had nonalcoholic parents. There was no significant difference in the elimination rate of ethanol.

It has been suggested that a genetic factor influencing the development of alcoholism might involve atypical liver alcohol dehydrogenase (ADH). Recent data (Stamatoyannopoulas, Chen, & Fukui, 1975) indicate a high frequency of ADH polymorphism among the Japanese. Analysis of 40 autopsied liver specimens showed that 34 had an atypical ADH phenotype. Since there appears to be a relatively low rate of alcoholism in Orientals, the fact that possibly 85% of Japanese carry an atypical liver ADH suggests that alcohol sensitivity may result from increased acetaldehyde formation in individuals carrying an atypical ADH gene and that, conversely, non-Orientals with a low incidence of atypical ADH may be more "at risk" for alcoholism than are Orientals.

Genetic marker studies

An association of alcoholism with characteristics known to be inherited would support a biological factor in the etiology of alcoholism. The presence of other components within blood types is a comprehensive field within modern medical science. Certain investigators have compared alcoholism with specific blood types and with other characteristics. Results in these studies have varied widely. Topics in which an association between genetic markers and alcoholism is explored include the following.

BLOOD TYPE GROUPINGS

Nordmo (1959) reported a high degree of association between blood group A and alcoholism in a population of 939 alcoholics in Pueblo, Colorado. Achte (1958), however, found no difference in the distribution of blood groups between 212 alcoholics and 1,383 healthy persons in Finland. Swinson and Madden (1973), studying 448 alcoholic inpatients, also failed to find an association between blood group types and alcoholism.

Hill, Goodwin, Cadoret, Osterland, and Doner (1975) investigated one of the blood marker groups and reported that it (the homozygous "SS" of the MNSs system) was more frequently found in nonalcoholic families than in their alcoholic relatives. In another study, the same authors found that all the alcoholics and nonalcoholic relatives tested had a phenotype that, from available population data, should appear in only 54% of the general population. However, in a subsequent study, Winokur, Tann, Elston, and Go (1976) found no evidence of an association between alcoholism and specific markers, including those that were previously reported by Hill and her colleagues (1975).

Results of a comparative analysis of serum haptoglobin levels in alcoholic and nonalcoholic human subjects revealed that levels of haptoglobin were significantly higher in the alcoholic group, but genetic typing revealed no differences in the frequency of the HP2 allele in either group (De Torok & Johnson-Decrow, 1976). Thus, it was suggested that a regulator gene may be present prior to the onset of heavy drinking and that the elevated haptoglobin levels in the alcoholic sera may help explain the atypical iron overload in alcoholics.

In a group of male alcoholics, Kojic, Stojanovic, Dojicinova, and Jakulic (1977) studied palmar and finger print characteristics, as well as blood characteristics. In comparison with the normal population, alcoholics showed an increased occurrence of whorls and arches on the fingers, a decrease in total finger ridge count, sharpening of the atd angle, and separation of the lower from the upper transverse line. Genetic markers in the blood of alcoholics showed greater frequencies of A, Lewis ab+, Lewis a-b, Duffy a-, Duffy a+, SS, and M blood groups; Ccd-ee, Hp1-1, Hp2-1 phenotypes; and HLA-5, HLA-7, w10, w16, and w5 antigens.

SALIVARY SECRETIONS

Camps and Dodd (1967) found a remarkable increase in nonsecretors of salivary ABH blood group substances among alcoholic patients, especially those of blood group A. Reid (1903), studying a group of 100 cirrhotic patients, did not find this association. However, Swinson and Madden (1973), in their study of 448 alcoholics, also found a highly significant correlation of alcoholism with nonsecretors of salivary ABH substance. As was true in the study by Camps and Dodd, this association was predominantly in subjects of blood group A.

TASTE RESPONSE

Peeples (1962) tested 52 alcoholics and 70 controls to find that the alcoholics had a significantly greater percentage of nontasters of phenylthiocarbamide (PTC) than did the controls (PTC taste response is inherited as an autosomal dominant trait). No effort was made, however, to determine the possible effects of long continued ingestion of alcohol on this test.

SEX-LINKED TRANSMISSION

Cruz-Coke and Varela (1966) found that color blindness, cirrhosis, and alcoholism were associated, leading them to advance the hypothesis that alcoholism was transmitted by an X-borne recessive gene. Failkow, Thuline, and Fenster (1966) reported an association between alcoholism and cirrhosis with color blindness, but, they also found that the color blindness usually disappeared after the acute alcoholic symptoms had subsided. They concluded that color blindness in alcoholics probably reflected the toxic or nutritional effects of heavy drinking, rather than a genetically determined condition. Smith and Brinton (1971) came to the same conclusion and also found that color blindness in alcoholics was generally reversible. In two other studies by Thuline (1967) and Dittrich and Neubauer (1967) of a possible relationship of alcoholism or cirrhosis to color blindness, the first found a relationship, the second did not.

Varela, Rivera, Mardones, and Cruz-Coke (1969), discussing these inconsistent results, concluded that they may be attributable to variable sensitivity of color blindness tests and so, repeated their original study, using a more sensitive test (the Fansworth-Munsell 100-Hue Test). The visual defect, they found, mainly involved the Tritan and Tetartan axis. More importantly, they discovered that male nonalcoholic relatives of alcoholics did not differ significantly from male controls, but that female relatives differed significantly from control females in the Tritan and Tetartan axis, indicating that sex-linked recessive genes affecting blue-yellow discrimination ability were associated with alcoholism.

The genetic marker studies are intriguing, however inconsistent their findings. One reason for the inconsistency undoubtedly arises from the still primitive state of population genetics. Genetic factors influencing taste, color vision, blood factors, etc., vary so widely from population to population that deciding what is "normal" becomes highly arbitrary. Phenotype, moreover, is influenced by environment, so that in the case of color blindness, for example, it is virtually impossible to distinguish a sex-linked genetic defect from an acquired impairment, unless color blindness is studied in family members. Varela et al. (1969) studied family members of color-blind alcoholics and found a familial pattern of color blindness consistent with sex-linked recessive transmission. The study needs replication; if confirmed by other investigators, it would provide the strongest evidence available to date that a genetic factor exists for at least certain types of alcoholism.

As of now, however, the sex-linked hypothesis appears improbable on clinical grounds. As Winokur (1967) has pointed out, if the hypothesis were true, 50% of the brothers of alcoholic biological parents should also be affected, since the mother's x-linked recessive alcoholism gene and normal gene would be equally distributed among her sons. If fathers were also alcoholic, 50% of the sisters would be alcoholic, since this percent of sisters would have received a recessive gene for alcoholism from their fathers and their heterozygous mothers. Clinical data are inconsistent with these expectations. Family studies of alcoholics are unanimous in showing a high prevalence of alcoholism among the fathers of alcoholics, but not among their sisters.

The finding by two groups of investigators of a statistically significant increase in group A nonsecretors also warrants further investigation. To be sure, the finding, if replicated in other studies, may represent an acquired change rather than constitute a genetic marker. However, as Swinson and Madden (1973) point out, it is difficult to see why the excessive intake of alcohol should affect the secretion of ABH substance in the saliva of blood group A alcoholics only. To rule out the possibility that nonsecretion of ABH substances by alcoholics is an acquired change, sibship studies would be helpful; or alternatively, a prospective study of people of known blood groups and secretor status before they become alcoholics would be needed.

Role for genetics in the future

The findings in the Danish and other adoption studies show that children of alcoholics are approximately four times more likely to be alcoholic than are children of nonalcoholics, whether they are raised by their families or not. Therefore, the evidence supporting a nonexperiential (whether strictly genetic or not) factor in alcoholism has grown stronger, calling for further research in the following areas:

TYPOLOGY

The time, perhaps, has come to follow the suggestion of Jellinek and Jolliffe (1940) that alcoholism be separated into two varieties—familial and non-familial. The former would be manifested by alcoholism in blood relatives, by early onset of alcoholism, and by a rapid development and fulminating course of the disease, requiring early treatment. Therefore, in future studies of alcoholism, it may be profitable to divide alcoholics into familial and non-familial types to determine whether a consistent pattern separating the two along both biological and psychosocial variables emerges. The separation of alcoholics into familial and non-familial groups would result in samples of fairly equal size, as about one-half of patients in most series do not report having alcoholic relatives (assuming they have maintained close enough contact to know).

Studies of special subgroups of alcoholics could provide further leads to an understanding of the mode of transmission. The children of female alcoholics should be compared to the children of male alcoholics, both those who were separated from their parents and those who were not. Children who have two alcoholic parents should be studied, and also, the children of alcoholics who do not become alcoholic.

The half-sib method can be used for research, especially when adoption records are unavailable. This method, in brief, presupposes that full sibs of an index case will more often be alcoholic than half sibs, since they share the genetic loading for alcoholism to a larger extent. Given the rate of divorce in the United States, there should be a potentially large number of sample groups available for study by this method.

TOLERANCE

One thing that definitely can be said about alcoholics is that they drink large amounts of alcohol with minimal adverse effects, particularly early in their drinking history. Some human and animal studies indicate that this tolerance may be more innate than acquired. Therefore, presumably, it has a biological basis.

What is the nature of this tolerance? One possibility is that what is inherited is not tolerance, but rather a *lack of tolerance*. Millions of people have a sensitivity to alcohol that makes it difficult if not impossible for them to consume more than a small amount of alcohol without suffering ill effects, such as headache, nausea, or vertigo. Recent studies, for example, indicate that two-thirds or more of adult Orientals develop a cutaneous flush after drinking very small amounts of alcohol. This flush is associated with subjective distress, such as dizziness, nausea, dysphoria, and a strong disclination to continue drinking. In a very real sense, it would appear that Orientals are protected from becoming alcoholic because their unpleasant reactions to alcohol are strong deterrents to excessive drinking. Many non-Orientals also experience symptoms of distress (with or without a flush) after modest amounts of alcohol. Informal surveys suggest that women and Jews develop these symptoms more often than do gentile males. These observations are highly unsystematic and for corroboration require studies similar to those being conducted with Orientals.

One goal of the Oriental studies is to determine if the flushing-dysphoric response can be correlated with biochemical alterations. Practically, if we knew the biochemical basis for the flushing-dysphoric response in Orientals, quite possibly we could decrease the tolerance of alcohol-tolerant individuals by chemical intervention. From the standpoint of understanding why alcoholism develops in some individuals, but not in others, such studies might suggest that the only factor "inherited" is lack of *intolerance* to alcohol. Other factors—cultural, psychosocial, biological—may be required also, but lack of intolerance seems at least a prerequisite for the development of alcoholism.

ALCOHOL MEDIATORS

How alcohol affects the brain to produce euphoria and other effects is not known. Brain levels of monoamines have been studied extensively, and there is some evidence that they are involved in elevation and depression of mood. Other substances, especially gamma aminobutyric acid and cyclic nucleotides, are apparently involved in neurotransmission. The effect of alcohol on these substances has been explored in numerous animal studies, with highly inconsistent and conflicting results. Part of this may be due to species-specificity, differing dose levels, and methodological differences. After 15 years of research, therefore, it is impossible to say whether alcohol consistently affects monoamines or other chemicals to change cognitive and mood states.

Contradictions in the literature, however, should not discourage research in this direction. It appears likely that ethanol does not exert its effects directly, but rather through a mediator or mediators. Identifying these mediators is important. For one thing, some people experience more euphoria from alcohol than do others. Some experience more dysphoria. These responses may be determined by genes that control substrates and enzymes in the brain. If we knew why some people respond one way to alcohol and some another, we would be getting closer to a genetic explanation for alcoholism.

One obstacle to investigating the possible role of biological factors in alcoholism is the lack of an animal model for alcoholism. Preliminary reports suggest that miniature swine (Tumbleson, Dexter, Hutcheson, & Middleton, 1977) may spontaneously drink sufficient amounts of alcohol and react to alcohol in other ways to qualify as "alcoholic." If this is confirmed, then extensive studies should be carried out to determine how "alcoholic" pigs differ from "nonalcoholic" pigs.

HIGH RISK STUDIES

Korsten, Matsuzaki, Feinman, and Lieber (1975) reported that alcoholics have higher levels of acetaldehyde than do nonalcoholics after ingestion of alcohol. If this were confirmed it would suggest that perhaps alcoholics maintain their drinking in order to overcome the unpleasant effects of acetaldehyde, following a model of addiction suggested by Wikler (1973). This investigator stresses the seesaw nature of addictive drugs, whereby euphoric effects are followed by dysphoric effects, leading to repeated attempts to overcome the latter by increasingly heavy use of the drug. The aversive stimuli then become generalized, which explains why relapses occur long after the drug has been discontinued. In any case, the acetaldehyde study needs to be replicated. Confirmation of the data would not, however, eliminate this further question: Is the higher level of acetaldehyde in alcoholics a reflection of many years of heavy drinking (particularly the effects of alcohol on the liver) or are alcoholics genetically predisposed to higher levels of acetaldehyde after drinking?

Only a study of high-risk individuals could answer these questions. These are individuals who are particularly prone to becoming alcoholic, at an age before they begin to drink seriously. Since children of alcoholics apparently become alcoholic about four times more often than children of nonalcoholics, they constitute a high risk group unlikely to be identified elsewhere. As with acetaldehyde, many differences have been reported between alcoholics and nonalcoholics, but it is usually impossible to tell whether the differences resulted from heavy drinking or whether they preceded heavy drinking or were incidental associations.

One important example is the frequent finding that alcoholics with a history of heavy drinking exhibit subtle types of intellectual impairment, particularly in abstracting ability. Conceivably, such differences could have preceded the development of alcoholism and, indeed, contributed to the drinking problem. Only a high risk study could also answer this important question.

Clinical applicability

When Jellinek and Jolliffe (1940) reviewed the literature on possible genetic influences in alcoholism, they concluded that alcoholism ran in families, but that the cause was probably not genetic. Their reason was that if the illness were genetic it would be untreatable.

This strange logic is still offered occasionally by people who view genetic disorders as intrinsically untreatable. This, of course, is not true. Adult-onset diabetes, essential hypertension, coronary artery disease, and some other illnesses that run in families and that are almost certainly influenced by heredity, can be treated. Insulin, a low-salt diet, avoiding cigarettes, respectively, often modify symptoms, course, and outcome.

There is no specific treatment for alcoholism in the sense that insulin is a treatment for diabetes, but as more is learned about the illness, the more likely it is that such a treatment will emerge.

Meanwhile, the families of alcoholics should be cognizant of the familial nature, if not the genetic basis, of at least many cases of alcoholism. Children of alcoholics can be taught to recognize early symptoms of alcoholism and become aware that their chance of becoming alcoholic is perhaps four or five times greater than for children of nonalcoholics. Just as children of diabetics should have their urine checked periodically for sugar, children of alcoholics should exercise special caution in their use of alcohol. The government, public schools, and media can help provide this education.

Alcoholic sons of alcoholics appear to have an earlier onset and more severe forms of the disease than do alcoholic sons of nonalcoholics (it is not clear whether this is also true of alcoholic daughters of alcoholics). For them, early intervention becomes especially important. Professionals who work with disturbed children, adolescents, and young people should be alert to alcoholism developing at an early age in patients who have alcoholic relatives.

"Familial alcoholism" does not appear to be associated with an increased risk of other psychiatric disorders; when the "familial" alcoholic stops drinking, he or she will not necessarily manifest another psychiatric disorder. Abstinence, in whatever way achieved, may be the sole goal of treatment. Alcoholics without a family history of alcoholism, on the other hand, may turn out to have an affective disorder, sociopathy, or other psychiatric illness independent of their drinking problem, which needs to be dealt with separately from their problems associated with alcohol. It may turn out (although it has not yet been proven) that Antabuse (disulfiram) is a more useful treatment for familial alcoholics than for other alcoholics.

A definitive treatment of alcoholism, of course, must await knowledge of the biochemical and psychological factors responsible for the addiction.

References

Achte, R. Korreloitovatko ABO-veriryhmat ja alkoholismi (Correlation of ABO blood groups with alcoholism). *Duodecim*, 1958, *74*, 20–22.

Bohman, M. Some genetic aspects of alcoholism and criminality: A population of adoptions. *Archives of General Psychiatry*, 1978, *35*, 269–276.

Cadoret, R. & Gath, A. Inheritance of alcoholism in adoptees. *British Journal of Psychiatry*, 1978, *132*, 252–258.

Camps, F. & Dodd, B. Increase in the incidence of nonsecretors of ABH blood group substances among alcoholic patients. *British Journal of Medicine*, 1967, *1*, 30–31.

Cruz-Coke, R., & Varela, A. Inheritance of alcoholism. *Lancet*, 1966, *2*, 1282–1284.

De Torok, D. & Johnson-Decrow, C. Quantitative and qualitative plasma protein studies on alcoholics versus nonalcoholics. *Annals of the New York Academy of Science*, 1976, *273*, 167–174.

Dittrich, H. & Neubauer, O. Storungen des Farbsehens bei leberkrankeiten. *Munchener Medizinische Wochenschift en Espanol*, 1967, *109*, 2690–2693.

Failkow, P., Thuline, M., & Fenster, L. Lack of association between cirrhosis and the common types of color-blindness. *New England Journal of Medicine*, 1966, *275*, 584–587.

Forsander, O. & Eriksson, K. Forekommer det etnologiska skillnader i alkoholens amnesomsattningen. *Alkoholpolitik*, 1974, *37*, 315.

Goodwin, D., Schulsinger, F., Hermansen, L., Guze, S., & Winokur, G. Alcohol problems in adoptees raised apart from alcoholic biological parents. *Archives of General Psychiatry*, 1973, *28*, 238–243.

Goodwin, D., Schulsinger, F., Knop, J., Mednick, S., & Guze, S. Alcoholism and depression in adopted-out daughters of alcoholics. *Archives of General Psychiatry*, 1977, *34*, 751–755.

Goodwin, D., Schulsinger, F., Moller, N., Hermansen, L., Winokur, G., & Guze, S. Drinking problems in adopted and nonadopted sons of alcoholics. *Archives of General Psychiatry*, 1974, *31*, 164–169.

Hill, S., Goodwin, D., Cadoret, R., Osterland, C., & Doner, S. Association and linkage between alcoholism and eleven serological markers. *Quarterly Journal of Studies on Alcohol*, 1975, *36*, 981–992.

Jellinek, E. & Jolliffe, N. Effect of alcohol on the individual: Review of the literature of 1939. *Quarterly Journal of Studies on Alcohol*, 1940, *1*, 110–181.

Jonsson, A. & Nilsson, T. Alkoholkonsumtion hos monozygota och dizygota tvillingar. *Nordisk Hygienisk Tidskrift,* 1968, *49,* 21–25.

Kaij, L. Studies on the etiology and sequels of abuse of alcohol. Department of Psychiatry, University of Lund, 1960.

Kaij, L. & Dock, J. Grandsons of alcoholics. *Archives of General Psychiatry,* 1975, *32,* 1379–1321.

Kojic, T., Stojanovic, O., Dojicinova, A., and Jakulic, S. Possible genetic predisposition for alcohol addiction. *Advances in Experimental Medicine and Biology,* 1977, *65,* 7–24.

Korsten, M., Matsuzaki, S., Feinman, L., & Lieber, C. High blood acetaldehyde levels after ethanol administration. *New England Journal of Medicine,* 1975, *292,* 386–389.

Loehlin, J. Analysis of alcohol-related questionnaire items from the National Merit twin study. *Annals of the New York Academy of Science,* 1972, *197,* 119–120.

Nordmo, S. Blood groups in schizophrenia, alcoholism and mental deficiency. *American Journal of Psychiatry,* 1959, *116,* 460–461.

Partanen, J., Brunn, K., & Markkanen, T. *Inheritance of drinking behavior.* New Brunswick, New Jersey: Rutgers University Center of Alcohol Studies, 1966.

Peeples, E. *Taste sensitivity to penylthiocarbamide in alcoholics.* Unpublished master's thesis, Stetson University, Weland, Florida, 1962.

Reid, G. Human evolution, with especial reference to alcohol. *British Medical Journal,* 1903, *2,* 818–820.

Roe, A. The adult adjustment of children of alcoholic parents raised in foster homes. *Quarterly Journal of Studies on Alcohol,* 1944, *5,* 378–393.

Schuckit, M., Goodwin, D., & Winokur, G. A study of alcoholism in half siblings. *American Journal of Psychiatry,* 1972, *128,* 1132–1136.

Smith, J. & Brinton, G. Color-vision defects in alcoholism. *Quarterly Journal of Studies on Alcohol,* 1971, *32,* 41–44.

Stamatoyannopoulas, G., Chen, Shi-Han, and Fukui, M. Liver alcohol dehydrogenase in Japanese: High population frequency of atypical form and its possible role in alcohol sensitivity. *American Journal of Human Genetics,* 1975, *27,* 789–796.

Swinson, R. & Madden, J. ABO blood groups and ABH substance secretion in alcoholics. *Quarterly Journal of Studies on Alcohol,* 1973, *34,* 64–70.

Thuline, H. Color blindness and alcoholism. *Lancet,* 1967, *1,* 274–275.

Tumbleson, M., Dexter, J., Hutcheson, D., & Middleton, C. Clearance, intolerance and withdrawal from intragastric infusion of ethanol in Sinclair (S-1) miniature swine. Unpublished abstract, 1977, University of Missouri, Columbia, Missouri.

Utne, H., Hansen, F., Winkler, K., & Schulsinger, F. Ethanol elimination rate in adoptees with and without parental disposition towards alcoholism. (Personal communication).

Varela, A., Rivera, L., Mardones, J., & Cruz-Coke, R. Color vision defects in nonalcoholic relatives of alcoholic parents. *British Journal of Addiction,* 1969, *64,* 67–73.

Vesell, E., Page, J., & Passananti, G. Genetic and environmental factors affecting ethanol metabolism in man. *Clinical Pharmacology and Therapeutics,* 1971, *12,* 192–201.

Wikler, A. Dynamics of drug dependence: Implications of a conditioning theory for research and treatment. *Archives of General Psychiatry,* 1973, *28,* 611–616.

Winokur, G. X-borne recessive genes in alcoholism. *Lancet,* 1967, *2,* 466.

Winokur, G., Reich, T., Rimmer, J., & Pitts, F. Alcoholism: Diagnosis and familial psychiatric illness in 259 alcoholic probands. *Archives of General Psychiatry,* 1970, *23,* 104–111.

Winokur, G., Tanna, V., Elston, R., & Go, R. Lack of association of genetic traits with alcoholism: C3, Ss and ABO systems. *Journal of Studies on Alcohol,* 1976, *37,* 1313–1315.

9. Antisocial personality disorder

Raymond R. Crowe

Introduction

The past decade has seen substantial progress in our understanding of genetic risk factors in antisocial personality disorder. Evidence for such risk factors dates to early family and twin investigations demonstrating a high prevalence of antisocial behavior in the immediate relatives of criminals and antisocials, but these observations have to be tempered by the fact that the relatives always shared a common environment with the antisocial proband. Recently, the use of adoption strategies to examine individuals separated in infancy from their biological relatives have allowed us to draw conclusions about both genetic and nongenetic risk factors in a design that separates the effects of the two factors. Thus, the hypothesis of genetic influences in antisocial personality disorder has once again become a valid scientific question to be empirically tested and answered. The purpose of this chapter is to review the original genetic data from family and twin studies, to cover in some depth adoption studies and their major conclusions, and finally, to review the results of recent analyses of these data in which sophisticated mathematical models of familial transmission were used.

behind the twin strategy is that monozygotic (MZ) twins have all of their genes in common and dizygotic (DZ) twins are genetically no more alike than ordinary siblings; therefore, a higher concordance rate among MZ twins is evidence of genetic factors. Using the probandwise method of computing concordance rates (Rosenthal, 1970), across the nine studies the MZ twins ranged from 41 to 100%, with a weighted mean of 67.6%; and the DZ twins ranged from 0 to 69.7%, with a weighted mean of 33.2%.

It should be noted that these DZ twins are same sex, and that in the six studies that examined opposite sex DZ twins, the concordance rates were always lower than among the same sex DZ twins.

Two of the studies are of special interest because they were based on national twin and police registers and in this way they avoided the selection biases that plagued the earlier studies (i.e., selecting more severe cases by ascertaining twins from prisons). Moreover, both studies employed more reliable means of zygosity testing. In the Christiansen (1970) study, the concordance rate among 81 MZ twins was 50% and that among 137 DZ twins 19.7%. The respective rates in the Dalgard and Kringlen (1976) study, using a strict definition of criminality, were 41.0% for 31 MZ and 25.8% for 54 DZ twins. In both these studies, the criminality rates were lower than the overall mean of the nine studies, probably reflecting the fact that sample selection was not biased.

The fact that the six studies reporting concordance rates for opposite sex DZ twins all found lower rates than for same sex DZ twins is sometimes cited as evidence for environmental factors. This does not necessarily follow. Whenever one sex is more frequently affected, as in antisocial personality, the index twin will more often be of the more frequently affected sex. The co-twin, being of the opposite sex, is less likely to be affected than if the pair were same sex DZ, thus producing the observed discrepancy.

Although the twin studies support a hypothesis of genetic risk factors in antisocial personality disorder, the evidence cannot be considered definitive because of the possibility that MZ twins may have a more common environment than DZ twins. In fact, Dalgard and Kringlen (1976) attempted to control this factor and found that it practically eradicated the MZ–DZ difference in their study. To truly test the genetic hypothesis, a design that maintains shared genes, but eliminates shared environment, is needed and the adoption studies answered this need.

Genetics of antisocial disorder

Family studies

Although the familial nature of antisocial behavior has been comm
on by numerous observers, the only investigation of this phenon
meeting rigorous standards for a psychiatric family study (i.e., struct
interviews and operational diagnostic criteria) is the one conducted
Guze (1976), at Washington University. This was a family study of
male and 66 female felons of which 78% of the male felons and 65%
the female felons were diagnosed as sociopathic (having an antisoci
personality disorder).

The principal finding was a high rate of antisocial personality disorder
among the relatives. This was diagnosed in 9% of the relatives of the male
felons (19% of the male and 3% of the female relatives). Among the interviewed relatives of female felons, sociopathy was diagnosed in 18% (31%
of the men and 11% of the women). In addition to the diagnoses of sociopathy, hysteria (somatization disorder) was found frequently in the female relatives; 5% of the female relatives of the male felons and 22% of
the female relatives of the female felons. Another disorder overrepresented
in these families was alcoholism, present in 15% of the relatives of male
felons (34% of the male and 5% of the female relatives) and 29% of the
relatives of female felons (50% of the male and 19% of the female relatives).

These data document the familial nature of antisocial personality disorder, as well as its higher prevalence in men, and demonstrate an
association between antisocial personality disorder in the male and
somatization disorder in the female. Alcoholism is frequently found
among the relatives. Finally, the relatives of female antisocials appear
to have a greater risk of developing each of these disorders than the relatives of male antisocials.

Twin studies

Additional data in support of genetic risk factors comes from nine investi-
gations of criminal twins (Borgstrom, 1939; Christiansen, 1970; Dalgard
& Kringlen, 1976; Kranz, 1936; Lange, 1929; LeGras, 1933; Rosanoff,
Handy, & Plesset, 1934; Stumpfl, 1936; Yoshimasu, 1961). The rationale

Adoption studies

The adoption strategy is based on the rationale that adoptees share a proportion of their genes in common with their biological relatives, but have no common environment with them. Therefore, concordance between adoptees and their biological relatives is evidence for genetic factors and concordance between adoptees and their adoptive families is evidence for environmental factors. In this way, suspected genetic and environmental risk factors can be examined independently. Several variations on this design have been employed, but the two most frequently encountered are the *adoptees family study* and the *adoptees study* (Rosenthal, 1970). In the former, the biological and adoptive families of affected adoptees are studied; in the latter, the adopted offspring of an affected parent. Of course, in either case an appropriate group of control adoptees is necessary for comparison.

The first adoption study of antisocial personality disorder was a Danish study of "psychopaths" by Schulsinger (1972). Danish adoption and hospital registers were used to identify an index group of 57 adoptees who had been hospitalized and whose records supported a diagnosis of "psychopathy." Fifty-seven control adoptees were chosen to match for age and sex, and the biological and adoptive relatives of both groups were checked through the hospital register. Based on hospital records, the investigator blindly diagnosed subjects as having any mental disorder falling within what he considered the "psychopathy spectrum" (criminality, drug abuse, alcoholism, and hysterical character disorder, in addition to psychopathy) or as having frank psychopathy. The principal finding was that significantly more of the 305 index biological relatives were found in all three categories: 19% with mental disorder, 14% with psychopathy spectrum disorders, and 4% with psychopathy. The respective rates for 285 control biological relatives were 13%, 7%, and 1.4%, which were comparable to the respective rates found among both groups of adoptive relatives.

Although the 4% rate of psychopathy among the index biological relatives appears low when compared with rates previously cited, it is undoubtedly an underestimate because the study was based on hospital records and antisocials who were not hospitalized would have been missed. Also, one would expect to find more psychopathy among the male relatives, as seen above. If one examines the 66 male relatives in the

Schulsinger study, 6 to 9% were diagnosed psychopaths. These data suggest a definite genetic contribution to antisocial personality disorder.

A second adoptee family study was based on Danish criminal records (Hutchings & Mednick, 1975). A group of 1,145 male adoptees in Copenhagen and an equal number of matched non-adopted controls, as well as all biological and adoptive parents, were checked through a register of criminal offenses comparable to indictable offenses in this country. Records were found on 16% of the adoptees compared with 9% of the non-adopted controls, the latter figure being the same as the population rate in Copenhagen. The corresponding figures for adoptive and control fathers were 13 and 11%, respectively, but 31% of the adoptees' biological fathers had records. When the analysis was narrowed to focus on criminal adoptees, the percentage of adoptive fathers with records increased from 9% to 22%. However, the percentage of biological fathers registered also increased, from 31 to 49%. Thus, criminality in the adoptee correlated with criminality in both the biological and the adoptive father.

The authors pursued this lead by studying 143 criminal adoptees, matching them with a control group of adoptees, and searching for criminal and psychiatric records on the biological and adoptive relatives of both groups. A multiple regression analysis of criminal outcome against a number of variables, both genetic and environmental, indicated that three factors correlated independently with a criminal outcome in the adoptee: criminality in a biological parent, criminality in an adoptive parent, and a psychiatric diagnosis in the biological mother.

Since the above data suggested the importance of both the biological and the adoptive parents in leading to a criminal outcome, the investigators used a cross-fostering design to examine these factors. Among adoptees born to criminal biological fathers, but reared by non-criminal adoptive parents, the rate of criminal offenses was 21%. By contrast, among adoptees born to non-criminal biological fathers, but reared by criminal adoptive fathers, the rate was 12%. Although the finding was in the direction of the genetic influence being stronger, the difference was not statistically significant. For comparison, the criminality rates among the other two groups of adoptees were (a) neither biological nor adoptive father criminal, 10% and (b) both adoptive and biological father criminal, 36%.

An adoptee study from the United States examined 52 adoptees, 27 male and 25 female, born to women offenders in correctional institutions, 90% of whom were felons (Crowe, 1972, 1974). The index adoptees were matched for age and sex with a control group of adoptees and at follow-up the subjects ranged in age from 15 to 45 years (mean=26). Positive assortative mating for criminality occurred in at least one-third of the parents, creating a considerable genetic loading for antisocial personality.

The initial follow-up was based on arrest records and psychiatric hospital records from the state in which they were born. The arrest records revealed 18 offenses by eight index subjects compared with two offenses by two controls. Moreover, 13% of the index adoptees had been convicted of at least one offense, 12% had spent time in correctional institutions, and 15% had been evaluated at psychiatric facilities, usually at the request of the courts. These last three figures were all significantly higher than the respective ones for the controls, which were 2, 0, and 4%.

The final follow-up was limited to the 46 adoptees in each group who were over 18 years of age by the end of follow-up and involved interviews by the author plus collateral data from sources such as orphanages, hospital correctional facilities, and mental health centers. Although the interviewer knew the status of the subjects, the material was reviewed blindly by three clinicians who diagnosed antisocial personality in 13% of the index adoptees (six subjects) compared with 2% of the controls (one male diagnosed "probable antisocial personality"). One of the clinicians also used the Feighner et al. (1972) research criteria, which are more consistent with the present DSM-III diagnosis of antisocial personality disorder, finding that all six index antisocials met the criteria, whereas none of the control subjects did.

The early environment of the antisocials was found to differ from the environment of the other adoptees in that longer periods of time were spent in temporary care (orphanges and temporary foster homes) prior to final placement. Since the index and control adoptees did not differ significantly on this variable, the index adoptees may have responded differently than the controls. This question was examined by comparing the index and control adoptees who spent over one year in temporary care, the cut-off that seemed to be associated with antisocial personality among the index adoptees. Five of seven such index subjects, but none of the four controls, became antisocial. Despite the small numbers, the trend was in the expected direction.

A large Swedish study (Bohman, 1971, 1972) compared sizable groups of adoptees (163), babies released for adoption, but returned to their biological mothers (205), and children reared in foster homes (124).

The study is of interest because one-third of the biological fathers appeared in the criminal register: 27%, 34%, and 40% of the three groups, respectively. The foster home group contained many children who were difficult to place for adoption due to physical handicaps, developmental retardation, or heredity. The children were followed up at 10 to 11 years of age by means of interviews with parents and teachers, as well as by a rating of their overall development. In the adopted group, no correlation was found between a criminal biological father and subsequent maladjustment. In particular, juvenile antisocial behavior (i.e., destructiveness, theft, truancy, vagrancy, lying) was not more frequent than among a matched control group of school children. In the other two groups, the girls born to criminal fathers tended to have less favorable adjustments than those born to non-criminal fathers, but the trend did not hold for the boys. The negative finding for the boys is surprising in view of the fact that the group contained many unadoptable children, as well as boys given up by their mothers because of the biological fathers' criminality.

Bohman (1972) looked at the effect of early rearing (up to 14 months) in an institution on adjustment and found that girls spending over six months in institutions made poorer overall adjustments than those spending less time, but again the trend did not hold for the boys. However, these comparisons of institutional rearing were made on the overall groups of children and were not limited to the subjects of criminal fathers.

Bohman (1978) followed up this study with a large adoptee family study of adults based on the Swedish adoption, criminal, and alcohol offense register. A population of 2,324 adoptees born between 1930 and 1949 was used for a series of analyses. The first of these analyses examined registrations for alcoholism and criminality in male adoptees whose biological fathers had been registered for either of these offenses or for neither (the controls). When the biological father was registered for a criminal offense, the adoptee rates of criminality (8.9%), alcohol abuse (7.6%), and both (3.6%) were not different from rates found among the controls (5.0, 6.6, and 7.0%, respectively). However, when the biological father was registered for alcohol abuse, the adoptee rates were criminality 4.5%, alcohol abuse 22.5%, and both 16.9%. These results supported a genetic hypothesis for the transmission of alcoholism, but not criminality and, moreover, suggested that criminality may be secondary to alcoholism.

In order to examine these questions further, Bohman (1978) selected, respectively, 50 male and 50 female adoptees from biological fathers and equal numbers from biological mothers with the most severe records of alcohol abuse and of criminal behavior, matching each of these eight groups with a respective control group (some of the groups contained slightly less than 50, due to difficulty filling the cells). Only the male probands had rates high enough for statistical comparison and their results supported the previous analysis. The adoptees born to criminal fathers experienced rates of criminality (6%) and criminality and alcoholism (2%) that were identical to those of their controls (8 and 0%, respectively). However, the former group experienced a 16% rate of alcoholism compared with 4% among their controls. The male adoptees born to biological fathers registered for alcohol abuse had criminality rates of 2%, alcohol and criminality 12%, and alcohol abuse 8%. These differences lie in the same direction as the previous analysis, but the numbers are small and the differences not statistically significant. Bohman (1978) also looked at the age at final placement in the adoptive home and found that there was no association between late placement and risk of either alcoholism or criminality.

Cadoret (1978) used adoption records in Iowa to obtain a series of 246 adoptees; 84 were 18 years old or older and 162 were 10–17 years old. Eighteen of the adult adoptees were born to biological parents diagnosed as antisocial based on information in the adoption agency files. Of these 18 adoptees, 14 received a psychiatric diagnosis and 5 were diagnosed antisocial personality disorder. These rates were both significantly higher than those found among the control group of 25 adoptees born to parents judged free of psychopathology, seven of whom received a psychiatric diagnosis, but none of whom were considered antisocial.

Turning next to the child sample, the incidence of total psychiatric diagnosis and conduct disorder was identical for the 24 children born to biological parents with antisocial behavior and the 70 control adoptees. However, childhood psychosomatic symptoms were significantly over-represented among the female offspring of the antisocials (6 of 9) when compared with the female controls (9 of 41).

The adult and child samples were combined in a multiple regression analysis to examine the effect of a number of genetic and environmental variables on antisocial outcome. These included diagnosis of biological parents, diagnosis of adoptive parents, SES level of adoptive family, time spent in temporary foster care, and sex of the adoptee. The factors found to correlate independently with an antisocial outcome in the adoptee were antisocial biological background, alcoholic biological background, psychiatric problems in the adoptive parent, and sex of the adoptee. Time spent in foster care revealed a non-significant trend in the expected direction ($p = .09$). A similar analysis was performed using psychosomatic symptoms as the dependent variable and the only independent variable to correlate was a biological background of antisocial behavior.

In a more detailed analysis (Cadoret & Cain, 1980), the effect of sex on the biological and environmental predictors of antisocial outcome was examined, using this same group of adoptees. In the overall group, a multiple regression analysis identified four variables as predicting an antisocial outcome. These were antisocial biological background, alcoholic biological background, adverse influences in the adoptive home (divorced or separated, adoptive parents; parental or sibling psychopathology) and discontinuous mothering (23 adoptees were temporarily placed in a home where they were cared for as babies by a large number of university students). However, when the sample was subdivided by sex, the pattern of factors correlating with antisocial outcome differed. Among the 110 females, the important biological factors were antisocial behavior and mental retardation in the biological parents, whereas none of the environmental factors were statistically significant. Among the 136 males, alcoholism in the biological parents was a significant predictor as was adverse environment in the adoptive home.

In an attempt to synthesize the findings of these five adoption studies, three issues need to be addressed. The first of these is that of genetic factors. With the exception of the Bohman material, the adoption studies are in agreement in demonstrating a genetic influence in the development of antisocial personality. The reason for the discrepant result in the Bohman (1978) study is unclear, particularly since this study would appear to be essentially a replication of the Hutchings and Mednick (1975) investigation. The Bohman data suggest that alcoholism may be the primary illness being transmitted in these families and that antisocial and criminal behavior may be secondary to it. However, Cadoret's finding that an antisocial outcome correlates independently with an antisocial background (Cadoret, 1978), as well as the failure to find an excess of alcoholism among the adoptees in the Crowe (1974) study, argues against this hypothesis. An interview study of Bohman's (1978) adoptees might help to clarify the problem.

A second issue raised by the adoption studies is that of the "spectrum" of disorders associated with antisocial personality. Two diagnoses are logical candidates: alcoholism and somatization disorder. The association between alcoholism and antisocial behavior in the Bohman material has already been commented on. It appeared in Schulsinger's (1972) "Psychopathy Spectrum," and Cadoret (1978) found a correlation between alcoholic biological background and antisocial outcome. In interpreting these data, two facts need to be kept in mind. The first is that antisocials frequently have significant drinking histories; the second that alcoholism may appear in the families of antisocials through assortative mating (Robins, 1966; Guze, 1976). In fact, Cadoret (1978) found that alcoholism in adoptees correlated with alcoholism in biological families and not with antisocial background.

The second candidate for an antisocial spectrum disorder is somatization disorder (hysteria). The association between this disorder and antisocial personality in family studies has already been mentioned, and, in fact, Guze (1976) has suggested that it is a female equivalent of antisocial personality disorder in the male. This hypothesis finds some support in the Cadoret (1978) study in which a high rate of somatic complaints among the female offspring of antisocial biological parents was found. In fact, Cadoret noted similar findings in a previous adoption study of children based on a different sample (Cadoret, Cunningham, Loftus, & Edwards, 1976). The other adoption study capable of providing data on this question is the one by Crowe (1974), which, unfortunately, failed to confirm it. No diagnoses of hysteria were made among the 19 women in that study, despite the fact that subjects were screened for that diagnosis.

The final issue raised by the adoption studies is the question of nongenetic risk factors. The Hutchings and Mednick (1975) and the Cadoret (1978) material stressed the importance of psychopathology in the adoptive family as well as the biological. Moreover, males may be more susceptible to these effects, a point made by Wolkind and Rutter (1973), which would help explain why antisocial personality is more prevalent among males. Length of time spent in temporary care, a significant factor in the Crowe (1974) study, was not found to affect outcome in Bohman's (1978) or Cadoret's (1978) material. However, the more specific influence of disruptive mothering was a significant factor (Cadoret & Cain, 1980).

Genetic models of antisocial personality disorder

The previous section has dealt with the evidence for both genetic and environmental risk factors in the development of antisocial personality and the problem of which diagnoses should be included in the spectrum

of antisocial disorder. This section will take up the application of recently developed mathematical transmission models that attempt to utilize these observations to explain the genetic-demographic data reviewed
in the first section. (For a more detailed presentation of transmission
models the reader is referred to Chapter 2 by Suarez, Rice, and Reich.)

The relevant observations are the following: The population prevalence
of antisocial personality in males exceeds that of females, and somatization disorder is found almost exclusively in females. Similarly, among biological relatives of male and female antisocials and women with somatization disorder, antisocial personality disorder rates in males exceed those
in females, whereas somatization disorder is found exclusively in females
(Guze, 1976). Cloninger and his associates (Cloninger, Reich, & Guze,
1975a, b) analyzed these findings using the Reich multifactorial multiple
threshold model of disease transmission (Reich, Cloninger, & Guze, 1975).
The model postulates that the liability to a disorder is a normally distributed variable contributed to by both genetic and environmental factors, each of which has a small additive effect. Persons whose liability
exceeds a theoretical threshold are phenotypically affected, and those
below the threshold appear normal. A disorder such as antisocial personality, in which one sex is more frequently affected than another, can
be viewed as a continuous liability distribution with two thresholds,
which differ for the sexes, the more frequently affected sex having a
threshold closer to the population mean such that a greater proportion of
the distribution would lie to the right of the threshold (i.e., a higher
prevalence of the disorder in that sex). Returning to antisocial personality, the model would predict that the relatives of females (the less
frequently affected sex) would experience higher rates of the disorder
than the relatives of males, and that, in each set of relatives, males would
be more frequently affected than females. These are essentially the same
findings reported by Guze (1976). The model is tested in the following
way. Three parameters, the population prevalence of the disorder in
males, the population prevalence of the disorder in females, and its
heritability, are sufficient to predict the remaining observed values,
namely, the male and female prevalence in first-degree relatives of male
and female probands, respectively. A computer program is used to suc-
cessively substitute multiple values for the first three parameters and to
test for the goodness of fit to all observed values (the male and female
prevalence rates in the population and in relatives of male and female
probands, respectively). The best-fitting parameter set generates a chi-

square value, which if non-significant, indicates an acceptable fit. When the model was applied to the observed data on personally interviewed first-degree relatives of white antisocials, the best-fitting parameters were a population prevalence of 3.6% for men, 0.7% for women, and a correlation of .56. The expected rates among relatives of 24.9% among male and 7.6% among female relatives of male probands, and 37.9% and 14.3% among the respective relatives of female probands were close to the observed values ($p > .90$), which indicated a good fit. Next, somatization disorder was included in the model, since this condition has been considered a variant of antisocial personality. This model led to a set of 12 observations: the prevalence of antisocial personality in men and women and of somatization disorder in women in the first-degree relatives of each of these three classes of affected subjects, plus the population. This model is defined by the three population prevalences and the heritability. When it was fit to observed data it provided a close fit ($p > .4$), which gave population prevalences of 3.8% for antisocial men, 0.5% for antisocial women, and 3.0% for women with somatization disorder. The finding that including somatization disorder does not affect the goodness of fit and leads to essentially the same expected prevalences is consistent with Guze's (1976) hypothesis.

The multifactorial model was next used to test the hypothesis that the sex differences in antisocial personality are due to extrafamilial environmental factors affecting the two sexes differently (Cloninger, Christiansen, Reich, & Gottesman, 1978). If this is the case, the correlation between females would differ from that found between males. If extrafamilial environmental factors act equally on both sexes, then the two correlations should be equal. The analysis yielded a male–male correlation of $0.43 \pm .07$ and a female–female correlation of $0.44 \pm .16$, indicating that extrafamilial environmental factors are not the cause of the sex differences in antisocial personality disorder.

The transmission model studies indicate that all the demographic observations on antisocial personality disorder and somatization disorder can be accounted for by a unitary hypothesis assuming a normally distributed liability with sex thresholds. The liability may be entirely genetic, entirely environmental, or more likely, a combination of the two. However, the fact that the model provides a satisfactory fit does not mean that it is the mode of transmission. The disorders in question may prove to be genetically heterogeneous, with different subtypes transmitted in different ways, or other transmission models may be shown to fit equally well. Despite these reservations, the multifactorial model does do a surprisingly good job of accounting for a number of otherwise unexplainable findings in the families of antisocials.

References

Bohman, M. A comparative study of adopted children, foster children and children in their biological environment born after undesired pregnancies. *Acta Paediatrica Scandinavica* (Suppl. 221), 1971.

Bohman, M. A study of adopted children, their background, environment, and adjustment. *Acta Paediatrica Scandinavica*, 1972, *61*, 90–97.

Bohman, M. Some genetic aspects of alcoholism and criminality: A population of adoptees. *Archives of General Psychiatry*, 1978, *35*, 269–276.

Borgstrom, C. Eine serie von kriminellen zwillingen. *Archiv Fur Rassen-und Gesellschaftsbiologie*, 1939, *33*, 334–343. (Cited in O. Dalgard and E. Kringlen, *British Journal of Criminology*, 1976, *6*, 213–232.)

Cadoret, R. Psychopathology in adopted-away offspring of biological parents with antisocial behavior. *Archives of General Psychiatry*, 1978, *35*, 176–184.

Cadoret, R. & Cain, C. Sex differences in predictors of antisocial behavior in adoptees. *Archives of General Psychiatry*, 1980, *137*, 1171–1175.

Cadoret, R., Cunningham, L., Loftus, R., Edwards, J. Studies of adoptees from psychiatrically disturbed biological parents: III. Medical symptoms and illnesses in childhood and adolescence. *American Journal of Psychiatry*, 1976, *133*, 1316–1318.

Christiansen, K. Crime in a Danish twin population. *Acta Geneticae Medicae et Gemellologiae*, 1970, *19*, 323–326.

Cloninger, C., Reich, T., & Guze, S. The multifactorial model of disease transmission: II. Sex differences in the familial transmission of sociopathy (antisocial personality). *British Journal of Psychiatry*, 1975a, *127*, 11–22.

Cloninger, C., Reich, T., & Guze, S. The multifactorial model of disease transmission: III. Familial relationship between sociopathy and hysteria (Briquet's syndrome). *British Journal of Psychiatry*, 1975b, *127*, 23–32.

Cloninger, C., Christiansen, K., Reich, T., & Gottesman, I. Implications of sex differences in the prevalences of antisocial personality, alcoholism, and criminality for familial transmission. *Archives of General Psychiatry*, 1978, *35*, 941–951.

Crowe, R. The adopted offspring of women criminal offenders: A study of their arrest records. *Archives of General Psychiatry*, 1972, *27*, 600–603.

Crowe, R. An adoption study of antisocial personality. *Archives of General Psychiatry*, 1974, *31*, 785–791.

Dalgard, O. & Kringlen, E. A Norwegian twin study of criminality. *British Journal of Criminology*, 1976, *16*, 231–232.

Feighner, J., Robins, E., Guze, S., Woodruff, R., Winokur, G., & Munoz, R.

Diagnostic criteria for use in psychiatric research. *Archives of General Psychiatry*, 1972, *26*, 57–63.

Guze, S. *Criminality and psychiatric disorders*. New York: Oxford University Press, 1976.

Hutchings, B. & Mednick, S. Registered criminality in the adoptive and biological parents of registered male criminal adoptees. In R. Fieve, D. Rosenthal, & H. Brill (Eds.), *Genetic research in psychiatry*. Baltimore: Johns Hopkins University Press, 1975.

Kranz, N. *Lebensschicksale krimineller zwillinge*. Berlin: Springer, 1936. (Cited in O. Dalgard, and E. Kringlen, *British Journal of Criminology*, 1976, *16*, 213–232.)

Lange, J. *Verbrechen als schicksal. Studien an kriminellen zwillingen*. Leipzig: Thieme, 1929. (Cited in O. Dalgard and E. Kringlen, *British Journal of Criminology*, 1976, *16*, 213–232.)

LeGras, A. Psychose und kriminalitat dei zwillingen. *Zentralblatt fuer Die Gesamte Neurologie und Psychiatrie*, 1933, *144*, 198–222.

Reich, T., Cloninger, C., & Guze, S. The multifactorial model of disease transmission: I. Description of the model and its use in psychiatry. *British Journal of Psychiatry*, 1975, *127*, 1–10.

Robins, L. *Deviant children grown up*. Baltimore: Williams & Wilkins, 1966.

Rosanoff, A., Handy, L., & Plesset, I. Criminality and delinquency in twins. *Journal of Criminal Law and Criminology*, 1934, *24*, 923–934.

Rosenthal, D. *Genetic theory and abnormal behavior*. New York: McGraw-Hill, 1970.

Schulsinger, F. Psychopathology, heredity and environment. *International Journal of Mental Health*, 1972, *1*, 190–206.

Stumpfl, F. *Die ursprunge des vervrechens, dargestellt am lebenslauf von zwillingen*. Leipzig: Thieme, 1936. (Cited in O. Dalgard & E. Kringlen, *British Journal of Criminology*, 1976, *6*, 213–232.)

Wolkind, S. & Rutter, M. Children who have been "in care"—an epidemiological study. *Journal of Child Psychology and Psychiatry*, 1973, *14*, 97–105.

Yoshimasu, S. The criminological significance of the family in the light of the studies of criminal twins. *Acta Criminologiae et Medicae Legalis Japonica*, 1961, *27*, 117–141. (Cited in O. Dalgard and E. Kringlen, *British Journal of Criminology*, 1976, *6*, 213–232.)

10. Affective disorders

Robert E. Smith and George Winokur

The bipolar-unipolar distinction

The separation of the affective disorders into different categories is a relatively recent advance within psychiatric nosology. Kraepelin's (1921) placement of recurrent depressions along with depressions plus manic episodes in the category of manic-depressive disorders dominated psychiatric thinking for decades. However, with the recent introduction of DSM-III (American Psychiatric Association, 1980), the affective disorders have been divided into bipolar illness and major depressive disorder (unipolar illness). Current research has borne out the validity of this subdivision by defining homogeneous groups of patients experiencing the same disease process.

Leonhard (1957) first suggested that patients exhibiting only recurrent depressions could be classified differently than patients demonstrating depressions in addition to undergoing manic episodes. The distinction was based on such variables as number of episodes of illness, chronicity, and treatment response. In the mid-1960's, three independent groups of investigators working in different countries produced data that supported Leonhard's distinction. Winokur and Clayton (1967), in the United States, separated affectively ill patients on the basis of presence or absence of a familial history of affective illness. Those who were manic at admission were likely to come from families in which there were two generations of affective illness. On the other hand, those who were depressed at admission were not likely to have familial histories of illness. Perris (1966), in Sweden, and Angst and Perris (1968), in Switzerland, also separated patients into two groups: those with depressions alone and those with depression and mania. They found that mania clustered in the families of probands who had experienced manic episodes. Thus, in the initial investigations, symptom patterns and family history distinguished the bipolar disorders, characterized by episodes of mania and depression, from depression, characterized by episodes of depression only. Subsequent research has confirmed these findings and, in addition, revealed many differentiating features between these two conditions.

Differential behavioral profiles for unipolar and bipolar illness

The current literature suggests that there are numerous differences between the characteristics of unipolar and bipolar depression that can assist the clinician in making diagnoses. Sleep disturbances characterize the depressed phase of all affective disorders. However, the type of sleep disturbance tends to distinguish the two types of affective disorder. For example, Detre and his colleagues (Detre, Himmelhoch, Swartzburg, Anderson, Byck, & Kupfer, 1972) found that patients with unipolar depression typically experienced insomnia, whereas bipolar patients more commonly experienced hypersomnia. Attempted and completed suicides are more likely in bipolar than in unipolar patients (Dunner, Gershon, & Goodwin, 1976). Beigel and Murphy (1971), in a study of anger, anxiety, and somatic complaints in bipolar and psychotic unipolar patients, found that anxiety did not differentiate the two groups. Anger was characteristic of the unipolar group, but was rarely found in the bipolar group. The anger was directed at the patients themselves, as well as displaced outward toward relatives and treating staff members. Of the unipolar patients, 68% also had higher ratings for somatic complaints when compared to their matched bipolar patient.

Disturbances of psychomotor activity are also common during depression. These take two main forms: psychomotor agitation (e.g., pacing, handwringing, pulling or rubbing on skin or clothing, outbursts of complaining or shouting, incessant talking) and psychomotor retardation (e.g., slowed speech, increased pauses, low or monotonous speech, muteness, slowed body movements). Beigel and Murphy (1971) investigated pacing as a differentiating clinical sign and found it to be both more frequent and more severe in the unipolar patient group. Bunney and Murphy (1973), in a later study, found that prolonged periods of psychomotor retardation characterized the depressed phase of bipolar illness. These general observations have subsequently been confirmed by other investigators (Kupfer, Weiss, Foster, Detre, Delgado, & McPartland, 1974; Dunner, Dwyer, & Fieve, 1976).

Several attempts have been made to differentiate the clinical courses of unipolar and bipolar affective illness according to age of onset of illness, number of episodes, and prognosis. Winokur, Clayton, and Reich (1969) found that bipolar illness often had an early onset; over 50% of the patients they studied suffered their first episode of illness before the age of 30. Angst and his colleagues (Angst, Baastrup, Grof, Hippius, Poldinger, & Weiss, 1973) studied over 1,000 patients and found that the median age of onset was 43 years in unipolar patients, but only 30 years in the bipolar patients. In long-term follow-up, the unipolar patients were observed to reach a limit of four to six recurrent episodes, whereas the bipolar patients had as many as seven to nine episodes. Evidence for more impairment between episodes in the bipolar group was also noted.

Although these unipolar-bipolar comparisons reflect differentiating characteristics, there is, nonetheless, sufficient overlap between these two disorders to limit application to individual patients in diagnosis. Despite this limitation, the clinical picture that emerges in unipolar depression patients is that of more anger directed at themselves or others, more somatic complaints while depressed, more hyposomnia, and higher levels of psychomotor agitation than in bipolar patients, who during depressive episodes have minimal anger, fewer somatic complaints, more hypersomnia, and more psychomotor retardation. Age of onset, frequency of episodes, suicide attempts, and inter-episodic impairment also appear to distinguish the two groups. Thus, it can be concluded that the clinical features of unipolar affective illness are quite different from that found in the bipolar condition.

Familial, genetic, and adoption data for unipolar and bipolar illness

The most compelling evidence for separating bipolar and unipolar illness has come from familial and genetic studies, demonstrating that relatives of patients differ in both the frequency and type of psychiatric disorder as a function of the classification of the proband.

FAMILIAL INVESTIGATIONS

Studies of the familial nature of affective disorders have been undertaken to ascertain the degree to which bipolar and unipolar groups "breed true" within a given family and to determine the ratio of ill to well individuals. As noted above, Winokur and Clayton (1967) and Angst and Perris (1968) found that individuals experiencing episodes of both depression and mania clustered within families of index cases of mania. In another study of the family histories of 59 mania patients, Reich, Clayton, and Winokur (1969) observed that the prevalence of affective disorder was higher in the families of bipolar than of unipolar patients. James and Chapman (1975) replicated these findings and also observed that affective illness in relatives of manics was usually of the unipolar type. In both of the above studies, the percentage of relatives with unipolar illness was found to be over twice the percentage of relatives with bipolar illness. These data are incompatible with the hypothesis that bipolar affective disorder "breeds true." However, the fact that familial studies have demonstrated that unipolar patients do not have a family history of bipolar illness can be interpreted as supporting the dichotomy between these two disorders.

Further support for a dichotomy was provided by Angst (1979), who reported that the age-corrected morbidity risk (defined as the percent estimate of individuals who develop a disorder if they survive the period of risk for that disorder) for bipolar illness in relatives of unipolar probands was 0.13, compared to an estimated 0.1 in the general population.

Again from Angst's data (1979), a morbidity risk of 14% was found for affective psychosis in parents and siblings of bipolar probands, whereas it was 26% for the combined spectrum of affective illnesses. In relatives of unipolar probands, however, the respective morbidity risks were 5% and 12%. Thus, the presence of bipolar illness in a family member places the child at much greater risk for developing an affective disorder than the presence of a unipolar illness.

The ratio of males to females among those who develop affective disorders remains an unsettled question. When all affective disorders are combined, female patients predominate (Helgason, 1964; Weissman & Klerman, 1977). However, the results are less conclusive with bipolar illness alone. Angst and Perris (1968), Hays (1976), and Angst (1979) concluded that for bipolar index cases, the number of male and female relatives affected is about equal. Reich, Clayton, and Winokur (1969),

James and Chapman (1975), and Mendlewicz and Rainer (1974), however, concluded that females outnumber males by approximately 2:1.
This sex difference was not present in the bipolar ill relatives of bipolar
index cases, but rather was produced solely by an excess of unipolar ill
females (Mendlewicz & Rainer, 1974).

TWIN STUDIES

Upon reviewing the twin studies pertaining to affective disorders, Allen
(1976) concluded that concordance and discordance rates distinguished
the two forms of affective illness. Monozygotic (MZ) bipolar twins were
found to have a concordance rate of 72% in comparison to only 40% for
MZ unipolar twins. Dyzygotic (DZ) bipolar twins had a concordance
rate of 14% in contrast to 11% for DZ unipolar twins. These results indicate that there is a greater genetic contribution in the etiology of bipolar
illness, whereas unipolar illness is more influenced by environmental
factors. Alternatively, it is possible that unipolar illness is simply a more
heterogeneous disorder and, thus, its etiology varies more.

LINKAGE STUDIES

Familial investigations suggested an X-linked mode of transmission for
bipolar illness, since disproportionate sex ratios among affectively ill
relatives and the absence of father-son transmission of the affective illnesses have been observed. In one study, Gershon, Targum, Matthysse,
and Bunney (1979) attempted to demonstrate linkage between bipolar
illness and the X-linked trait of red-green color blindness. Close linkage
was ruled out from their data, leading them to conclude that bipolar illness is not transmitted by a single major gene that is close to the region
of the X-chromosome, which transmits color blindness. On the other hand,
Mendlewicz and his colleagues (Mendlewicz, Linkowski, Guroff, & Van
Pragg, 1979) found evidence of linkage and concluded that a subgroup
of patients develop bipolar illness through an X-linked dominant genetic
transmission. Conflicting findings have also been reported for other
genetic markers on the X-chromosome (Leckman, Gershon, McGinnis,
Targum, & Dibble, 1979; Mendlewicz & Fleiss, 1974). Although these
investigations are far from conclusive, the value of this type of research
is apparent. If linkage does exist, then the individual at risk for the
development of bipolar illness can be identified by the linked trait. Conversely, absence of the trait would suggest minimal risk for that individual.

Since twin and linkage studies have not determined the relative contributions of genetic and environmental factors in the etiology of affective
disorders, adoption studies have been undertaken. So far, only a few
reports have been published, since there are considerable difficulties in
conducting adoption studies of the affective illnesses. The number of
affectively ill parents who place offspring for adoption is small compared
to parents with other psychiatric disorders, and those who do relinquish
their children are frequently either mentally retarded, alcoholic, antisocial, or schizophrenic, in addition to being depressed. Technical difficulties, such as access to the adoption register, selection bias, and morbidity of the subjects, also abound in adoption studies.

The first report of an adoption study of affective illness was published
by Mendlewicz and Rainer (1977). Their subjects were the adoptive
and biological parents of bipolar ill adoptees. Controls comprised the
biological parents of non-adopted bipolar patients, the adoptive and
biological parents of non-ill adoptees, and parents of patients suffering
from the disabling illness of poliomyelitis. The major finding was that
psychopathology in the biological parents of the bipolar ill adoptees
exceeded that found in the adoptive parents. The difference in the frequencies of affective spectrum illnesses (defined by the authors as bipolar
illness, unipolar illness, schizoaffective psychosis, and cyclothymia) in
these two groups was significant at the 0.025 level ($\chi^2 = 5.10$). The frequency of affective illness in the biological parents of the ill adoptees was
no different from the frequency in the parents of non-adopted bipolar
patients. Conversely, the lower frequency of illness in the adoptive
parents of the bipolar probands was similar to the frequency in the
other two control groups. These findings further support the role of
genetic factors in the etiology of bipolar illness.

Adoption studies have also been used to examine the incidence of
suicide in the biological and adoptive families of adoptees with depression. Kety (1979) and Schulsinger, Kety, Rosenthal, and Wender (1979)
found that the incidence of suicide in biological relatives was 3.9% (15
completed suicides in 381 relatives of 71 probands), whereas in adoptive
relatives it was 0.5% (1 suicide in 166 relatives). It was not clear whether
the authors separated unipolar and bipolar illness in these two investigations; however, further reports from these investigators are pending and
should clarify this vital issue.

In another study, Cadoret (1978) evaluated 83 adoptees who had a biological parent suffering from a psychiatric disorder. Eight of the adoptees had a primary affective disorder (5 bipolar and three unipolar). The incidence of depression was found to be significantly higher in the adoptees with a biological parent who had an affective disorder than in those whose biological parent had other psychiatric disorders.

Subtypes of unipolar depression

In the early 1970's, a study was published that suggested that unipolar depressive illness could be separated into two or more familially defined subgroups. In this study, Cadoret, Winokur, and Clayton (1970) found a preponderance of illness among daughters in families in which the mother was affectively ill, whereas the sex distribution for ill children was about equal in families in which the father was affectively ill.

A subsequent study (Winokur, Cadoret, Dorzab, & Baker, 1971) examined 100 inpatients with a Research Criteria Diagnosis of primary depression, but with no history of mania or hypomania in themselves or in any extended family member. The family study method was used to systematically evaluate 129 first-degree relatives. The familial pattern of illness revealed that first-degree female relatives were more likely to have a diagnosis of depression than male relatives. When probands were compared according to sex and time of illness onset, a disparity between the first-degree relatives of the early-onset depressed female patients and depressed male patients was observed. This disparity was not seen in the families of late-onset female patients or male patients. When the kinds of psychiatric illnesses that occurred in the relatives of the males and late-onset depressives were examined, alcoholism or sociopathy replaced the proportion of cases otherwise reflected as depression in the families of the female and early-onset groups.

When the probands were separated into early onset and late onset and male and female, a disparity between the incidence of depression in first-degree relatives was not noted. Higher familial incidences of depression were seen in the early-onset and female probands. From this study, the authors postulated two types of unipolar depressive illnesses. The first type has an early onset in females and is associated with depression in female relatives and more alcoholism or sociopathy in male relatives. This disorder was called "depressive spectrum disease" because of the link with other psychiatric illnesses in the families. The second type of

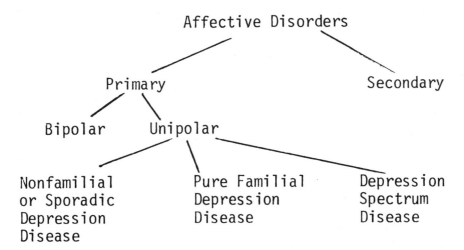

Fig. 10–1. Classification of depression based on familial constellations.

unipolar depression was labeled "pure depressive disease," since no psychiatric illness, other than depression, appeared in the families.

The distinction between subtypes of unipolar depression has been supported by subsequent research (Winokur, 1972; Winokur, Morrison, Clancy, & Crowe, 1973). Recently, investigators at the University of Iowa (Winokur, Behar, Van Valkenburg, & Lowry, 1978) were able to identify a third group of unipolar depressed patients: those with no family history of depression or other psychiatric illness. These patients, who had sporadic or nonfamilial depression, differed from other types of unipolar depressive patients on such variables as course and severity of illness. Thus, on the basis of the available evidence, a tripartite classification of unipolar depression based on familial constellations is proposed; the classification is diagrammatically represented in Figure 10-1.

Depression spectrum disease

Depression spectrum disease is a familial syndrome in which persons suffering from depression that meets rigorous diagnostic criteria have a first-degree relative with alcoholism or sociopathy and may or may not have a relative with depression. We believe that this syndrome is manifested as depression in some family members and as alcoholism or antisocial personality in others. Family members with depression are mostly women (2 to 1 ratio), whereas those with alcoholism and sociopathy are almost always men.

CLINICAL DEPRESSION

Since individuals with depression spectrum disease may suffer from depression, alcoholism, or sociopathy as adults (a recent study by Tanna, Winokur, Elston, & Go, 1976, gave less support to the association with sociopathy), clinical descriptions of each form of presentation are needed. The alcoholic family members are difficult to diagnose as also having depression because of symptom overlap (e.g., poor appetite, decreased concentration, low libido, low energy, disturbed sleep, thoughts of suicide), but they may well also be depressed. The depressed individuals are not alcoholic, nor do they have histories of antisocial behavior. However, they do have premorbid histories of problems that generally fall into the personality disorder realm, though these symptoms are not severe enough to warrant a strict diagnosis of personality disorder (Van Valkenburg & Winokur, 1979).

The first depressive episodes occur relatively early in life. Patients typically become depressed in their early 30's (Schlesser, Winokur, & Sherman, 1979; Winokur, Behar, Van Valkenburg, & Lowry, 1978). Once depressed, these patients do not appear to differ from patients with other subtypes of unipolar depression or with bipolar depression. The severity of depression as measured by the Hamilton Depression Scale is the same for the three proposed subtypes of unipolar depression (Schlesser et al., 1979); however, it should be noted that this conclusion is based on a comparison of global scores that did not include an analysis of either the individual symptoms or the six factor scores described by Cleary and Guy (1975).

The presence or absence of 25 depressive symptoms in depression spectrum and pure depressive patients was investigated by Van Valkenburg and colleagues (Van Valkenburg, Lowry, Winokur, & Cadoret, 1977). The spectrum patients differed significantly from the pure depressive patients in that they were much less likely to have lost interest in usual activities ($p < .005$); a finding that, the authors hypothesized, was due to chance. The spectrum group exhibited trends in the direction of increased hypochondriasis, anxiety attacks, and blaming others, whereas the pure depression group tended toward a more diurnal variation in mood. In light of the differences in behavioral profiles between bipolar and unipolar patients, the possibility that the symptomatic behavior of patients with one or the other subtype of unipolar depression resembles that of patients with bipolar depression warrants further research.

The prognosis for patients with depression spectrum disease, as reflected by the number of acute episodes, appears to be better than that for patients with either pure or sporadic depression. As a group, depression spectrum patients report about one-half the number of episodes of illness than do patients suffering from pure depression (Van Valkenburg et al., 1977).

BIOCHEMICAL DIFFERENTIATION OF DEPRESSION SPECTRUM DISEASE

Endocrine differences between the subtypes of unipolar depression have been recently reported. Using the dexamethasone suppression test in a study of 86 unipolar depressed patients, Schlesser, Winokur, and Sherman (1979) found that suppression characterized the spectrum group, whereas nonsuppression characterized the group with pure depression. Thus, spectrum patients have identical clinical pictures of depression when compared to familial pure depression patients, but exhibit different familial constellations and divergent responses to an endocrinological assessment of their hypothalamic-pituitary-adrenal functioning.

LINKAGE STUDIES OF DEPRESSION SPECTRUM DISEASE

Upon screening for several genetic markers in depression spectrum patients, Tanna and colleagues (1976; 1977; 1979) reported evidence of linkage with the third component of complement (C_3) and alpha-haptoglobin. These findings, however, should be viewed as tentative, until replicated by other investigators.

Familial pure depression disease

As previously noted, this syndrome involves an episode of depression that is diagnosed by rigorous criteria in a person who has a depressed first-degree relative, but whose family has no history of bipolar illness, alcoholism, or antisocial personality. It has been estimated that 25 to 33% of depressed patients belong to this group (Schlesser et al., 1979; Winokur et al., 1978).

CLINICAL DESCRIPTION

The mean age of onset of symptoms at 33.4 years (Winokur et al. 1978) differs both from those patients classified as having depression spectrum disease and from those exhibiting sporadic depressive disease. Other studies have confirmed the early age of onset in pure depressive disease (Andreasen & Winokur, 1979; Schlesser et al., 1979). In addition, Andreasen and Winokur (1979) have reported that the sex ratio in the pure depression type was comparable to the depression spectrum and the sporadic depression types.

The symptomatic profile and premorbid personalities of patients with pure depression have been examined in several studies. There is general agreement that no differences exist between the subtypes of unipolar depression when precipitating factors, endogenous phenomenology, and personality traits are considered.

Non-familial or sporadic depression disease

The diagnosis of non-familial or sporadic depressive disease is made when depressed persons do not have a family history of bipolar illness, alcoholism, sociopathy, or unipolar depression. The average age of onset and the age of index admission in these persons is much later than that found in patients with spectrum or pure depressive disease. Winokur et al. (1978) found that the mean age of onset was 41.2 years, almost 10 years later than the other groups. Patients suffering from sporadic depression disease fell between the pure depressives and spectrum depressives for mean number of prior admissions and acute episodes. Follow-up data did not differentiate the sporadic group from the pure depressives in regard to the number of subsequent episodes or hospitalizations, but there was a trend for less chronicity in the sporadic group. Results of the dexamethasone suppression test were intermediate (Schlesser et al., 1979). Also, the symptomatic profile was essentially the same as found in the other groups.

High risk research in affective disorders

Stress and life events

Much has been published in the psychiatric literature on the relationship between stress, separation or loss, and other life events, acting both as immediate precipitating causes and as more remote predisposing factors on the subsequent development of affective illness. However, generalizations about the etiology of psychiatric disorders are valid only if it can be demonstrated that the incidence of mental disorders is greater among individuals who experience similar life events than those who experience different life events.

Renaud and Estess (1955) studied the life histories of 100 normal males and found "as many traumatic events and pathogenic factors as are ordinarily elicited in interviews with many psychiatric patients." Oltman, McGarry, and Friedman (1952) investigated the significance of parental deprivation and broken homes for both normal and psychiatrically ill individuals. They found that normal and manic-depressive individuals did not differ with respect to the incidence of these life events. Pitts and colleagues (Pitts, Meyer, Brooks, & Winokur, 1965) systematically examined 748 consecutive psychiatric admissions for evidence of parental deprivation, using consecutive medical or surgical admissions to the same hospital as a control group. There were no significant differences in parental deprivation in childhood for the psychiatrically ill group, as a whole, or for any diagnostic subgroup, including affective disorders. Thus, when the base rate in the general population is controlled, the presumed predisposing factor of parental loss does not distinguish the child who is at risk for affective illness.

These studies do not address the issue of heterogeneity in affective illnesses. Since genetic and family studies indicate that affective disorders can be meaningfully subtyped, the significance of life events and various stressors needs to be examined in each "homogeneous" subtype to elucidate the role of environmental precipitating and predisposing factors. Some preliminary studies have been made in this area. Perris (1965), for example, reported more unfavorable home situations in early life for bipolar than for unipolar patients and more somatic factors in unipolar than in bipolar patients. Cadoret and co-workers (1972) examined the relationship between life events and the onset of illness in unipolar depressed patients grouped as early onset and late onset. They controlled the base rate of life events by determining the corresponding rate in non-ill relatives. An increased incidence of real or threatened personal losses in the year preceding hospitalization was noted in the early-onset subgroup. This subgroup probably constituted patients exhibiting depressive spectrum disease, suggesting that life events may play an important role in this type of unipolar depression.

How may we now apply these findings concerning life events to the problem of identifying the child at risk for affective disorder? It is apparent that the incidence of traumatic life events occurring in childhood does not distinguish those who develop affective illness from those who

do not. On the other hand, if genetic predisposition were the sole etiological factor, one would expect a hereditary pattern as definite as that
of Huntington's chorea. An individual possessing the abnormal gene
would develop the illness in any environment. Differences in age of onset, rate of progression, and symptomatic profiles would reflect different
genetic strains among afflicted kin (Davenport & Muncey, 1916). Twin
studies do support the role of genetic factors in the etiology of affective
disorders, but a 28% rate of discordance for bipolar illness in MZ twins
and a 60% rate of discordance for unipolar illness indicate the importance of environmental factors as well (Allen, 1976).

The retrospective method of tracing back from "effect" toward "cause"
has not been very helpful in elucidating environmental factors in depression. On the other hand, prospective investigations involving the general
population, or a subpopulation that has experienced various adverse life
events, are prohibitively costly to conduct. Any attempt to identify the
risk factors for affective disorders, when only 2 to 4% of the general
population are afflicted, would require an enormous sample size. Instead,
it is proposed that a better strategy would be to utilize familial and genetic data in selecting a subpopulation at risk for developing an affective
disorder. Within this high risk group, the impact of other factors on the
subsequent development of an affective illness could then be delineated.

High risk research methods

Longitudinal and cross-section designs are the two basic methodologies
in prospective research. In the longitudinal design, data on target and
control groups are collected at intervals over a period of time. Collection
of data is started well in advance of the onset of illness and is terminated
when a final assessment of outcome can be made. The major advantage
of this procedure is the opportunity to observe the onset and sequential
development of pathology. The disadvantages include a time commitment that can exceed three decades, high cost, restriction of sampling
to cooperative individuals who must also be available for follow-up, high
attrition, and the inability to incorporate into the study scientific advances as they develop. In a cross-sectional design, target and control
groups are sampled at one or more points in time and then are compared
on a number of variables. This design requires less time between collection and analysis of data. There are also lower costs, less attrition, and
less conceptual and technical obsolescence than a longitudinal investiga-

tion. The major disadvantage is that it is not possible to observe the sequential development of pathology.

A convergent design, which combines the best of both strategies and is applicable in high risk research on affective disorders, can be used. This involves a series of overlapping, cross-sectional follow-up studies in which the subjects in each study are from different, evenly spaced age groups. Each group's data set bridges with the next older group so as to provide a continuous evaluation over a wide age span. By using genetic criteria to select the high risk groups, comparable analogous samples can be obtained. This technique, however, is not without its limitations. For example, the problem of obtaining comparable assessments across the differently aged samples is difficult. Nonetheless, this paradigm affords the opportunity for obtaining meaningful data within a relatively limited time period.

We have already described how the use of genetic criteria in selecting subjects for studies of bipolar affective disorder, unipolar pure depression, and unipolar depressive spectrum disorders can facilitate the identification of high risk individuals. Genetic criteria, however, do not appear to be helpful in identifying sporadic depression disorder. For the bipolar, pure depressive, and depressive spectrum disorders, the morbid risk for children of ill parents can be accurately estimated. Thus, given a knowledge of expectancy rates, follow-up studies, generated in appropriately selected samples, utilize repeated measurements. By conducting such a prospective investigation of the subtypes of affective disorders, a better understanding of the state variables will evolve, and ultimately one or more trait variables will be delineated to identify the child at risk.

References

Allen, M. Twin studies of affective illness. *Archives of General Psychiatry*, 1976, *33*, 1476–1478.

American Psychiatric Association. *Diagnostic and statistical manual of mental disorders* (Third Ed.). Washington D.C., 1980.

Andreasen, N. & Winokur, G. Newer experimental methods for classifying depression. *Archives of General Psychiatry*, 1979, *36*, 447–452.

Angst, J. The reliability of morbidity risk figures in affective disorders: Results of a reinvestigation. In J. Mendlewicz & B. Shopsin (Eds.), *Genetic aspects of affective illness*. New York: SP Medical & Scientific Books, 1979.

Angst, J. & Perris, C. Zur nosologie endogener depressionen. *Archiv fur Psychiatrie und nervenkrankheiten*, 1968, *210*, 373–386.

Angst, J., Baastrup, P., Grof, P., Hippius, H., Poldinger, W., & Weiss, P. The course of monopolar depression and bipolar psychoses. *Psychiatrica, Neurologica et Neurochirurgia*, 1973, *76*, 489–500.

Beigel, A. & Murphy, D. Unipolar and bipolar affective illness: Differences in clinical characteristics accompanying depression. *Archives of General Psychiatry*, 1971, *24*, 215–220.

Bunney, W. & Murphy, D. The behavioral switch process and psychopathology. In J. Mendels (Ed.), *Biological psychiatry*. New York: Wiley-Interscience, 1973.

Cadoret, R. Evidence for genetic inheritance of primary affective disorder in adoptees. *American Journal of Psychiatry*, 1978, *135*, 463–466.

Cadoret, R., Winokur, G., & Clayton, P. Family history studies: VII. Manic depressive disease versus depressive disease. *British Journal of Psychiatry*, 1970, *116*, 625–635.

Cadoret, R., Winokur, G., Dorzab, J., & Baker, M. Depressive disease: Life events and onset of illness. *Archives of General Psychiatry*, 1972, *26*, 133–136.

Cleary, P. & Guy, W. *Factor analyses of the Hamilton Depression Scale*. Paper presented at the International Symposium on the Evaluation of New Drugs in Clinical Psychopharmacology, Pisa, Italy, September, 1975.

Davenport, C. & Muncey, E. Huntington's chorea in relation to heredity and eugenics. *American Journal of Insanity*, 1916, *73*, 195–222.

Detre, T., Himmelhoch, J., Swartzburg, M., Anderson, C., Byck, R., & Kupfer, D. Hypersomnia and manic-depressive disease. *American Journal of Psychiatry*, 1972, *128*, 1303–1305.

Dunner, D., Dwyer, T., & Fieve, R. Depressive symptoms in patients with unipolar and bipolar affective disorder. *Comprehensive Psychiatry*, 1976, *17*, 447–451.

Dunner, D., Gershon, E., & Goodwin, F. Heritable factors in the severity of affective illness. *Biological Psychiatry*, 1976, *11*, 31–42.

Gershon, E., Targum, S., Matthysse, S., & Bunney, W. Color blindness not closely linked to bipolar illness. *Archives of General Psychiatry*, 1979, *36*, 1423–1430.

Hays, P. Etiological factors in manic-depressive psychoses. *Archives of General Psychiatry*, 1976, *33*, 1187–1188.

Helgason, T. Epidemiology of mental disorders in Iceland. *Acta Psychiatrica Scandinavica*, 1964, *40* (Suppl. 173, p. 258).

James, N. & Chapman, C. A genetic study of bipolar affective disorder. *British Journal of Psychiatry*, 1975, *126*, 449–456.

Kety, S. Disorders of the human brain. *Scientific American*, 1979, 202–214.

Kraepelin, E. *Manic-depressive insanity and paranoia*. Edinburgh, Scotland: Livingstone, 1921.

Kupfer, D., Weiss, B., Foster, G., Detre, T., Delgado, J., & McPartland, R. Psychomotor activity in affective states. *Archives of General Psychiatry*, 1974, *30*, 765–768.

Leckman, J., Gershon, E., McGinnis, M., Targum, S. & Dibble, E. New data do not suggest linkage between the Xg blood group and bipolar illness. *Archives of General Psychiatry*, 1979, *36*, 1435–1441.

Leonhard, K. *Aufteilung der endogenen psychosen* (First Ed.), Berlin: Akademieverlag, 1957.

Mendlewicz, J. & Fleiss, J. Linkage studies with X-chromosomal markers in bipolar and unipolar illness. *Biological Psychiatry*, 1974, *9*, 261–294.

Mendlewicz, J. & Rainer, J. Morbidity risk and genetic transmission in manic-depressive illness. *American Journal of Human Genetics*, 1974, *26*, 692–701.

Mendlewicz, J. & Rainer, J. Adoption study supporting genetic transmission in manic-depressive illness. *Nature*, 1977, *268*, 327–329.

Mendlewicz, J., Linkowski, P., Guroff, J., & Van Praag, H. Color blindness linkage to bipolar manic-depressive illness. *Archives of General Psychiatry*, 1979, *36*, 1442–1447.

Oltman, J., McGarry, J., & Friedman, S. Parental deprivation and the "broken home" in dementia praecox and other mental disorders. *American Journal of Psychiatry*, 1952, *108*, 685–694.

Perris, C. A study of bipolar (manic-depressive) and unipolar recurrent depressive psychoses. *Acta Psychiatrica Scandinavica* (Suppl. 194), 1966, *42*, 15–189.

Pitts, F., Meyer, J., Brooks, M., & Winokur, G. Adult psychiatric illness assessed for childhood parental loss, and psychiatric illness in family members—a study of 748 patients and 250 controls. *American Journal of Psychiatry* (Suppl.), 1965, *121*, 1–10.

Reich, T., Clayton, P., & Winokur, G. Family history studies: V. The genetics of mania. *American Journal of Psychiatry*, 1969, *125*, 1358–1369.

Renaud, H. & Estess, F. Life history interviews with 100 normal American males: Pathogenicity of childhood. *American Psychologist*, 1955, *10*, 371.

Schlesser, M., Winokur, G., & Sherman, B. Genetic subtypes of unipolar primary depressive illness distinguished by hypothalamic-pituitary-adrenal axis activity. *Lancet*, 1979, *1*, 739–741.

Schulsinger, F., Kety, S., Rosenthal, D., & Wender, P. A family study of suicide. In M. Schou & E. Stromgen (Eds.), *Origin, prevention and treatment of affective disorders*. New York: Academic Press, 1979.

Tanna, V., Go, R., Winokur, G., & Elston, R. Possible linkage between group-specific component (Gc protein) and pure depressive disease. *Acta Psychiatrica Scandinavica*, 1977, *55*, 111–115.

Tanna, V., Go, R., Winokur, G., & Elston, R. Possible linkage between alpha-haptoglobin (Hp) and depression spectrum disease. *Neuropsychobiology*, 1979, *5*, 102–113.

Tanna, V., Winokur, G., Elston, R., & Go, R. A linkage study of depression spectrum disease: The use of the sib-pair method. *Neuropsychobiology*, 1976, *2*, 52–62.

Van Valkenburg, C., Lowry, M., Winokur, G., & Cadoret, R. Depression spectrum disease vs. pure depressive disease. Clinical, personality and course differences. *Journal of Nervous and Mental Disease*, 1977, *165*, 341–347.

Van Valkenburg, C. & Winokur, G. Depression spectrum disease. *Psychiatric Clinics of North America,* 1979, *2,* 469–482.

Weissman, M. & Klerman, G. Sex differences and the epidemiology of depression. *Archives of General Psychiatry,* 1977, *34,* 98–109.

Winokur, G. Types of depressive illness. *British Journal of Psychiatry,* 1972, *120,* 265–266.

Winokur, G. & Clayton, P. In J. Wortis (Ed.), *Recent advances in biological psychiatry* (Vol. 9). New York: Plenum Press, 1967.

Winokur, G., Behar, D., Van Valkenburg, C., & Lowry, M. Is a familial definition of depression both feasible and valid? *Journal of Nervous and Mental Disease,* 1978, *166,* 764–768.

Winokur, G., Cadoret, R., Dorzab, J., & Baker, M. Depressive disease: A genetic study. *Archives of General Psychiatry,* 1971, *24,* 135–144.

Winokur, G., Clayton, P., & Reich, T. *Manic depressive illness.* St. Louis: C. V. Mosby, 1969.

Winokur, G., Morrison, J., Clancy, J., & Crowe, R. The Iowa 500: Familial and clinical findings favor two kinds of depressive illness. *Comprehensive Psychiatry,* 1973, *14,* 99–106.

11. Neurotic conditions

H. J. Eysenck

Neurosis and neuroticism

The concept of "neurosis" is inevitably somewhat ambiguous, so ambiguous in fact that the term has been officially dropped by the American Psychiatric Association in favor of more highly specific neurotic disorders. If the term neurosis is used in the context of a medical model of disordered human behavior, that is, with obvious implications of specific etiology and treatment, then such a diagnosis may be reasonable. However, most psychologists reject the medical model of neurotic conditions and prefer to look upon neurotic disorders as learned behavior patterns that are probably acquired through a process of conditioning, and subject to extinction (Eysenck, 1979, 1980a). This latter point of view is best conceptualized in terms of a dimensional system of description, in contrast to the medical view of separate "diseases" that are qualitatively different from each other (Eysenck, 1970a, b). Such a dimensional system is conceptualized best in relation to the "diathesis-stress" theory that is widely accepted in connection with neurotic disorders. Figure 11-1 represents the theory diagrammatically. The abscissa represents varying degrees of predisposition to the formation of neurotic symptoms ("neuroticism"), whereas the ordinate represents the proportion of people in the population manifesting the varying degree of predisposition. The distribution need not be normal, of course, but the evidence suggests that it does not depart very far from normality (Eysenck & Eysenck, 1969).

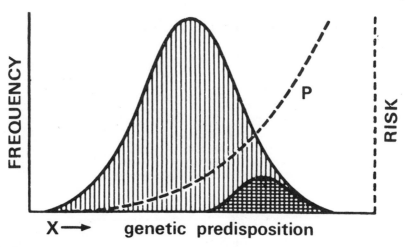

X   Genetic predisposition

|||| Frequency distribution in the population

P   Likelihood of being affected at a particular level of x

▦   Frequency distribution of affected individuals

Fig. 11–1. Diagrammatic representation of the diathesis-stress model of mental disorder.

The line marked *p* reflects the increasing probability that a person at a given position on the abscissa (that is, having a given score on a test of neuroticism) would actually suffer a neurotic disorder. The cross-hatched distribution curve at the right-hand end of the abscissa indicates the subpopulation actually diagnosed as suffering from a neurotic disorder at a given time. The diagram is strongly idealized, since in real life the congruence between neurosis and neuroticism (that is, diathesis or predisposition) and actual disorder would not be as close. Nevertheless, Figure 11-1 illustrates how neurosis is conceived of as occurring in predisposed individuals with the degree of predisposition being normally distributed in the population.

In order to accommodate all the various *kinds* of neurotic disorder that are commonly recognized, we require more than one descriptive dimension. Jung (1924) recognized this need by postulating that "hysterical" disorders differed profoundly from "psychasthenic" ones. He suggested that these types of disorder were related to his concepts of introversion

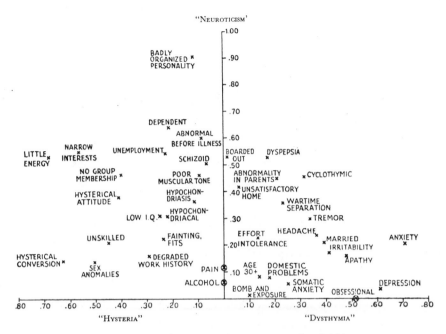

Fig. 11–2. The two aspects of neurosis. (From Eysenck, 1947.)

and extraversion, with hysterics being more extraverted and psychasthenics being more introverted. Eysenck (1947) tested this hypothesis in a factor analytic study of 700 neurotic military service patients whose symptoms were intercorrelated. The results are presented in Figure 11-2. The introverted constellation of symptoms was named "dysthymia," since the term "psychasthenia" had become obsolete. It can be seen that dysthymic disorders involved mainly anxiety, depression, obsessional features, apathy, and irritability. The hysterical disorders, on the other hand, consisted of hysterical attitudes, conversion symptoms, narrow interests, little energy, and hypochondriasis. Later work revealed that antisocial and psychopathic behavior are also characteristic of this group (Eysenck, 1977).

In another study, the behaviors of 2,113 boys were intercorrelated and factor-analyzed. Similar patterns were obtained (Eysenck, 1970a). The extraverted group of disorders emerged as "conduct problems," with antisocial behaviors highly represented, whereas the introverted group presented mainly "personality problems." Figure 11-3 indicates clearly

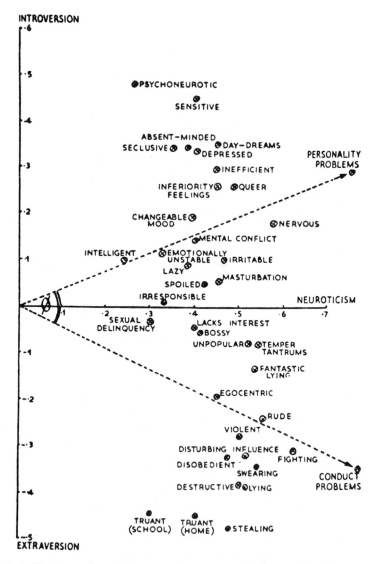

Fig. 11–3. Extraverted and introverted patterns of neurotic behavior in children. (From Eysenck, 1970a.)

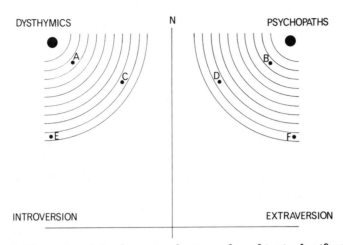

Fig. 11–4. Illustration of the dimensional system of psychiatric classification.

that the two sets of problems are themselves correlated, justifying the postulation of a "neuroticism" dimension.

Eysenck and Rachman (1965) provided a detailed account of the nature of what they called "disorders of the first and second kind"; that is, the introverted and extraverted disorders, respectively. It is not suggested that all neurotics must be either one kind or the other. The majority are expected to lie somewhere in the middle (ambivert), with complex symptoms involving divergent functions. Figure 11-4 illustrates what is involved. Certain combinations of neuroticism and extraversion produce the "ideal" psychopath. Similarly, a particular combination of neuroticism and introversion produces the "ideal" dysthymic. These two conditions can be diagnosed with considerable reliability by different psychiatrists, but such "ideal" combinations of neuroticism and extraversion are rare. Far more frequent are combinations indicated by persons A, B, C, D, E, and F; and how these are diagnosed depends very much on chance or the particular idiosyncratic ideas of the individual psychiatrist. A detailed discussion of these problems is given in successive editions of Eysenck's *Handbook of Abnormal Psychology* (1961, 1973).

This type of analysis has, however, been criticized. Foulds (1965), in a detailed discussion of neurotic disorders, makes a clear distinction between traits and attitudes and signs and symptoms. Three major differences are proposed to illustrate the distinctions:

1. Traits and attitudes, unlike symptoms and signs, are universal
2. Traits and attitudes are relatively ego-syntonic, whereas symptoms and signs are distressful
3. Traits and attitudes (particularly the former) are relatively enduring

In this conceptualization it is argued that hysteria could not merely be a combination of high extraversion (E) and high neuroticism (N), or dysthmia a combination of low E and high N. He views the emergence of these conditions as involving more complex processes and, in so doing, distinguishes between traits and attitudes and signs and symptoms. The distinction Foulds (1965) makes, although it is appealing in the abstract, is less clear cut in the concrete. For example, whereas traits such as "worrying" are universal and relatively enduring, they are also characteristic of neurotic disorders, but are certainly not ego-syntonic. Should such traits be regarded rather as symptoms and signs? The answer must surely be that there is no obvious distinction between the two sets of concepts; extreme introversion, for example, is certainly a personal trait, but it is also experienced by the person concerned as distressful and non-ego-syntonic. Thus, although Foulds (1965) identifies the problem, he does not offer a satisfactory solution.

The difficulty with making a clear distinction between normal personality traits and abnormal signs and symptoms is readily illustrated with another example provided by Foulds. He states: "A trait, or attitude, may be *common,* if the position on the particular variable is one that is shared by many other people; or it may be uncommon, if it is rarely found in the same degrees in others—for example, extreme conscientiousness. Reference is to inter-individual variation. It should be noted that a change from even extreme conscientiousness to over-conscientiousness is not a linear extension, but a step-function. Over-conscientiousness implies that the individual finds his preoccupation with rectitude distressful. The step is from an attitude to a symptom."

The issue is somewhat question-begging. Of course extremes along a continuum are less common than intermediate steps; extreme overconscientiousness is less common than average degrees of conscientiousness. Does this simple statistical fact require us to posit a qualitative change? Consider the problem of identifying the hyperactive child. To what extent is such a child merely the extreme on a continuum, and to what extent is he to be regarded as a psychiatric problem, differing qualitatively from other children (Satterfield, 1978)? Ultimately, the answer must be found in terms of statistical models and experimental testing of these models along the lines of criterion analysis (Eysenck, 1950). Results so far obtained suggest that the distinction posed by Foulds is not observed in neurotic and psychotic patients, since we find continuity instead of discontinuity (Eysenck, 1952). Neurosis, as we shall see, can best be regarded as a temporary exacerbation of latent traits, catalyzed by specific events (stresses) leading to the establishment of autonomic conditioned responses. As such, it fits well into the model illustrated in Figure 11-1 as occupying an extreme position on the diathesis variable.

We may conclude this section by stating briefly that neurosis is conceptualized here in terms of a diathesis-stress model of disorder. In this view, neurosis is considered to be the outcome of predisposition (diathesis) and environmental stress. Two major kinds of disorder can be distinguished: disorders of the first kind and disorders of the second kind, but these are merely extremes on a set of continua, with many intermediate symptomatologies. No categorical system of diagnosis, based on the medical model of disease entities, can do justice to the complexity of facts. Dimensional models of the kind outlined are required. Before turning to the origin of neurotic disorders, we will discuss the genetics and psychophysiology of neuroticism and extraversion–introversion.

Genetics of polygenic traits

Although it has been widely accepted for some time that physique and intelligence were determined to a large extent by genetic factors, there was little evidence for such a genetic determination for personality. Observed inter-individual differences were almost entirely attributed to environmental influences. Insofar as there was speculation about the nature of these environmental influences, they were usually believed to be of the *between family* kind, rather than of the *within family* kind. This is an important distinction, with far-reaching implications. Two children born into different families may differ from each other because of the differing socioeconomic status of their parents, their different schooling, and the differing methods of child upbringing practiced by their parents. These are *between family* environmental determinants. On the other hand, two children born into the same family may differ from each other because of accidental features of their lives, such as that one has a good teacher, the other a bad one, although they go to the same school; that one is frequently ill and misses much schooling; that one chances upon a sex partner early on, the other one not; and so forth. These are *within family* environmental factors making for personality differences, and, as stated above, have usually been neglected by psychologists in favor of between family determinants. As it happens, the traditional emphasis on environmental factors to the almost complete exclusion of genetic ones and the emphasis on *between family* factors to the almost complete exclusion of *within family* influences are contrary to the best available evidence. Personality, like intelligence, has approximately 75% of the total variance accounted for by genetic factors, and 25% by environmental contribution, of which the latter are almost entirely due to within family rather than to between family factors. A thorough review of the methods and results of recent genetic work in the area of personality is provided elsewhere (Eysenck, 1976a; Fulker, 1980).

The difficulty in presenting a comprehensive discussion of genetic methodology is that the field is a very technical one and psychologists are typically not familiar with the basics of modern behavioral genetics. In a biometrical genetical analysis (Mather & Jinks, 1971), use is made of a number of strategies, such as that furnished by the study of twins separated at an early age and brought up in different environments; comparisons between monozygotic (MZ) (identical) and dizygotic (DZ) (fraternal) twins; resemblance of adopted children to either their biological or their adoptive parents; familial similarity as a function of consanguinity; inbreeding depression produced by the parents being themselves related; and genetic regression to the mean, to mention a few of the more common techniques. It is quite erroneous to think of genetic studies as relying exclusively on comparisons between MZ and DZ twins; although these can be very informative, they are by no means the only, or even necessarily the preferred method of obtaining information. In fact, no single method of data collection is free of assumptions and possible criticisms. It is because the different methods yield congruent results that we infer that the quantitative estimates presented here have some claim to validity. Unfortunately, it is not possible here to enter into detailed technical accounts of the methods employed. Readers searching for such a discussion are referred to Fulker (1980).

One crucial concept is *heritability,* defined as the proportion of phenotypic variance attributable to genetic factors. By commencing with the measurement of a particular character (trait, ability, attitude, etc.), the task is then to break down the total variance of the phenotype into various components that have genetic meaning. The general formula for this can be described as follows:

$$V_P = (V_G + V_{AM} + V_D + V_{EP}) + (V_E + Cov_{GE} + V_{GE}) + V_e$$
$$= V_H \text{ (Heredity)} + V_E \text{ (Environment)} + \text{(Error)}$$

In this formula, V_P denotes phenotypic variance and V_G denotes additive genetic variance. The non-additive components are given by V_{AM} (assortative mating), V_D (dominance), and V_{EP} (epistasis or interaction among genes at two or more loci); V_E denotes environmental variance and V_e denotes error variance (unreliability). There are two terms denoting interaction between environment and heredity: Cov_{GE} denotes the covariance of heredity and environment and it arises when genotypic values and environmental values are correlated in the population, as, for instance, when genotypically bright children are reared in homes with superior environmental advantages. Some geneticists include Cov_{GE} as part of the total genetic variance, rather than as part of the environmental variance because the causal element is genetic. *Statistical interaction,* V_{GE}, reflects the fact that different genotypes may respond differently to the same environmental effect. Most formulae for the estimation of heritability include V_e as part of the environmental variance, but strictly speaking this is incorrect. An appropriate correction for unreliability in the measuring instument should always be made, or alternately the portion of the total phenotypic variance due to error should be specified.

The major variance components in the above formula can be further partitioned into a between family component and a within family component. The between family component, G_2 in the case of the genetic variance, is that proportion of the variance relatives have in common by virtue of common ancestry. The within family component, G_1, is that proportion of the variance they do not share in common, since relatives receive a random selection of genes from their ancestral pool. The between family component E_2, in the case of the environmental variance, is shared in common by virtue of the individual being reared in the same family setting. The within family component E_1 is the variance not shared in common by individuals reared in the same family, since some environmental variation occurs within the family setting.

Given this definition and scope of heritability, it is possible to assess heritability narrowly by considering only the additive genetic variance or broadly by also including non-additive genetic variance. The formulae, accordingly, are as follows:

$$h^2_n = \frac{V_G}{V_P}$$

$$h^2_b = \frac{V_G + V_{AM} + V_D + V_{EP}}{V_P}$$

These formulae are widely used, but they do not in fact constitute proper genetic estimates of heritability, although the results are often presented as such. For example, the formulae prepared by Holzinger (1929), Neel and Schull (1954), and Nichols (1965) fall into this group. Proper formulations of the biometrical genetical analysis of human behavior have been developed by Mather and Jinks (1971), and a simplified account of these methods, together with an application to the analysis of the genetics of human intelligence and personality, can be found in Jinks and Fulker (1970). The essential point to grasp about the methods of genetic analysis now coming to the fore is that different kinds and degrees of kinship can be used to estimate the various terms of the general formula. In addition, it is sometimes possible to carry out direct studies to establish the likely amount of particular contributions. Thus, to illustrate the latter point, it is possible to study the degree of assortative mating (V_{AM}) taking place in a given population with respect to a particular trait by a direct study of the mating couples. To illustrate the former point, estimates of the dominance variance (V_D) can be obtained from a comparison of half siblings (of the same mother) and full siblings, or by looking for "inbreeding depression," that is, a lowering of scores found in the offspring of genetically related couples.

It should be clear that the aim of modern biometrical genetical analysis is not only, or even mainly, to discover the heritability of a given trait or ability. This is of interest only in the context of a wider study of genetic architecture. Rather, what we are interested in is the analysis of all the causal factors that enter into the variation observed in a given population that includes both genetic and environmental factors, additive and non-additive, and involves an analysis of the interactions and covariations between the genetic and environmental factors. This approach contrasts markedly with the environmentalistic bias so prevalent in modern sociology and social psychology, which disregards genetic hypotheses almost completely.

Thus, heritability cannot be interpreted as an absolute figure. It is a population statistic that refers to a given population and cannot be extrapolated to other populations. Studies carried out in the United States or in the United Kingdom (which give very similar results) do not necessarily tell us anything about the heritability of the traits or abilities in question in other countries, such as India or China. Neither do they necessarily tell us anything about the heritability of these traits in the United States or in the United Kingdom at some other period in history. Moreover, the fact that our heritability estimates refer to *populations* makes it impossible to apply the conclusions to particular *persons*. Because heritability accounts for 75% of the total variance in neuroticism or extraversion does not mean that for Mr. Smith or Mrs. Jones heredity accounts for the same proportion of their phenotype behavior! Nor can we say, because a particular type of behavior is strongly determined by genetic factors, that environmental factors will have no influence. For instance, phenylketonuria (PKU) is caused by a single recessive autosomal gene. Recognition that the disorder is due to the lack of one enzyme, which leads to toxic poisoning because of the inability of the body to convert phenylalanine to tyrosine, led to the practice of giving afflicted babies a low phenylalanine diet, thus bypassing the metabolic problem and avoiding brain damage in children with this disorder (Shields, 1973). A population in which routine determination of PKU is practiced, as well as the following of appropriate dietary measures, would yield an entirely different heritability coefficient for mental defect than one that fails to do so. Thus, a number of restrictions must be borne in mind in considering the interpretation of genetic data.

The inheritance of neuroticism

The view that personality was little influenced by genetic factors was originally expressed by Newman, Freeman, and Holzinger (1937). As a result of their investigations, they concluded that "physical characteristics are least affected by the environment, that intelligence is affected more; educational achievement still more; and personality or temperament, if our tests can be relied upon, the most. This finding is significant, regardless of the absolute amount of the environmental influence." There are good reasons for doubting the validity of the conclusion, as far as personality is concerned. Two main criticisms may be made of their study.

In the first place, the tests used would not now be regarded as either reliable or valid. They included the Kent-Rosanoff Scale, the Pressey Cross-Out Test, and the Downey Will-Temperament Test. Even if they could be regarded as reliable and valid, the question would still have to be asked, Valid for what? Of the tests used, the Woodworth-Matthews Inventory is the only one on which detailed statistics are presented. We discover that for MZ twins the intra-class correlation is .562, whereas for DZ twins it is .371; and for MZ twins brought up separately, it is .583. If we regard, as these authors certainly did, that this questionnaire is an inventory of neurotic tendency (neuroticism), then we would seem to have some indication of the importance of heredity, seeing that both groups of MZ twins are distinctly superior in intraclass correlation to the DZ twins. Moreover, the MZ twins brought up separately are more, rather than less, alike than are MZ twins brought up together. From these figures we can conclude that neuroticism has qiute a substantial heritability, particularly when the data are corrected for unreliability of the testing instrument, which undoubtedly was quite high. Oddly enough, the authors comment that "the Woodworth-Matthews Test appears to show no very definite trend in correlations, possibly because of the nature of the trait and also because of the unreliability of the measure." It is not clear to the present writer why this definite trend is denied; it seems fairly clear that MZ twins, whether brought up separately or together, are more alike than are DZ twins.

The second criticism is that the personality tests used in these studies were essentially tests for adults. The Woodworth-Matthews Inventory, for instance, was constructed specifically for selection purposes for the Army and in hospitals, and it is quite inadmissible to use tests of this kind on children (the average age of the whole group of MZ and DZ twins was only about 13 years). No details are given, but it is clear that there must have been children as young as eight or even younger in this group. It is thus doubtful whether a large proportion of the children were in a position to understand the terms used in the tests so as to give meaningful replies to them. The only conclusion one can draw from this study must be that there is some evidence for genetic determination of individual differences in neuroticism. The heritability figure, when corrected for unreliability of the measuring instrument, is almost certainly not less than 50%, and possibly is much higher.

A study by Carter (1935) yielded similar results for 55 pairs of MZ twins and 43 pairs of same sex DZ twins. For neuroticism, the intraclass correlations for MZ and DZ twins were .63 and .32, respectively. Many other studies, reviewed by Eysenck (1976a), exhibited similar trends.

A series of British studies emphasized the measurement of *super factors* rather than concentrating on the relatively minor primary ones. A study by Eysenck and Prell (1952) illustrates this approach. They argued that objective tests of behavior are superior to personality questionnaires, particularly when used on children. They also argued that such concepts as neuroticism are essentially based on the notion of *intercorrelated traits and measurements* and that twin studies carried out on single measures confound the issue by confusing variance due to the trait under investigation with specific variance relative to the test in question. They proposed, therefore, that a battery of tests be administered and factor-analyzed so that a score based on the combination of tests having the highest saturation for the factor in question could be utilized. In addition, they suggested that these factor scores be validated against some form of external control. In so doing they compared an experimental group of children under treatment at a child guidance clinic with normal children in school, demonstrating significant differences in neuroticism between the two groups (Eysenck & Prell, 1952).

Using this approach, Eysenck and Prell (1952) found that the factor score derived from all the tests yielded an intraclass correlation of .851 for MZ twins and .217 for DZ twins. This factor score showed a greater difference between MZ and DZ twins than any single constituent test, thus suggesting that it was indeed a general factor of neuroticism that was inherited rather than specific variance for any single test. The Holzinger h^2 coefficient revealed a hereditary determination of .810, if we are willing to assume that this coefficient can be used to determine hereditary estimation in this situation.

Of particular importance is the work of Shields (1962) in evaluating the thesis that heredity plays a larger part in the determination of personality traits than hitherto had been suspected. He investigated a sample of 44 separated MZ pairs of twins, 44 non-separated MZ control pairs, and 32 pairs of DZ twins, of which 11 pairs had been brought up apart. For neuroticism he found that the DZ pairs of twins had an intraclass correlation of only .11, whereas the MZ twins showed a correlation of .38 when brought up together and .53 when brought up separately. These results are similar, though much more definitive, than those obtained by

Newman et al. (1937), especially in their demonstration of greater intra-class correlation in the separated MZ twins than of those who were brought up together!

Shields' data were reanalyzed by Jinks and Fulker (1970). They found no evidence for an environment–heredity interaction or for correlated environments. The authors were able to fit a simple additive genetic and within family factors model to the data, showing that both were clearly significant. There was no evidence for assortative mating, and equally, there was no evidence for the presence of dominant gene action. This suggests that an intermediate level of neuroticism has been favored by natural selection, which constitutes a population optimum for this personality trait.

Further tests confirmed the adequacy of the model that has been found to fit the data extremely well. After correcting for unreliability in the measuring instrument, heritability has been found to exceed the 70% level. Cattell, Blewett, and Beloff (1955) employed the Cattell scales, of which two factors (C, or emotional stability, and Q4, or nervous tension) are closely related to neuroticism. These investigators assessed 52 pairs of MZ twins reared together, 32 pairs of DZ twins reared together, 91 pairs of full sibs reared togther, 31 pairs of full sibs reared apart, and 36 pairs of unrelated individuals reared together. Cattell applied an elaborate system of analysis, but unfortunately, conceptual and statistical problems render his analysis unreliable (Fulker, 1980). An elaborate reanalysis of the data by Fulker revealed heritabilities corrected for unreliability of .60 and .76, respectively, for the two neuroticism scores. This is broadly in line with the data surveyed so far.

A large-scale study was reported by Loehlin and Nichols (1976), who administered the California Personality Inventory (CPI) to 461 pairs of MZ and 312 pairs of DZ twins. Two broad second-order factors identified with Eysenck's neuroticism and extraversion factors were extracted from the test items. Again, a simple model provided an excellent fit to the data, giving heritability estimates between 50 and 60%. When a reliability of 0.75 was assumed, a corrected heritability of 69% for neuroticism was obtained. Thus, this study, though much larger than the others heretofore considered, yielded very similar results.

We now turn to a series of studies in which the personality questionnaires developed by Eysenck, and based on his personality theory, were employed. These studies obtained information from the extensive twin register maintained at the Institute of Psychiatry and, thus, involved much larger numbers of twin pairs than most other investigations have had access to. The subjects comprised many different genetic relationships and covered all 13 different kinds of relationships to be found in the augmented twin register (Eaves, 1978; Eaves and Eysenck, 1976a; Eysenck, 1976a; Fulker, 1980). With this much enlarged data base, it was observed that there was no indication for an influence from shared family environment in heritability. It was also observed that heritability found in the familial studies was somewhat lower than that in the twin analyses. Possibly, age differences between the related individuals in the familial studies, but absent among twins, were responsible for this lower heritability. If genetic expression changes with age, then genetic resemblance will decline as age differences between relatives increase.

In the Eaves and Eysenck (1976a) study, age was correlated with pair scores and pair differences for 402 sets of MZ twins and 212 sets of DZ twins. The results of the rather complex analysis suggested that additional genes controlling neuroticism may operate at later periods during an individual's life, a form of genetic × age interaction. However, only a longitudinal study could establish such effects unambiguously and differentiate between linear and non-linear regressions.

Although there are no relevant longitudinal studies, Eaves and Eysenck (1976b) were able to look at the stability of neuroticism by comparing responses to inventories given to 441 pairs of twins over a 2-year period. Although there was evidence for a significant subjects × occasions interaction, indicating genuine changes in neuroticism over the 2-year period, there was no clear evidence that twins resembled each other with respect to these changes. This finding, which rules out either a genetic or common environmental explanation of the changes, leaves only specific environmental effects to explain them. During this short period of 2 years, therefore, there was no evidence of the genetic × age interaction found in the previous studies involving much longer periods of time.

The latest, and by far the largest study ever to be conducted, was reported by Floderus-Myhred, Pedersen and Rasmuson (1980). They obtained data from 12,898 unselected twin pairs from the Swedish Twin Registry and tested them with the short forms of the Eysenck Personality Inventory. The internal reliability of this questionnaire was found to be .75 for neuroticism; heritability was found to be .50 for males, and .58 for females. When these figures were corrected for unreliability, they revealed a heritability of approximately .75, thus agreeing very closely with the investigations previously described. The authors also found little evidence for non-additive genetic variance.

It is important to emphasize the size of the sample and the fact that it was unselected. This has not always been recognized or appreciated when different models of gene action were being tested. The number of twins required to carry out an adequate test should be as high as possible. The usual type of analysis that samples fewer than 100 twins pairs makes it very difficult, if not impossible, to test quantitatively different models. Similarly, if volunteer twins are selected, it is possible that the sample may be biased, usually in favor of women and middle-class subjects. Because it is difficult to be certain if such a bias is operating, it is therefore of particular importance to note that in the above study the sample was unbiased, and conclusions similar to those reached by previous workers could be drawn. The age range of the twins tested was quite considerable, with birth dates varying over a period of 30 years. The heritabilities for different subgroups more homogeneous in age did not differ too widely for us to be able to accept the overall figures as reasonably representative for the total population, although the youngest group exhibited the highest heritabilities (.50 for men, .66 for women).

Briefly summarizing, we can state that the evidence unequivocally indicates that *neuroticism is strongly determined by heredity, probably to the extent of about 75% of the variance, with the remaining 25% of the variance due to environmental determinants.* These environmental determinants are almost certainly of the *within family* kind, since there is very little evidence in any of the studies for between family environmental effects. There is no evidence for dominance or for assortative mating, which suggests that the genetic influence is of the simple, additive kind. Thus, a very simple model of variability in neuroticism is able to explain almost all the observed data.

We have so far only considered neuroticism, but the evidence for *neurosis,* of both the first and second kind, is equally strong regarding the importance of genetic factors. In their reviews, Fieve, Rosenthal, and Brill (1975), Rosenthal (1970), Schepank (1974), and Shields (1973) all concluded that genetic factors play a crucial part in causing dysthymic disorders as well as psychopathic or antisocial behavior. The evidence has also been reviewed in detail by Eysenck (1977) and found to be quite convincing.

The inheritance of extraversion–introversion

In many of the studies reported in the previous section, extraversion was also investigated. The first major study, however, to assess the inheritance of extraversion–introversion was not connected with a study of neuroticism (Eysenck, 1956). The study was concerned with school children who were mostly between 145 and 185 months old. Self and teacher ratings, as well as sociometric measures, were obtained. Two sociability scores were derived from the sociometric examination. Several behavior tests were also administered, including a Rorschach test administered under standard conditions and objectively scored.

A factor-analysis disclosed three factors: extraversion–introversion, intelligence, and autonomic functioning. Factor scores, which turned out to be quite independent of each other, were computed. Intraclass correlations were separately calculated for the identical and fraternal twins on the three factors, and Holzinger h^2 heritabilities were calculated. These turned out to be .712 for intelligence, .624 for extraversion, and .748 for the autonomic factor; the latter might be regarded as a psychophysiological measure of neuroticism. It should be noted that the intraclass correlation for fraternal twins on extraversion had a negative sign, although this negative correlation was not significant. This fact, however, makes the calculation of h^2 rather doubtful, but as we shall see, later work confirmed the figure obtained.

Shields (1962), in his study of identical and fraternal twins, also used an extraversion scale derived from the Eysenck questionnaires. Intraclass correlations were .42 for the MZ twins brought up together, .61 for the MZ twins brought up separately, and −.17 for the DZ twins. Shields replicated Eysenck's original finding of a negative correlation between DZ twins, although here again the correlation was not significant and, therefore, may simply have reflected a chance deviation from zero.

Jinks and Fulker (1970) reanalyzed Shields' data and concluded that the best model to represent the data included additive genetic variance and within family environmental variance, but not between family environmental variance. There was also evidence for a certain amount of interaction between additive genetic and within family environmental factors. Introvert genotypes were more susceptible to environmental influences than were extravert genotypes. This finding is, of course, fully consistent with Eysenck's (1967) theory that the introvert is more conditionable than the extravert. Heritability was found to account for 67% of variance, but it should be noted that acceptance of this figure depends on certain assumptions, since a simple model did not fit the data as well as it did in the case of neuroticism. Jinks and Fulker (1970) raise the possibility that there is "competition" between the DZ twins; and both Eysenck's (1956) and Shields' (1962) data yielding negative intraclass correlations on environment for DZ twins support this hypothesis.

We next turn to the study of Cattell, Blewett, and Beloff (1965), who employed Cattell's Junior Personality Quiz. Two scales are relevant to extraversion, namely, scale A (reserved vs. outgoing), as a measure of sociability, and scale Q3 (uncontrolled vs. controlled), as a measure of impulsivity. The indices of heritability, corrected for unreliability, were 1.00 and .85. These values are almost certainly too high, the reason for this being that when reliabilities are very low, as in the Cattell scales, a certain amount of over-correction takes place.

The next study to be considered is the one by Loehlin and Nichols (1976), who used the California Personality Inventory. The estimate of heritability in this study was .59 ± .03. This value would, of course, have been much larger had a correction been applied for reliability. The final value as obtained is, nonetheless, very close to that reported by both Eysenck and Shields. In view of the very large number of twins used in their investigation, this is a crucial replication. They also did not find any influence of a between families component and concluded that being reared in a common family setting is unimportant, an observation that is consistent with the body of available evidence.

Several studies have been carried out at the Institute of Psychiatry, of which only the first one, by Eaves and Eysenck (1975), will be described here in detail. The study employed an 80-item personality inventory and involved an exhaustive analysis of two subscales of extraversion, sociability, and impulsiveness. In all, 837 pairs, both male and female MZ and DZ twins, as well as opposite sex DZ twins, were included. It was found that a simple additive genetic model, together with within family environmental variance, constituted a model that fitted the data surprisingly well. Heritability, corrected for unreliability, was found to account for 57% of the variance, which though less than earlier values, is probably not significantly lower than previously reported.

The study went on to examine the genetic architecture of extraversion–introversion in more detail by analyzing individual differences in the trait profiles of the sociability and impulsiveness subscales. Of particular interest was the relationship observed between sociability and impulsiveness. The analysis revealed genetic and environmental correlations between sociability and impulsiveness of .42 and .66, respectively. As Fulker (1980) points out: "These correlations suggest that the unitary nature of extraversion, so far as these two studies are concerned, owes more to environmental influences than to genetical ones."

The results reported by Eaves (1978), employing both adult and juvenile measures of neuroticism, have already been described. As in the case of neuroticism, Eaves found that the pedigree data gave a slightly lower estimate of heritability for extraversion than did the twin data. This was possibly due to the age difference between the related individuals used in the former analysis that was absent among twins.

To complete this brief account of the major genetic investigations of extraversion–introversion, we must again mention the very large-scale study of Floderus–Myrhed et al. (1980). The uncorrected heritability was found to be .54 for the men and .66 for the women, but it should be recalled that the scales were relatively short, and hence, not very reliable (the reliability for the extraversion scales was only .63). Correcting for unreliability would yield much higher values, but because of the risk of over-correction, no adjustment was made.

Unlike neuroticism, there is no evidence that in extraversion the younger groups have higher heritabilities. Younger males exhibit higher reliabilities than older males, but the oldest female group reveals the highest heritabilities of all, namely, .74. There is, accordingly, no evidence for any age-related difference in heritability of extraversion.

It can be seen from this brief review that there are many similarities in the heritability of extraversion and neuroticism. Both seem to fit into a very simple model, which explains differences in personality by two factors, namely, additive genetic variance and within family environmental variance. There is no evidence for between family environmental variance or for non-additive genetic factors such as assortative mating and dominance. In both cases, the evidence suggests that approximately 7% of the total variance is contributed by the additive genetic factors, leaving the residual variance for environmental influences. These estimates are, of course, fairly rough, but the results from the studies reviewed are remarkably congruent and indicate that, for the populations studied, the figures are highly replicable.

The psychophysiology of extraversion

The fact that both neuroticism and extraversion are strongly determined by genetic factors indicates that they must have a firm biological basis in anatomy, physiology, and neurology. Behavior as such is not inherited, rather it is only biological features of human morphology that are inherited, which, in interaction with the environment, form the basis for differences in habitual behavior.

Figure 11-1 illustrates, in diagrammatic form, the general theory of extraversion and neuroticism I have proposed as a basis for experimental work (Eysenck, 1967). It is hypothesized that the basis for individual differences in neuroticism are to be found in the differential degrees of lability of the limbic system or visceral brain, which governs the expression of emotions through the coordination of the sympathetic and parasympathetic autonomic nervous systems. Individual variation in extraversion–introversion is determined by differences in the degree to which the reticular activating system produces arousal in the cortex. Extraverts are postulated to manifest low degrees of arousal, whereas introverts demonstrate high degrees of arousal under resting conditions. The activity of the limbic and reticular systems are, in general, independent of each other (Routtenberg, 1968). However, in states of high emotional arousal, that is, when the limbic system is extensively involved with sympathetic innervation, this independence disappears both through direct innervation of the reticular formation from the limbic system and also through indirect cortical arousal as a function of the perceived results from sympathetic innervation. Thus, the concept of two separate arousal systems, one producing emotional excitement, the other cortical arousal, does not hold when emotional excitement is very strong. However, under most testing conditions, and in ordinary life situations, emotional arousal is relatively low and the two systems can be posited to be relatively independent. The anatomical substrate of emotional arousal is diagrammatically represented in Figure 11-5.

The widely accepted relationship between neuroticism and the autonomic nervous system will be discussed in the next section. The theory linking cortical arousal with extraversion–introversion, which is less widely accepted, will be discussed in more detail below.

First, we must note one or two important considerations that are relevant to the kinds of deductions that can be made from the general theory that link introversion–extraversion with cortical arousal. The first

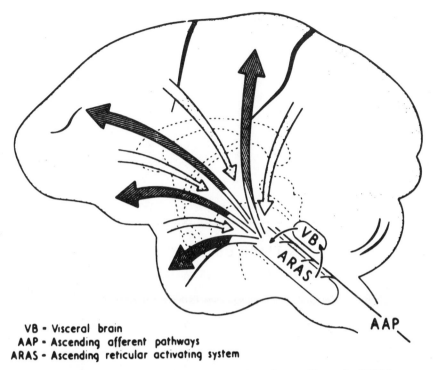

VB - Visceral brain
AAP - Ascending afferent pathways
ARAS - Ascending reticular activating system

Fig. 11–5. The physiological basis of personality. (From Eysenck, 1967.)

of these is concerned with the often observed inverse U-shaped function that performance competency is a function of arousal and motivation. The Yerkes–Dodson Law, advanced at the turn of the century, states that performance is best at intermediate levels of arousal or motivation and poorest when arousal or motivation is either very high or very low. The optimum point for successful performance is related to the complexity of the task; the more complex the task, the lower the required optimum level of arousal. Pavlov (1927) explained similar findings from animal research by advancing the concept of "transmarginal inhibition" or "protective inhibition." By this he meant that as the strength of the unconditioned stimulus is increased, conditioning is facilitated, but only up to a point. Once this point is passed, further increments in the strength of the unconditioned stimulus lead to less conditioning or even extinction. He explained this phenomenon by suggesting that cortical neurons react through inhibition in order to protect themselves from overload. Figure 11-6 illustrates an example of this phenomenon. What is dia-

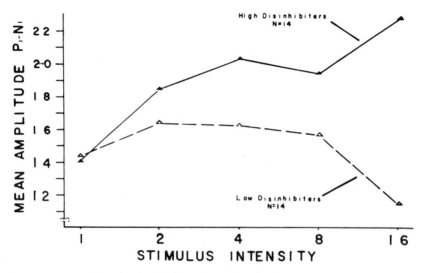

Mean AER amplitudes* for low and high Disinhibition scorers at each level of stimulus intensity.

*Amplitudes are in arbitrary mm deflection units. Each mm unit =.42 μV.

Fig. 11–6. Transmarginal inhibition in introverts (low disinhibitors). (From Zuckerman et al., 1974.)

grammed is the evoked potential of the EEG: that is, the amplitude of waves generated by such stimuli as sudden sounds delivered over ear- phones. The amplitudes of the waves increases with the intensity of the stimulus, and it will be seen that this is certainly true for the extraverted group. For the introverted group, however, there is a clear point beyond which an increase in intensity leads to a *decrement* in the amplitude of the evoked potential. Hence, in formulating hypotheses and testing in general theory, we must be careful to bear in mind the importance of transmarginal inhibition. The reason why introverts demonstrate trans- marginal inhibition earlier than extraverts is simply that their basal arousal (as the theory predicts) is much higher than that for extraverts, and hence, they require less intense stimuli to reach the cut-off point.

Another consideration to be borne in mind is the level of stimulation in the testing situation itself. It is obvious that the best results of condi- tioning are obtained when stimulation is relatively low. If the sensory and psychological stimulation is excessive or intense in the testing situa- tion, high levels of arousal will ensue, which then may lead to transmarginal inhibition in introverts. On the other hand, if the conditions of testing present insufficient stimulation, as under conditions of sensory deprivation, extraverts will react with an increase in arousal. This effect is opposite to transmarginal inhibition and has been labeled "transmarginal arousal" (Eysenck, 1967, 1980a). Thus, the conditions of testing must be carefully controlled and the parameters of the testing situation considered for the theory to be tested properly.

The necessity for doing this becomes apparent when we examine the relationship between personality and resting EEG activity. High arousal is correlated with low amplitude, fast frequency rhythms, whereas low arousal is characterized by high amplitude, low frequency waves. The prediction generated from the theory is that extraverts would manifest slow, high amplitude rhythms, and introverts would exhibit fast, low amplitude rhythms. This prediction was first verified by Savage (1964), but since then approximately 20 experiments have been conducted, with contradictory results. Much of the inconsistency stems from differences in recording and scoring methods as well as in subject selection. In reviews by Gale (1973) and Stelmack (1980), it was pointed out that the published studies were methodologically quite idiosyncratic in the electrode placements, as well as in the methods of analyzing the EEG data and defining the parameters of alpha activity. Similarly, the task demands on the subject varied from reclining in a semi-somnolent state, with eyes closed, to procedures during which the subject sat upright and performed difficult arithmetic problems. Moreover, sex differences were not controlled in a number of the studies reported, and in some studies, hand scoring techniques were used. Gale (1973) concluded from the studies reviewed that the results demonstrate high arousal for introverts under conditions that produce neither very high nor very low levels of arousal. When conditions are introduced that produce either very high or very low levels of arousal, the results are somewhat contradictory. On the whole, however, the EEG research tends to support the hypothesis.

We next turn to the relationship between personality and cortical evoked potentials. We have already mentioned that transmarginal inhibition in evoked potentials occurs much earlier in introverts than in extraverts. Shagass and Schwartz (1965) have found evidence for increased levels of cortical activity for introverts, as inferred from the somatosensory evoked potential. Since then, however, not all replications have been successful. This is possibly due to the tendency to correct for individual differences by applying different levels of stimulus intensity according to the subject's absolute threshold to somatic stimulation. Clearly, this procedure affects the results. Hendrickson (1973), and Stelmack, Achorn, and Michand (1977) have reported positive results that are more in line with theoretical requirements. Studies summarized by Stelmack (1980), in which drug effects were assessed, have also, on the whole, strongly supported the hypothesized prediction.

The orienting reflex (OR), first observed by Pavlov (1927), is also related to personality characteristics. Arousal increases during the first few presentations of a stimulus so as to facilitate its identification and analysis. It would, therefore, be expected that the OR produced by cortical arousal would be greater in introverts; a hypothesis that in the majority of studies has been confirmed. However, the review by Stelmack (1980) illustrates that the phenomenon is extremely complex when looked at from the point of view of stimulus parameters. Similar difficulties are extant in which the rapidity of habituation is found to correlate with extraversion. Although extraverts habituate more quickly than introverts, there is also considerable interaction with the conditions of the specific experimental situation. To cite one example, it has been frequently found in studies of the OR and habituation that the application of 1,000 Hz 60–75 db tones typically fails to differentiate introverts and extraverts, whereas differences are usually observed in the 75–90 db range. Stelmack (1980) concluded his survey by asserting that the "conditions which favor differentiating between extraversion groups with the electrodermal measures of the OR can be described as moderately arousing, a consideration which may serve as a rough guide in the selection of stimulus conditions." Therefore, the studies of the orienting reflex and habituation yielded results that closely resemble those obtained in the EEG investigations.

Significant differences between introverts and extraverts have also been observed on both tonic and phasic measures of electrodermal activity. Here again, there are many complexities relating to the choice of measures and stimulus conditions, but for the most part, the studies such as those conducted by Fowles, Roberts, and Nagel (1977), Desjardin (1976), Crider and Lunn (1971), and Nielson and Peterson (1976) have observed higher skin conductance in introverts, greater numbers of phasic responses to repetitive stimulation, and greater numbers of spontaneous electrodermal fluctuations, in comparison to extraverts. Stelmack (1980) summarized the evidence by stating that

Differences in electrodermal activity between introverts and extraverts have been demonstrated with both simple auditory stimuli of moderate intensity and visual stimulation, and usually under non-stressed conditions where more than passive participation is required. Electrodermal activity is typically greater for introverts than extraverts. Differences in phasic response, in particular, with introverts showing more persistent electrodermal responses to repetitive stimulation, has been the effect most frequently observed and concurs with O'Gormon's (1977) conclusion that extraversion is related to electrodermal habituation. . . . There is also some evidence that introverts demonstrate higher skin conductance levels and greater frequency of non-specific responses than extraverts. These observations imply differences in basic arousal processes and suggest that the effect is not exclusively stimulus-bound.

Pupillary responses have been related to extraversion by Holmes (1967), who reported that fast constrictors were less extraverted than slow constrictors. This finding was interpreted as reflecting the introvert's greater awareness of the environment and tendency toward more rapid conditioning. Frith (1977) and Stelmack and Mandelzys (1975) also obtained similar results.

There are well over 100 studies directly relating extraversion–introversion to psychophysiological mechanisms. The majority of studies are in accord with predictions generated from the theory. Negative results, when reported, can be traced to the conditions of testing or poor selection of scoring methods. This is not to deny that sometimes we do find contradictory results that are difficult to explain; however, such results do not make up more than at most 10% of the literature. The theory that introverts are characterized by higher resting levels of arousal is in general supported by the available evidence, although we do not as yet have an adequate understanding of all the conditions that must be met in demonstrating the postulated relationships.

It is also possible to test the theory by utilizing experimental psychological techniques. One such approach is Pavlovian conditioning. Until the level of transmarginal inhibition is reached, the higher the arousal, the better the conditioning. This leads to the postulation that introverts should condition better than extraverts. This has indeed been found, as indicated in Figures 11-7 and 11-8. When the strength of the unconditioned stimulus is too high, that is, when the point of transmarginal inhibition is passed, we would expect extraverts to condition better. Figure 11-9 shows that this is indeed the case. Thus, where there is a very strong unconditioned stimulus, extraverts condition better than introverts.

One other example taken from the field of perception may serve to il-

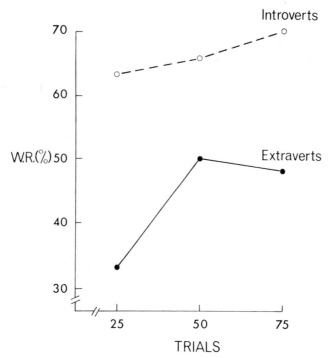

Fig. 11–7. Conditioned eyeblink performance of introverts and extraverts, respectively. (Unpuplished data.)

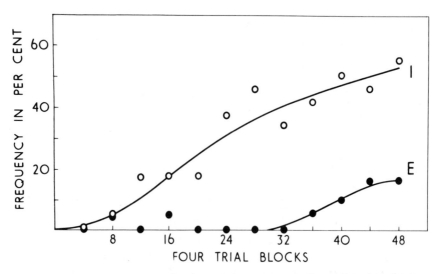

Fig. 11–8. Rate of eyelid conditioning for introverts and extraverts under conditions of 100% reinforcement, strong UCS, and long CS-UCS interval.

270

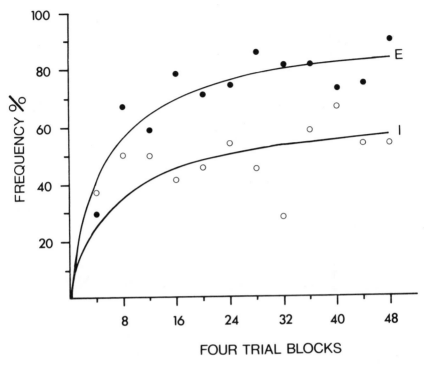

Fig. 11-9. Rate of eyelid conditioning for introverts and extraverts under conditions of 100% reinforcement, strong UCS, and long CS-UCS interval.

lustrate the point. Shigehisa and Symons (1973) have carried out a series of experiments on sensory thresholds and the changes that are induced by varying the intensity of irrelevant ambient stimulation. The general hypothesis was that increases in ambient illumination would reduce sensory thresholds for auditory stimuli by increasing the arousal level of the subject. Shigehisa and Symons (1973) argued that this effect might be due to individual differences that are related to transmarginal inhibition. In other words, as visual intensity increases, auditory thresholds should decrease until an optimal point is reached. Beyond this point, further increases in the intensity of illumination would lead to an increase in sensory thresholds. Furthermore, they predicted that this change in stimulation would be found earlier in introverts than in ambiverts, and, in turn, earlier in ambiverts than in extraverts.

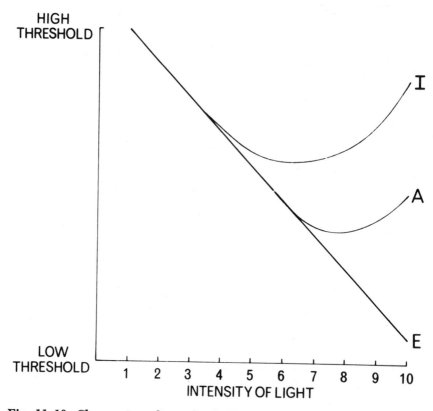

Fig. 11–10. Changes in auditory threshold with different intensities of illumination in introverts, ambiverts, and extraverts. (From Shigehisa
and Symons, 1973.)

Figure 11-10 presents the results of the experiment. Ten degrees of intensity of illumination are marked on the abscissa. It can be seen that
the prediction is precisely followed by the three groups. Introverts exhibit a very early point of transmarginal inhibition when the intensity of
the illumination is still relatively low. Ambiverts show a rather higher
turning point, requiring levels of illumination significantly higher than
observed in introverts. Extraverts do not reveal a change of direction
even at the highest level of illumination used in this experiment. Had
higher levels of intensity been used, they too would have undoubtedly
provided additional evidence for transmarginal inhibition.

The above experiment not only supports the general relationship between arousal and perception, but also demonstrates a point that this author has always considered particularly important—namely, that few psychological predictions and experiments are replicable unless we take care to incorporate personality variables in the design of the experiment. At higher levels of incidental illumination, introverts, ambiverts, and extraverts react in quite different ways to changes in the level of illumination. Introverts demonstrate an increase in sensory thresholds, ambiverts no change, and extraverts a decrease. In other words, no simple generalization can be advanced, since we obtain contradictory results from different groups of people depending on their personality characteristics. As has been emphasized elsewhere (Eysenck, 1967, 1980a), this is not an isolated or insignificant finding, but rather one that affects all areas of study, such as experimental psychology, social psychology, clinical psychology, educational psychology, and industrial psychology, in which personality is an important and often vital parameter. Frequently, it is impossible to replicate experiments because different populations manifest entirely different reactions, depending on their personality scores. Thus, personality study is an integral part of all experimental work in psychology, and its neglect by so many psychologists has had a very injurious effect on the replicability and evaluation of empirical studies in this field.

So far, we have considered experiments in which personality was essentially characterized in terms of questionnaire responses or ratings. Individuals showing extreme deviations from the mean on these scales are frequently described as disturbed and are thus clinically classified. For example, it has been found that people who score high on neuroticism and extraversion tend to indulge in psychopathic, hysterical, and antisocial behavior. Similarly, people scoring high on neuroticism and introversion are inclined to present evidence for neurotic behaviors of the anxious, phobic, or obsessive-compulsive types—the so-called dysthymic neuroses. In concordance with the theory proposed, we can presume that neurotics of this type are characterized by high levels of arousal, whereas psychopaths are characterized by low levels of arousal. The evidence (Eysenck, 1980b; Hare, 1970; Lader & Wing, 1966) suggests that this is indeed the case as assessed by direct psychophysiological measures as well as inferred through indirect psychological measures or measured in conditioning and perception paradigms. It would seem, therefore, that the proposed general theory of personality may have considerable social relevance by explaining, in part, the behavioral patterns of criminals, neurotics, drug abusers, and alcoholics, as well as other disturbed individuals.

An extensive review of this topic has been provided by Stelmack (1980). He points out that "the demonstration of differences in autonomic activation along the neuroticism dimension has proven to be more difficult [than the demonstration of differences in arousal between extraverts and introverts] and, in fact, few attempts have been made. Because of the significance of establishing the determinants of introverted (phobias, anxiety reaction) and extraverted (psychopathy, hysteria) neurosis, it is worthwhile to consider research issues on this problem which can contribute to the psychophysiology of neuroticism."

There are two ways of looking at the problem. First, differences between subjects scoring high and low on neuroticism scales can be interpreted in terms of differential thresholds for hypothalamic activity (Eysenck, 1967) and, in particular, to differences in responsivity of the sympathetic nervous system. In theory, high neuroticism scores are associated with greater autonomic responsivity. Second, the differences between corticoreticular arousal and autonomic activation can be derived (Eysenck, 1967). In the latter approach, it has been theorized that the distinction between autonomic activation and corticoreticular arousal may not apply for individuals who have experienced intense emotions over long periods of time. For these individuals, even mild stimuli can be emotionally activating (Eysenck, 1967). This approach can be investigated by comparing normal control subjects to various patient populations who are tested under moderate or low levels of stimulation.

In one study (Kelly & Martin, 1969), it was reported that there were significant differences between experimental and control groups differing in degree of neuroticism on measures of heart rate, blood pressure, and blood flow during a non-stressful period. This finding is consistent with the expectation of high sympathetic activity for high neuroticism subjects who have experienced chronic or reactive anxiety states. However, no differences in these measures were observed during a stressful mental arithmetic task, a result probably due to ceiling effect. A review of the literature in which anxiety-neurotic patients were studied (Lader, 1969) also tended to show that such patient groups are generally autonomically less reactive than controls. Not surprisingly, therefore, efforts to differentiate anxiety patients from control populations using electrodermal indices have not been successful (Stern & Jones, 1973).

In a non-psychiatric population, Nielsen and Peterson (1976) found significant positive correlations between neuroticism and habituation in a classical conditioning paradigm. They also found a relationship between neuroticism and the number of spontaneous electrodermal fluctuations throughout a series of manipulations that included a 105 db habituation series. Katkin (1975) made the interesting observation that, under high stress conditions (threat of shock), there were no differences between groups, but under moderate levels of stress (ego-involving threat), subjects with higher trait anxiety revealed a greater increase in the number of electrodermal responses than subjects with lower trait anxiety scores. Stelmack (1980) concludes, after reviewing the literature, that "successful differentiation between high and low neuroticism subjects may not only depend on selecting stressors which achieve maximum between subject variability of response without ceiling effects, but also distinguishing the neuroticism trait as it is manifested in normal or patient populations."

A neo-behaviorist theory of neurosis

Genetically determined differences in the limbic system and reticular formation may produce the dispositional diathesis that places children at risk for neurotic disorders of the first and second kind. However, there must be, in addition, life events that transform the disposition into an overt disorder. This section will be devoted to the presentation of a general theory of the origins of neurosis.

To summarize succinctly the major points of the proposed theory, it is hypothesized that neurotic symptoms are produced by a process of Pavlovian conditioning. This process frequently leads to incubation (enhancement) of anxiety as the product of the confrontation of unreinforced conditioned stimuli under certain specified conditions. These conditioned emotional reactions and behaviors can be eliminated by a process of extinction. It will be the purpose of this section to spell out some of the specific conditions under which enhancement and extinction of conditioned responses takes place.

The conditioning theory of neurosis, and the notion that the process of extinction would lead to the elimination of neurotic symptoms, was originally suggested by Watson and Rayner (1920). The earliest clinical application of these methods by Mary Cover Jones (1924a,b), in the treatment of fears, proved eminently successful. Mowrer (1939) elaborated upon Watson's theory (commonly referred to as the Watson–Mowrer theory) and in so doing presented the first systematic statement of the classical conditioning process as it relates to anxiety. However, despite these advances, a number of criticisms have been made over the years, and there have been many observations conditioning theory is incapable of assimilating.

The first, and most serious point to be considered is that unreinforced conditioned reactions extinguish quickly (Kimble, 1961). Thus, if neurotic reactions are classically conditioned, they should not be an exception to this rule. Kimmel (1975) has suggested that the non-occurrence of extinction in neurotic anxiety is sufficient reason to reject Watson's theory. Indeed, it is difficult to see how Watson's theory can be reconciled with the accepted facts of extinction. Neurotic subjects are exposed very frequently to the feared objects or situations, or they encounter them in symbolic or imaginary forms. Each such encounter should theoretically produce a modicum of extinction that would lead to complete elimination of the neurotic reaction. Although it is possible to account for the occurrence of spontaneous remission through a simple extinction paradigm (Eysenck, 1963), the question arises as to why not all neuroses remit spontaneously. This is a very grave difficulty for the Watson–Mowrer theory.

Other difficulties beset the Watson–Mowrer theory. In many neuroses, we not only fail to observe the expected extinction of the unreinforced CS, but we find an incremental (enhancement) effect, such that the unreinforced CS actually produces more and more anxiety (CR) with each presentation of the CS. In Pavlovian conditioning, there is no provision for CRs to achieve greater strength than UCRs; the dog never salivates more to the bell than to the food (McIntosh, 1974). This incrementation, so often observed in the history of a neurotic illness, is impossible to reconcile with the orthodox learning theory.

This point may be linked with another issue, namely, the absence of traumatic UCSs in the history of most neurotic illnesses (particularly those observed in peace time; in wartime, traumatic events often do produce neurotic reactions). As Lautsch (1971) and Gourney and O'Connor (1971) have pointed out, in the majority of cases there is some sort of insidious onset, without any single event that could be called "traumatic" even by lenient standards (Marks, 1969; Rachman, 1968). Accordingly, a distinctly subtraumatic event inaugurates the development of a neurotic disorder, which in the end, leads to CRs that are very

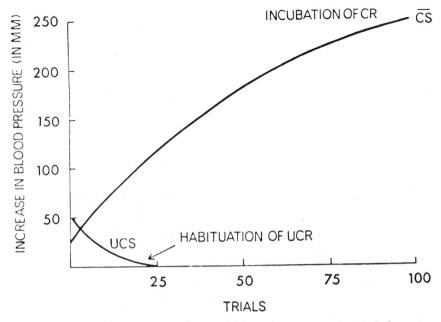

Fig. 11–11. Incubation of the unreinforced CR, as contrasted with habituation of UCR. (From Eysenck, 1976b.)

much stronger than those that were elicited to the original UCSs. This possibility is not envisaged by orthodox learning theory.

An alternative theory was advanced by Eysenck (1976b, 1979) to account for these problems within the context of laboratory investigations into the extinction process. The theory asserts that extinction is not a universal reaction to the presentation of the CS administered alone (without reinforcement). *Under certain conditions, the presentation of the unreinforced CS produces enhancement of incubation of the CRs, rather than extinction.* One example of this phenomenon can be derived from the study by Napalkov (1963), which was discussed in some detail by Eysenck (1967, 1968). Dogs were used as experimental subjects and increments in blood pressure were recorded after a pistol was fired behind the ear. As can be seen in Figure 11-11, the unconditioned stimulus did not produce a traumatic reaction. An increment of 50 mm of blood pressure is relatively slight, and after only 25 trials there was no elevation in blood pressure upon presentation of the UCS.

The fate of the conditioned response, however, is quite different. In Napalkov's experiment, the CS was paired only once with the UCS; after that the pistol was not shot again. At first, as can be seen in the figure, the CR is relatively slight, but it gradually increases as more and more CRs without reinforcement are given, until finally a very strong reaction, five times as strong as the original reaction to the UCS, is recorded. Napalkov mentions that these very strong CRs become chronic in some dogs and are very difficult to extinguish. Here we have an experimental example of the process of incubation or enhancement that is postulated to occur in the development of neurotic disorders. Many other examples from the laboratory literature can be found (Eysenck, 1976b).

What explanation can be advanced for this phenomenon that seems to fly in the face of the law of extinction? It may be useful to start with the two subclasses of classical conditioning as first distinguished by Grant (1964). He made an important distinction between what he called "Pavlovian A conditioning" and Pavlovian B conditioning." The first kind of conditioning is exemplified by the prototype of classical salivary conditioning, in which the sound of a bell, by being repeatedly presented before food was given, elicits salivation and orientation movements toward the feeding cups. The reference experiment for Pavlovian B conditioning, quoted by Grant, is one in which an animal is given repeated injections of apomorphine. The UCR to apomorphine involves severe nausea, profuse secretions of saliva, vomiting, and then profound sleep. After repeated daily injections, Pavlov's dogs would show severe nausea and profuse secretion of saliva at the first touch from the experimenter. "In Pavlovian B conditioning . . . the CS appears to act as a partial substitute for the UCS. Furthermore, the UCS elicits a complete UCR in Pavlovian B conditioning, whereas in Pavlovian A conditioning the organism emits the UCR of approaching and ingesting the food." Thus, in Pavlovian B conditioning, stimulation by the UCS is not contingent on the subject's instrumental acts, and hence, there is less dependence upon the motivational state of the organism.

What Eysenck's (1976b) theory suggests is simply that for certain types of conditioning situations (particularly Pavlovian B conditioning situations), the CR, by reproducing many of the components of the UCR, in fact provides for the reinforcement of the CS not accompanied by the UCS. Thus, a positive feedback process is set up, which, though starting out at a relatively low level CR, develops into a very strong CR without any further association with the UCS.

Another way of looking at this question is by postulating that Pavlovian B conditioning is particularly relevant to conditioned responses that have drive properties (Eysenck, 1976b). Pavlovian A conditioning, unlike type B conditioning, does not produce conditioned responses that can act as drives (Miller, 1951a,b). Thus, exposure of the subject to a CS that has been acquired through a process of Pavlovian A conditioning leads to extinction when the CS is presented without reinforcement by the UCS. On the other hand, exposure of the subject to a CS that has been acquired through Pavlovian B conditioning, in which the CR is a drive, may lead to extinction or enhancement of the CR when the CS is produced without the UCS. This process depends on certain parameters now to be discussed because they are crucial to any scientific understanding of the mechanism of extinction, whether in the laboratory or in the clinic.

The theory governing our approach is illustrated in Figure 11-12, which plots on the ordinate the strength of the conditioned response, and on the abscissa the duration of the unreinforced conditioned stimulus, using of course only stimuli acquired through Pavlovian B conditioning. It is hypothesized that a strong CR is evoked upon presentation of the CS; this CR is felt as fear or anxiety by the patient and is usually accompanied by behavioral and autonomic reactions. This CR habituates or extinguishes (curve A) as the presentation of the unreinforced CS is prolonged, just as the UCR would habituate or extinguish. When strong, the CR can act as a reinforcement in much the same way as the UCS does. Below a critical point, the CR is too weak to act in this manner; beyond this point we get only extinction, rather than enhancement of the CR.

The conditioning theory of neurosis thus posits that a neurosis of the first kind arises through a process of Pavlovian B conditioning, producing a positive feedback situation through the incubation or enhancement of the CR. Such CRs can be extinguished according to Pavlovian rules, leading to methods of treatment that can eliminate the neurosis, although, of course, the underlying diatheses (neuroticism, introversion) is unaffected.

Clinical applicability of research findings

It is suggested that a proper understanding of the genetic and environmental contributions to neurotic disorders, and a reasonable theory re-

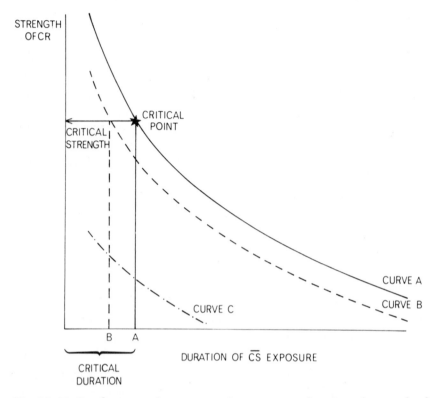

Fig. 11–12. Incubation and extinction of anxiety as a function of strength of
    CR and duration of CS exposure. (From Eysenck, 1979.)

garding the physiological, hormonal, and other biological factors underlying the development of neurotic disorders, is essential for both an
understanding of these disorders and the development of proper methods of treatment. Modern methods of behavior therapy and behavior
modification have been developed largely on the basis of the general
model here presented. There is now ample evidence that these new
methods of therapy work well, both with adults and children, and indeed
give better results than traditional approaches, whether psychoanalytic,
psychotherapeutic, or pharmaceutical. Many examples of comparisons
between the effects of behavior therapy and psychotherapy are given in
the recently published book *The Effects of Psychological Therapy* by
S. Rachman and G. T. Wilson; the major point that emerges is that very

important practical consequences follow from the theoretical considerations outlined in this chapter.

References

Carter, H. Twin similarities in emotional traits. *Character and Personality*, 1935, *4*, 61–78.

Cattell, R., Blewett, D., & Beloff, J. The inheritance of personality: A multiple variance analysis of determination of approximate nature-nurture ratios for primary personality factors in Q-data. *American Journal of Human Genetics*, 1955, *7*, 122–146.

Crider, A. & Lunn, P. Electrodermal lability as a personality dimension. *Journal of Experimental Research in Personality*, 1971, *5*, 145–150.

Desjardin, E. The effects of denotative and connotative linguistic meaning and work concreteness on the habituation of the skin conductance response: Extraversion and neuroticism as subject variables. Unpublished doctoral dissertation, University of Ottawa, 1976.

Eaves, L. Twins as a basis for the causal analysis of human personality. In W. Nance, G. Allen, & P. Parisi (Eds.), *Progress in clinical and biological research: Twin research, psychology and methodology (Part A)*. New York: Alan R. Liss, 1978.

Eaves, L. & Eysenck, H. The nature of extraversion: A genetical analysis. *Journal of Personality and Social Psychology*, 1975, *32*, 102–112.

Eaves, L. & Eysenck, H. Genotype × age interaction for neuroticism. *Behavior Genetics*, 1976a, *6*, 359–363.

Eaves, L. & Eysenck, H. Genetic and environmental components of inconsistency and unrepeatability in twins' responses to a neuroticism questionnaire. *Behavior Genetics*, 1976b, *6*, 145–160.

Eysenck, H. *Dimensions of personality*. London: Routledge & Kegan Paul, 1947.

Eysenck, H. Criterion analysis—an application of the hypothetico-deductive method to factor analysis. *Psychological Review*, 1950, *57*, 38–53.

Eysenck, H. Schizothymia-cyclothymia as a dimension of personality: II. Experimental. *Journal of Personality*, 1952, *20*, 345–384.

Eysenck, H. The inheritance of extraversion-introversion. *Acta Psychologica*, 1956, *12*, 95–110.

Eysenck, H. (Ed.), *Handbook of abnormal psychology: An experimental approach*. New York: Basic Books, 1961.

Eysenck, H. Behavior therapy, spontaneous remission and transference in neurotics. *American Journal of Psychiatry*, 1963, *119*, 867–871.

Eysenck, H. *The biological basis of personality*. Springfield, IL: C. Thomas, 1967.

Eysenck, H. A theory of the incubation of anxiety/fear responses. *Behavior Research and Therapy*, 1968, *6*, 309–321.

Eysenck, H. *The structure of human personality*. London: Methuen, 1970a.

Eysenck, H. A dimensional system of psychodiagnostics. In A. H. Mahrer

(Ed.), *New approaches to personality classification*. New York: Columbia University Press, 1970b.

Eysenck, H. (Ed.) *Handbook of abnormal psychology*. San Diego: Knapp, 1973.

Eysenck, H. Genetic factors in personality development. In A. R. Kaplan (Ed.), *Human behavior genetics*. Springfield, IL: C. Thomas, 1976a.

Eysenck, H. The learning theory model of neurosis—a new approach. *Behavior Research and Therapy*, 1976b, *14*, 251–257.

Eysenck, H. *Crime and personality*. London: Routledge & Kegan Paul. 1977.

Eysenck, H. The conditioning model of neurosis. *The Behavioral and Brain Sciences*, 1979, *2*, 155–159.

Eysenck, H. A neo-behavioristic (S-R) theory of behavior therapy. In C. M. Franks & G. T. Wilson (Eds.), *Handbook of behavior therapy*, New York: Guildford Press, 1980a.

Eysenck, H. Psychopathie. In U. Baumann, H. Barbalk, & G. Siedenstucker (Eds.), *Klinishe Psychologie: Trends in forschung und praxis* (Vol. 3). Wien: Hans Huber, 1980b.

Eysenck, H. & Eysenck, S. *Personality structure and measurement*. London: Routledge & Kegan Paul, 1969.

Eysenck, H. & Prell, D. A note on the differentiation of normal and neurotic children by means of objective tests. *Journal of Clinical Psychology*, 1952, *8*, 202–204.

Eysenck, H. & Rachman, S. *The causes and cures of neurosis*. London: Routledge & Kegan Paul, 1965.

Fieve, R., Rosenthal, D., & Brill, H. (Eds.) *Genetic research in psychiatry*. London: Johns Hopkins University Press, 1975.

Floderus-Myrhed, B., Pedersen, N., & Rasmuson, I. Assessment of heritability for personality, based on a short form of the Eysenck Personality Inventory: A study of 12,898 twin pairs. *Behavior Genetics*, 1980, *10*, 153–162.

Foulds, G. *Personality and personal illness*. London: Tavistock, 1965.

Fowles, D., Roberts, R., & Nagel, K. The influence of introversion-extraversion on the skin conductance response to stress and stimulus intensity. *Journal of Research in Personality*, 1977, *11*, 129–146.

Frith, C. Habituation of the pupil size and light response to sound. Paper presented at the American Psychological Association meeting, San Francisco, August, 1977.

Fulker, D. The genetic and environmental architecture of psychoticism, extraversion and neuroticism. In H. J. Eysenck (Ed.). *A model for personality*. New York: Springer, 1980.

Gale, A. The psychophysiology of individual differences: Studies of extraversion and the EEG. In P. Kline (Ed.). *New approaches in psychological measurement*. New York: Wiley, 1973.

Gourney, A. & O'Connor, P. Anxiety associated with flying. *British Journal of Psychiatry*, 1971, *119*, 159–166.

Grant, D. Classical and operant conditioning. In A. W. Melton (Ed.), *Categories of human learning*. New York: Academic Press, 1964.

Hare, R. *Psychopathy*. New York: Wiley, 1970.

Hendrickson, D. An examination of individual differences in cortical evoked response. London: Unpublished doctoral dissertation. University of London, 1973.

Holmes, D. Pupillary response, conditioning and personality. *Journal of Personality and Social Psychology*, 1967, 5, 98–103.

Holzinger, K. The relative effect of nature and nurture influences on twin differences. *Journal of Educational Psychology*, 1929, 20, 245–248.

Jinks, J. & Fulker, D. Comparison of the biometrical genetical, MAVA and classical approaches to the analysis of human behavior. *Psychological Bulletin*, 1970, 73, 311–349.

Jones, M. A laboratory study of fear: The case of Peter. *Pedagogical Seminar*, 1924a, 31, 308–315.

Jones, M. The elimination of children's fear. *Journal of Experimental Psychology*, 1924b, 7, 380–390.

Jung, J. *Psychological types*. London: Routledge & Kegan Paul, 1924.

Katkin, E. Electrodermal lability: A psychophysiological analysis of individual differences in response to stress. In I. G. Sarason & C. D. Spielberger (Eds.). *Stress and anxiety* (Vol. 2). New York: Wiley, 1975.

Kelly, D. & Martin, I. Autonomic reactivity, eyelid conditioning and their relationship to neuroticism and extraversion. *Behavior Research and Therapy*, 1969, 7, 233–244.

Kimble, G. *Hilgard and Marquis' conditioning and learning*. New York: Appleton-Century Crofts, 1961.

Kimmel, H. Conditioned fear and anxiety. In C. D. Spielberger & I. G. Sarason (Eds.). *Stress and anxiety* (Vol. 1). New York: Wiley, 1975.

Lader, M. Psychophysiological aspects of anxiety. In M. H. Lader (Ed.). *Studies of anxiety*. Ashford, Kent: Headley Bros., 1969.

Lader, M. & Wing, L. *Physiological measures, sedative drugs, and morbid anxiety*. London: Oxford University Press, 1966.

Loehlin, J. & Nichols, R. *Heredity, environment and personality*. Austin: University of Texas Press, 1976.

Lautsch, H. Dental phobia. *British Journal of Psychiatry*, 1971, 119, 151–158.

Marks, I. *Fears and phobias*. London: Heineman, 1969.

Mather, K. & Jinks, J. *Biometrical genetics*. London: Chapman & Hall, 1971.

McIntosh, N. *The psychology of animal learning*. London: Academic Press, 1974.

Miller, N. Learnable drives and rewards. In S. S. Stevens (Ed.). *Handbook of experimental psychology*. New York: Wiley, 1951a.

Miller, N. Comments on multiple process conceptions of learning. *Psychological Review*, 1951b, 58, 375–381.

Mowrer, O. A stimulus response analysis of anxiety and its role as a reinforcing agent. *Psychological Review*, 1939, 46, 553–565.

Napalkov, A. Information process of the brain. In N. Wiener & J. Sefade (Eds.). *Progress in brain research* (Vol. 2). Amsterdam: Elsevier, 1963.

Neel, J. & Schull, W. *Human heredity*. Chicago: University of Chicago Press, 1954.

Newman, H., Freeman, F., & Holzinger, J. *Twins: A study of heredity and environment*. Chicago: University of Chicago Press, 1937.

Nichols, R. The National Merit Twin Study. In S. G. Vandenberg (Ed.). *Methods and goals in human behavior genetics*. New York: Academic Press, 1965.

Nielson, T. & Peterson, K. Electrodermal correlates of extraversion, trait anxiety and schizophrenia. *Scandinavian Journal of Psychology*, 1976, *17*, 73–80.

O'Gorman, J. Individual differences in habituation of human physiological responses: A review of theory, method and finding in the study of personality correlates in non-clinical populations. *Biological Psychology*, 1977, *5*, 257–318.

Pavlov, I. *Conditioned reflexes*. London: Oxford University Press, 1927.

Rachman, S. *Phobias: Their nature and control*. Springfield, IL: C. Thomas, 1968.

Rachman, S. & Wilson, G. *The effects of psychological therapy*. New York: Pergamon Press, 1980.

Rosenthal, D. *Genetic theory and abnormal behavior*. London: McGraw-Hill, 1970.

Routtenberg, A. The two-arousal hypothesis: Reticular formation and limbic system. *Psychological Review*, 1968, *75*, 51–80.

Satterfield, J. The hyperactive child syndrome: A precursor of adult psychopathy? In R. D. Hare & D. Schalling (Eds.). *Psychopathic behavior*. New York: Wiley, 1978.

Savage, R. Electro-cerebral activity, extraversion and neuroticism. *British Journal of Psychiatry*, 1964, *110*, 98–110.

Schepank, H. *Erb-und uweltfaktoren bei neurosen*. New York: Springer Verlag, 1974.

Shagass, C. & Schwartz, M. Age, personality and somato-sensory evoked responses. *Science*, 1965, *148*, 1359–1361.

Shields, J. *Monozygotic twins brought up apart and brought up together*. London: Oxford University Press, 1962.

Shields, J. Heredity and psychological abnormality. In H. J. Eysenck (Ed.), *Handbook of abnormal psychology*. London: Pitman, 1973.

Shigehisa, T. & Symons, J. Effect of intensity of visual stimulation on auditory sensitivity in relation to personality. *British Journal of Psychology*, 1973, *64*, 205–213.

Stelmack, R. M. The psychophysiology of extraversion and neuroticism. In H. J. Eysenck (Ed.), *A model for personality*. London: Springer, 1980.

Stelmack, R. M. & Mandelzys, N. Extraversion and pupillary response to affective and taboo words. *Psychophysiology*, 1975, *12*, 536–540.

Stelmack, R. M., Achorn, E., & Michand, A. Extraversion and individual differences in auditory evoked response. *Psychophysiology*, 1977, *14*, 368–374.

Stern, J. & Jones, C. Personality and psychopathology. In W. F. Prokasy &

D. C. Raskin (Eds.). *Electrodermal activity in psychological research.* New York: Academic Press, 1973.

Watson, J. & Rayner, R. Conditioned emotional reactions. *Journal of Experimental Psychology,* 1920, *3*, 1–14.

Zuckerman, M., Murtaugh, T., & Siegel, J. Sensation seeking and cortical augmenting and reducing. *Psychophysiology,* 1974, *11*, 535–542.

Index